REVOLUTION AND ECONOMIC DEVELOPMENT IN CUBA

REVOLUTION AND ECONOMIC DEVELOPMENT IN CUBA

Arthur MacEwan

St. Martin's Press
New York

To my parents,
Alan MacEwan and Mary MacEwan
for many reasons

ISBN 0-312-67980-7

Library of Congress Cataloging in Publication Data

MacEwan, Arthur.
  Revolution and economic development in Cuba.

  Bibliography: p.
  Includes index.
1. Agriculture – Economic aspects – Cuba.
2. Cuba – Economic conditions – 1959–
3. Cuba – Social conditions – 1959–
4. Socialism in Cuba. I. Title.
HD1837.M3   1980   338.1′87291   80–11130
ISBN 0-312-67980-7

Contents

List of Tables

Preface

The Cuban revolution has cleared the way for economic progress. It has destroyed the old political, economic and social structures which held the country in a condition of underdevelopment.

The revolution has also created. And creating the new structures has been at least as difficult as destroying the old ones. It has been a process with notable achievements, but it has also been a process fraught with difficulties and setbacks. Indeed, the successes themselves have often created new problems, as Cuban society has moved toward socialism and discovered new contradictions.

Moreover, old structures may have been destroyed in form, but they live on in their influence on today's social relations and attitudes. History is never destroyed, and Cuba's history of underdevelopment and domination by imperialism is continually present in the problems of the new society.

This essay is an examination of the progress and continuing problems in the Cuban economy. It focuses particularly on the changes that have taken place in Cuban agriculture since 1959, when the revolutionary government came to power, and on the relation of those changes to the Cuban economy generally.

Agriculture has played a central role in Cuba's economic history, and it has continued to play an important role throughout the revolutionary process. But Cuban agriculture is not something separate from the rest of the nation's economic and social life. The policies and problems of agriculture are policies and problems of the whole economy, and vice versa. By concentrating attention on agriculture, it is thus possible to learn a good deal about the entire development process in Cuba.

In any nation, but especially in Cuba, economic development means social change. The changes that have taken place in Cuban agriculture— the restructuring of class relations, the formation of new production programmes, the reorganisation of labour—are part of a change from one social system to another. So in discussing agriculture and development in Cuba, this essay is designed to provide insights on the process of the transition toward socialism, both as it has been experienced in Cuba and as a general phenomenon.

ORGANISATION AND CLASSES IN CUBAN DEVELOPMENT

In Cuba, as in other nations where a transition toward socialism has been initiated by a successful military struggle, socialist forces have been confronted with an underdeveloped economy. Underdevelopment in Cuba was characterised by a weak national capitalist class, extreme inequality and social injustice, economic stagnation and political instability. Through such characteristics, underdevelopment facilitated the ascendency of Cuba's socialist forces.

But the country's underdevelopment has also made the task of socialist development particularly onerous. The nation's position of dependency in the world economy, the very tangible conditions of poverty, economic imbalance, and technological backwardness have constituted serious, concrete obstacles to economic advancement in Cuba. Moreover, Cuba's history of underdevelopment did little to prepare the working people for the task of administering a new system of economic organisation.

Since coming to power at the beginning of 1959, the Cuban revolutionaries have been engaged in a continuous struggle against their inheritance of underdevelopment. They have attained some major successes. The government has been able to attain control over the nation's economic surplus and direct it towards expansion. High investment rates have moved the country well ahead on at least one basic development front: the task of capital accumulation.

There is, however, another fundamental task of development which seems more difficult to accomplish. Economic development is primarily a problem of creating new forms of social organisation, in particular of creating new ways of organising and coordinating work processes. Furthermore, in any particular society, the relation among social classes—the functioning of power in the society—is dialectically bound up with the social process which constitutes economic development.

Capitalist development requires that a bourgeoisie assert its control over economic and political organisation, use its power to create a disciplined work force, and thereby bring about a transformation of society's productive forces. In so doing, of course, it further enhances its own power. Capitalist underdevelopment—the situation in pre-1959

Cuba—can be understood in contrast to this pattern of successful capitalist development.

Socialist forces that come to power in Cuba and elsewhere face the problem of accomplishing what capitalism failed to do. Cuban revolutionaries have needed to find new ways of organising and coordinating work processes so as to achieve economic expansion. The context of a society attempting a transition towards socialism means that this task is undertaken with a collective consciousness that is lacking in a capitalist society; socialist development is a planned process. Moreover, if the transition is to be successful, the transformation must be carried out so as to establish socialist social relations—especially economic democracy and equality—as well as to achieve economic expansion.

As with capitalist development, socialist development is dialectically bound up with a particular relation among classes. But in socialist development it is the working class (perhaps in alliance with other toiling groups) which asserts control over political and economic organisation, which uses its power to organise the society in its own interests, and which thereby enhances its own power. The interests of the working class are different from those of the bourgeoisie and the organisational forms which lie at the base of socialist development will be different from those of capitalist development. Nonetheless, the problem of creating new forms of socialist organisation remains the crux of the process and, accordingly, constitutes a central theme of this essay. It will become evident that, while Cuba's success in establishing effective organisation has been slow and uneven, events of the 1970s indicate some very significant accomplishments.

STRUCTURE OF THE ESSAY

I shall proceed to examine the Cuban economy with a dual purpose. I want to interpret the Cuban experience from the general perspective of viewing socialist development in terms of changing social organisation and class relations. I also want to expand this general perspective on socialist development by the examination of the Cuban experience.

To accomplish my purpose, it is useful to give some attention to the pre-1959 situation. This is done in Part One. I provide a brief description of the role of agriculture in the pre-revolutionary Cuban economy and offer some comparisons with other revolutionary situations (Chapter 1). I then examine the history of imperialism and underdevelopment in

Cuba in order to analyse the nation's class relations and to begin to gain an understanding of the pre-1959 economic stagnation (Chapter 2). This lends into a discussion of the economic nature of the large estates (Chapter 3). Having analysed the material background of the Cuban revolution, I then turn to the revolutionary process itself, in order to develop a picture of the role of different classes and their potential for participation in socialist organisation (Chapter 4). Finally, in Part One, I introduce some important aspects of post-revolutionary economic changes (Chapter 5).

While economic and social changes are continuing processes in Cuban agriculture, the most fundamental changes—those that set the stage of economic development for years to come—took place in the period immediately following the seizure of power by the revolutionary forces. Consequently, I give the events of those years considerable attention in Part Two and Part Three.

In Part Two, I discuss the first agrarian reform—implemented between 1959 and 1961. In connection with each aspect of the reform— the process of land take-over (Chapter 6), the creation of the public sector (Chapter 7), the restructuring of the private sector (Chapter 8), and the formation of a national agricultural-production policy (Chapter 9)—I attempt to focus on contradictions associated with the agricultural transformation. This allows me to develop a foundation for interpreting the production crisis of the early 1960s and later policy formulations and production problems.

In Part Three, I discuss the various events that set the framework for the formation of Cuba's agriculture-based development strategy of the mid- and late 1960s. First, I focus on the second agrarian reform, implemented at the end of 1963 (Chapter 10). Second, I discuss the set of social reforms implemented in Cuba during the early 1960s (Chapter 11). I give most attention to the literacy campaign, partly because it had such a profound impact on rural society, and partly because its execution illustrates important patterns in the Cuban approach to social transformation. Third, I provide a description of the changes of income distribution in Cuba, which, I will subsequently argue, were especially important in affecting the course of later events (Chapter 12).

In Part Four, I discuss the substance of and rationale behind the Cuban development strategy of the 1960s. This is the policy which centred on the goal of harvesting 10 million tons of sugar in 1970 and was based on an effort to alter the system of work incentives. I first examine the sectoral focus of the plan (Chapter 13) and then turn to matters of incentives and planning (Chapter 14). I then describe the 'big push' in investment and labour mobilisation, which the government viewed as a key to its policy (Chapter 15). Finally, I describe the failure of the strategy to achieve the goals which had been set (Chapter 16).

My task in Part Five is to explain the problems that dominated the Cuban economy in the 1960s, the deficiencies in the formulation of development strategy, and the failure of the effort to harvest 10 million tons of sugar in 1970. In explaining these matters, I am able to focus directly on issues of organisation and social transformation (Chapter 17) and to examine their relation to such issues as the effectiveness of investment (Chapter 18), the design of the strategy (Chapter 19), and the formation of incentives (Chapter 20). Finally, I argue that the economic difficulties of the 1960s were bound up with political weaknesses of the revolution in that period (Chapter 21).

The Cuban experience in the 1970s, however, has been substantially different from that of the earlier years. In Part Six I turn attention to the economic expansion of the early 1970s and discuss the policy changes of those years. To begin with, I introduce some of these changes, emphasise the dual nature of the political and planning changes that were made, and suggest reasons for the changes having their particular political character (Chapter 22). I then focus on two institutions which had long played a role in Cuban development and were continuing factors of importance in the development and extension of organisation in the 1970s: the educational system and the special programmes (Chapter 23). Then I turn in more detail to the reorganisation of the political process (Chapter 24) and the restructuring of labour incentives and planning (Chapter 25). All this gives me a good basis from which to examine the overall redirection of the economy and the particulars of events in agriculture (Chapter 26). Finally, I discuss economic events of the most recent period—since 1975—and attempt to delineate the direction in which the Cuban economy is currently moving (Chapter 27).

The essay provides the foundation for drawing some lessons from the experience of agriculture and development in Cuba. These lessons are the subject of Part Seven (Chapter 28). Following a discussion of the overriding importance of the rural–urban contradiction in Cuba (and in socialist development generally), I take up the matter of agriculture's weakness as a leading sector. This leads into a consideration of the role of external assistance in Cuba's development. Finally, I conclude with a summation of the role of equality in Cuban development and an attempt to make some generalisations regarding the relation between equality and economic growth.

A LIMITATION OF THE ESSAY

Before proceeding, it will be useful to warn the reader of one of the important limitations of this essay. There is a serious lack of information available on the Cuban economy. There are gaps in the aggregate- and commodity-production data, and there are numerous topics on which no systematic data are available. For example, there are no reliable national accounts for 1959–61, and data on agricultural production after 1959 do not include that share of private production not collected by the state agencies. There are no comprehensive studies of income distribution, for either the pre- or post-1959 periods, and there are no studies of agricultural pricing and procurement. Also there is considerable delay in the availability of data; in particular, information on the course of the economy since 1975 is rather limited. There are ways in which these and the numerous other deficiencies of information can be (and have been) finessed, but it must be recognised that the data problem poses a serious limitation on a general study of this sort.

Most of the information that is available, however, is readily available. A few studies of the Cuban economy have gone a long way to provide the informational foundation for this essay. My debts to the works of James O'Connor, José Acosta, Dudley Seers, Andres Bianchi, Archibald Ritter, and Carmelo Mesa-Lago will be apparent from the references. In addition, I have relied heavily on a few major documents published by the Cuban government and on the writings and speeches of Cuban political leaders. The reader should, accordingly, not expect to find any wealth of new and important information in this essay.

Instead, my attempt here has been to make a contribution of synthesis and interpretation. I have been successful if I have been able to pull together information so as to offer some useful insights on agriculture and development in Cuba.

Acknowledgements

My work on Cuba has developed over a number of years. I first visited the country at the end of 1960, and my first debt is to the many Cubans who were eager to explain to me and show me what was happening in their country. On later visits—in 1968, 1969 and 1972—I benefited greatly from discussions with many people at the Universidad de la Habana, especially in the Instituto de Economia. Also, numerous government officials, workers, peasants, enterprise administrators, union officials, Communist Party cadre, and people in the streets were generous in giving me information and ideas. There is no way I could name them all, but to them all I am extremely grateful. I must, however, give special thanks to Nestor Garcia, who did so much to facilitate my work in Cuba, while the discussions I have had with him over the years have also been very enlightening.

As I have been preparing the present manuscript, numerous friends have given me special advice and assistance in a variety of ways: Jean-Pierre Berlan, Sam Bowles, Jim Campen, Margery Davies, David Evans, Tom Hexner, David Hunt, Azizur Rahman Khan, Mary MacEwan, Samir Radwan, Dudley Seers, Sandy Shea, Michele Urann and Andy Zimbalist. To each, my thanks.

During the course of this work, Crux Inc, of Cambridge, Massachusetts, provided me with some valuable assistance for which I am appreciative. Also, I would like to acknowledge a grant from the Social Sciences Research Council which I received in 1972–3 and which was helpful in giving me the time to gather information and develop my ideas at an early stage of this project.

The support I received from my family was essential for the preparation of this book. Margery, Karla and Anna—and, in the final moment, Peter too—had to put up with a lot, and I am grateful for their forbearance. Margery was especially generous in giving me the time I needed to plough through the project: thanks!

The author and publishers wish to thank the following who have kindly given permission for the use of copyright material: the University of North Carolina Press, for the tables and extracts from *Cuba: The*

Economic and Social Revolution, edited by Dudley Seers, © University of North Carolina Press; and the editor of *Socialist Revolution*, for the extracts from the author's article, 'Incentives, Equality and Power in Revolutionary Cuba', which originally appeared in no 23, April 1975.

None of the above mentioned organisations or people should be held responsible for any errors, poor analysis or opinions put forth in what follows.

Part One

Prelude to Socialist Development

1 The Agricultural Setting of the Cuban Revolution

When the Cuban revolution triumphed at the beginning of 1959, a majority of Cuba's population—about 53 per cent—lived in the urban areas. Yet the Cuban economy was dominated by rural, agricultural activity. Agriculture, particularly sugar, determined the ups and downs of the nation's business, and the problems and conflicts of the rural areas were at the centre of Cuba's economic life.

Agriculture directly accounted for about a quarter of national income and employed over 40 per cent of the work force in pre-1959 Cuba. In manufacturing, the largest industries were those directly tied to agriculture. The sugar industry alone accounted for 5 per cent of total domestic product, or about a quarter of all manufacturing activity.

The dominance of agriculture, especially sugar, was particularly pronounced in the annual cycle of the economy. The period of harvest (the *zafra*) from November until March was relatively active, and the rest of the year was known as the dead season (*el tiempo muerto*). In 1957, for example, the unemployment rate fluctuated between 9.1 per cent in March and 15.1 per cent in August; these figures do not take account of so-called disguised unemployment which was especially severe in *el tiempo muerto*.

Furthermore, Cuba was highly dependent on foreign trade, and agriculture-based exports accounted for the lion's share of foreign-exchange earnings. Sugar sales alone made up 75–80 per cent of export earnings. The next largest component of export earnings was the 7 per cent or so provided by tobacco.

In some nations much less urbanised than Cuba, the modern industrial sector is more independent of agriculture. In those economies, agriculture is to a large extent small-scale subsistence production. The agricultural surplus is small, the role of the market in the rural areas is limited, and the principal commodities—for example, food grains—do not tie in with extensive industrial processing. Class relations in the

3

country are quite distinct from those in the city, and the central forces of social and economic development operate in rather different ways.

But such an economic structure of sharp separation and distinction between town and country did not exist in Cuba. To begin with, Cuba's main crop, sugar, was one which is entirely processed and marketed. Moreover, the growing of sugar cane was directly and thoroughly tied to the sugar mills not only in the production process but often in common-ownership bonds or contract relations as well. Workers in the cane fields were wage labourers or peasants who depended on wages for a significant portion of their income. Consequently, cane workers depended on the market to provide them with their daily needs. In cattle ranching, Cuba's other large-scale agricultural activity, the system of organisation and the ties to the rest of the economy were similar to those in sugar (although cattle production was a much less labour-intensive activity).

In the parts of agriculture which were operated as small-scale peasant production—tobacco, coffee and food crops—farming was specialised and commercially oriented. To a great extent, peasants in Cuba produced for the market, and depended on the market for their own consumption needs. Thus, both large plantations and ranches and small peasant plots in pre-revolutionary Cuba were part of the nation's capitalist network, in which agriculture was the central activity.

SOCIALIST REVOLUTIONS AND HISTORICAL STRUCTURES

This structural setting in which the Cuban revolution took place was in sharp contrast to the situations in other countries which have experienced socialist revolutions. It is useful to note the differences in order to avoid stereotypical views of revolution and socialist agriculture.

The situation in Russia prior to 1917, in particular, was much more one of separation between town and country. No more than 20 per cent of Russia's pre-First World War population lived in urban areas. Industry was based not on agricultural processing, but on heavy-goods sectors such as machinery and metallurgy, which grew to meet the needs of the railways and the czar's armies. Most agricultural workers were peasants, who did produce a small marketable surplus of grain, but who also produced for their own needs. Large estates were the primary surplus producers, but they relied on sharecroppers and other labourers who were primarily peasants themselves; wage labour was a secondary form of exploitation.

While Russian agriculture was as much dominated by remnants of feudalism as by capitalism, the industrial sector was rapidly modernising and creating an urban proletariat. As a consequence of this distinction between rural and urban life, the Russian Revolution itself took on a double character. The politically dominant working-class-based revolution in the urban areas was anti-capitalist and guided by socialist organisation, aspirations and ideology. The numerically dominant revolution in the countryside was more simply anti-landlord, and it was guided by the peasants' aspirations for control of the land, often on an individualistic basis.

Thus the particular historical structure of the Russian economy set the context for the two-sided character of the revolution. Out of this situation emerged many of the particular conflicts, institutions and problems of Soviet agriculture (and, indeed, Soviet society). The historical structure was very different from that of Cuba, and consequently any effort to use the Soviet experience in order to generate generalisations applicable to Cuba would, at best, have serious limitations.

Of course, the historical structure of a nation's economy in itself—the separatness or closeness of town and country *per se*—does not determine the course of revolutionary developments. The pre-revolutionary Chinese economy was similar to that of Russia in terms of the relation between the cities and rural areas. However, the degree of conflict between the rural and urban populations that characterised socialist development in Russia was largely absent in China because the political centre of the Chinese Revolution was established early on within the numerically dominant rural population. Consequently the socialist development emerging from the historical structure of China's economy was very distinct from that of the Soviet Union.

And Cuban socialist development has been a far cry from that of either of the classical Soviet or Chinese experiences. Cuba's own economic structure and its own particular political history have created different sorts of problems and different sorts of solutions. As we shall see, for example, Cuban agricultural development has been able to proceed since 1959 with the continued existence of a large private sector; yet conflict between the private and public sectors appears to have been minimal. Also, within the public sector, Cuba moved extremely rapidly in the formation of state farms.

There are, to be sure, similarities between Cuba's socialist development and the experiences of other nations. Likewise, there are important
similarities in historical structure. Regardless of differences in the
relation between agriculture and industry, Cuba, like pre-1917 Russia
and pre-1949 China, was a nation in the periphery of the international
capitalist system. All three countries were characterised by certain basic
features of underdevelopment.

STAGNATION OF CUBAN AGRICULTURE

In Cuba, as elsewhere, one basic feature of underdevelopment was the
stagnation of agricultural production. Per capita agricultural production was actually lower on the eve of the triumph of the revolution
than it had been at the beginning of the 1950s, though the late 1950s did
show a notable improvement as compared to the middle of the decade
(see Table 1.1).

TABLE 1.1 Agricultural production, 1949–58

Year	Total ag. production (quantum indices, 1952–6 = 100)	Ag. production per capita	Sugar harvest (metric tons)
1949	90.53	101.3	5.1
1950	100.60	110.1	5.4
1951	101.27	108.3	5.6
1952	118.08	123.5	7.2
1953	96.90	99.0	5.0
1954	96.71	96.7	4.8
1955	92.43	90.5	4.4
1956	95.85	91.8	4.6
1957	108.00	101.0	5.7
1958	107.00	98.0	5.8

SOURCE
Ritter (1974) p. 113. The figures are based on various UN documents. Ritter notes they are
'fragmentary and incomplete'. The 1949 sugar-harvest figure is from International Bank
for Reconstruction and Development's *Report on Cuba* (1951) p. 799.

Sugar production accounted for roughly 40 per cent of farming
income, and cane fields covered 60–70 per cent of cultivated land. A
record sugar production of 7.2 million tons was achieved in 1952, but no
trend in sugar output was apparent during the decade (see Table 1.1). In

the livestock sector, there were 15 per cent fewer head of cattle in 1959 than in 1940. (There does, however, appear to have been some upward trend in the cattle stock during the early 1950s, and the longer-run decline in cattle was somewhat offset by an increased number of hogs.)

In other sectors of Cuban agriculture, the situation was not so bleak. Tobacco production grew substantially in the post-Second World War period, and coffee production showed signs of growth. Nonetheless, the overwhelming importance of sugar and livestock (see Table 1.2) meant that their poor showings were not offset by these limited developments.

TABLE 1.2 Composition of farm income and farms, classified according to principal source of income in Cuba, 1945

Principal source of income	Number of farms in 000s	% of all farms	% share in total farm income	% of income from principal crop or activity*
Sugar cane	29.1	18.2	41.6	86.6
Livestock	28.8	18.0	20.9	82.2
Tobacco	22.8	14.2	10.2	75.9
Cereals and Beans	26.8	16.8	9.4	63.8
Root crops	15.7	9.8	6.7	60.7
Coffee	9.3	5.8	2.7	75.6
Tree fruit	4.8	3.0	2.0	70.6
Garden truck	1.2	0.9	0.9	62.1
Other crops	11.4	7.1	5.0	73.9
Forest products	0.9	0.6	0.6	79.3
	9.1†	5.6†		
Totals	159.9	100.0	100.0	

NOTES
* That is, the percentage of the total income of farms of each type which comes from their principal crop or activity. For example, farms whose principal crop was sugar obtained 86.6 per cent of their income from sugar; farms whose principal activity was cattle raising obtained 82.2 per cent of their income from cattle—and so on.
† No income reported.

SOURCE
Bianchi (1964) p. 81, based on Cuban Agricultural Census, 1946.

The stagnation of Cuban agriculture was part of a general stagnation of the Cuban economy. A sugar-led economic expansion during the first quarter of the century had been thoroughly terminated by the great depression. While there were ups and downs in the subsequent decades and some significant expansion of investment during the 1950s, no continuing expansion of production took place. An explanation of Cuba's agricultural and general economic stagnation may be found in the country's history of underdevelopment.

2 Imperialism, Class Power and Cuban Underdevelopment

The long domination of Cuba by imperialist powers and the consequent nature of class relations within Cuba were central factors effecting the nation's underdevelopment. Most nations outside Europe and North America have had the course of their development shaped by imperialist domination. But few have experienced the degree of subjugation suffered by Cuba during its 400 years under formal Spanish control as a colony and its 60 years under the *de facto* control of the United States.

From the end of the eighteenth century on, sugar was the primary mechanism connecting Cuba to the world economy, and the expansion of the sugar nexus was a major determinant of the country's class structure. Thus, to a large extent, the modern economic history of Cuba may be told as the history of sugar. In particular, two features of the class structure that was formed in the colonial era deserve special emphasis: the weakness of the national capitalist class and the large size of the wage-labour force.

FORMATION OF CLASS STRUCTURE
IN THE COLONIAL ERA

Sugar became established as a major Cuban export crop during the last decades of the eighteenth century, and rode to unchallenged ascendency on the great expansion of world trade that took place in the first half of the nineteenth century. Between 1800 and 1850, sugar exports expanded almost nine-fold, from 26,000 tons to 223,000 tons. Politically, the growing economic importance of sugar placed the owners of sugar estates and mills in the seats of power; they formed a 'sugar oligarchy' which, in alliance with the Spanish crown, dominated the island's political affairs.

9

The development of other groups which might contend for power—most particularly the nascent manufacturers—was severely restricted. In the first place, manufacturing was directly restricted by regulations imposed by Spain in its attempt to maintain some market, however limited, for the products of its own industry. But perhaps of greater importance, Cuban manufacturing was pre-empted by foreign competition. Spain had been forced by international pressure to ease trade restriction from 1818 onward, and the consequence was the continual growth of foreign activity—particularly from the US and the UK—in the Cuban economy. The rising importance of Cuban trade with the US and the UK during the nineteenth century is indicated by the figures in Table 2.1, showing Cuban exports to various nations.

TABLE 2.1 Cuban exports to selected countries, 1800s

| | Millions of pesos | |
	1826–30	1856–60
United States	3.72	18.37
Spain	2.80	5.31
England	1.54	8.66
France	1.16	2.58
Germany	1.68	2.48
Latin America		0.97

SOURCE
Pino-Santos (1964) p. 95.

The expansion of manufacturing and the rise of a nationally oriented capitalist class would have required, at the very least, some protection and state support—for example, by way of infrastructure development. Yet, with the sugar oligarchy firmly in control of the political apparatus and with its interest in free trade, the nineteenth century saw no movement in that direction. Indeed, the sugar interests quite naturally pursued policies which exacerbated a lopsided national development. The organisation of roads and other aspects of the infrastructure, for example, was defined by the need of transporting sugar to export centres rather than by any efforts to meet the needs of internal commerce. And policies were adopted which allowed Cuba's forests to be devoured in the boilers of the sugar mills.

To establish its position, a national capitalist class in Cuba would have had to undertake a political struggle against the sugar oligarchy. On its own, it was never powerful enough to enter into such a struggle. Afraid of the potential power of Cuba's growing working class, national capitalists opted—and in the coming years would continue to opt—for subservience to sugar and foreign interests.

The large size of Cuba's wage-labour force is the second feature of the nation's class structure which deserves emphasis. While the dominance of sugar had subverted the rise of a modern national capitalist class, it had nonetheless created a modern proletariat. During its period of ascendency, sugar production had been based on slave labour. When slavery was abolished in 1886, former slaves were quickly transformed to wage labourers. Moreover, as it grew, the sugar complex pushed the small peasants off the land, undermined the markets of the small craftsmen, and drew small farmers and craftsmen alike into the ranks of sugar-dependent wage labourers. However, the process was not always complete, especially among the small farmers, many of whom both cultivated their own plots and worked in the sugar complex. Nonetheless, the process was a powerful one, receiving the following description from Manuel Moreno Fraginales:

> In its dramatic upsurge the sugarmill absorbed all the small peasantry raising tobacco and minor crops, the shipyard and foundry workers, and innumerable other small artisans. It is on record how the growing white populations of Guines, Santiago, and Bejucal were either drawn into the sugarmills by the high wages or forced into them by the destructive violence of the sugar producers.

While the weakness of Cuba's national bourgeoisie was typical of many poor countries, the large size of its proletariat, though not unique, was somewhat unusual. More often, underdeveloped nations are characterised by a higher percentage of working people being small peasants. But the nature of sugar production—plantation agriculture plus large rural industrial units (the sugar mills)—led to the creation of a particularly large proletariat in Cuba. The division between town and country was thus not nearly so sharp in Cuba as in many underdeveloped nations. Even among the Cuban peasantry, there were considerable ties to the proletariat, through those family members and poorer peasants who worked—at least part of the year—on the plantations and constituted a 'semi-proletariat'. (I discuss in Chapter 4 below the political significance of this minimal rural–urban distinction among working people. It should be noted that the Spanish had completely obliterated Cuba's indigenous pre-Colombian population. Thus there was little basis in Cuba for a sharply distinct, traditional peasant culture as, for example, in many other parts of Latin America.)

The structure of the labour force established in the nineteenth century would continue to characterise the Cuban economy up to the time of the Cuban Revolution. As Table 2.2 indicates, in 1952, 63.6 per cent of Cuba's agricultural labour force consisted of wage labourers (though there is some controversy over the validity of these data—see notes to Table 2.2).

TABLE 2.2 Agricultural labour force in Cuba, 1952

	Thousands of persons	%
Farm labourers	596.8	72.9
Paid workers	520.9	63.6
Unpaid family workers	66.7	8.1
Administrators and foremen	9.2	1.1
Ranchers and farmers	221.9	27.1
Total agricultural labour force	818.7	100.0

SOURCE
Bianchi (1964) p. 80 from *Censos de Población, Viviendas y Electoral,* 1953.

NOTE
Pollitt, in various writing cited in the references to Chapter 1, has called into question the widely held view that Cuba's rural labour force was so thoroughly proletarianised. While Pollitt makes a strong case that the data such as these may overstate proletarianisation, there seems little doubt that as compared to most other poor countries, Cuba's rural labour force was far more one characterised by wage labour.

THE ERA OF THE REPUBLIC AND US INFLUENCE

With the successful culmination of the military struggle for independence in 1898 and the formation of the Cuban republic, the dominant foreign interests in Cuba were those of the US. In fact, the importance of the US in Cuban affairs had been rising throughout the century and had grown especially rapidly after Spain had been forced to grant various trade concessions following the first phase of the independence struggle (1868–78). Just before independence, US investments in Cuba totalled $50 million. With the open door provided by independence, the value of US assets rose to $160 million in 1906, $205 million dollars in 1911, and $1.2 billion in 1923. (Note, however, that these data are not fully consistent with data for later years – see Table 2.3. The apparent decline between 1923 and 1929 is, most likely, an artefact resulting from inconsistent data.)

The growing US investment was concentrated in the sugar industry. By 1920 US-owned sugar mills manufactured 48 per cent of Cuba's sugar, and by 1927 they produced 70–75 per cent. The mills, it may be assumed, owned or controlled a somewhat lesser—but also large—share of the cane-producing land. During the 1920s, US investments extended into other areas of the Cuban economy: a large share of electric utilities, the telephone system and the principal port facilities of Havana were in US hands by the late 1920s; the railway system of Cuba was dominated by US concerns, along with one major British operation (though many sugar mills had their own private networks); and US banks held $100 million of Cuban government debt (not to mention private debt). Nonetheless, more than half of US business investments remained in sugar; and in 1929 US investments outside the sugar industry, agriculture, and services accounted for only 6 per cent of the total (see Table 2.3). (It is worth noting that total US direct foreign investment was $7.5 billion in 1929; so that in Cuba amounted to 12 per cent of the total. Also, Cuba accounted for 26 per cent of US direct investment in Latin America at that time—see Table 2.3).

TABLE 2.3 Direct investment by US business in Cuba, 1929–58 (book value in US $ millions)

	1929	1950	1958
1 Agriculture, including sugar industry	575	263	265
2 Services	290	305	386
3 Manufacturing	45	54	80
4 Petroleum and mining	9	35	270
5 Total US direct investment in Cuba	919	657	1001
6 Total US direct foreign investment	7500	11800	29700
7 Total US direct investment in Latin America	3500	4600	9000
8 (5) as a % of (6)	12.3%	5.6%	3.4%
9 (5) as a % of (7)	26.3%	14.3%	11.1%

SOURCE
Cuba data from Seers (1964) p. 16, based on *US Investment in Latin America* (US Dept. of Commerce). Other data from Weisskopf (1972) from various US Dept. of Commerce sources.

The non-industrial bias of foreign investment in Cuba had several roots: the lack of an infrastructure for industrial development, the limited market resulting from the extremely unequal distribution of income, and political instability. Yet these factors could not be altered while there was no Cuban class with the strength and interest to undertake the lead in national development. And no such class could emerge while foreign interests dominated the economy.

US businesses themselves had little interest in Cuba's development. As it was, Cuba provided them with useful avenues for investment. The steps required for development would have threatened even more political instability, upset the labour-supply system in agriculture, and had only distant pay-offs. In addition, US industry had access to the Cuban market through trade and thus little impetus for industrial investments.

Various trade agreements between Cuba and the US, especially the Reciprocal Trade Agreement of 1934, assured the continuous access of US business to the Cuban market. The Reciprocal Trade Agreement, which remained in effect (with some modifications) until the revolution, lowered Cuban duties on many items and specified that duties would not be raised for a long list of goods; it reduced internal taxes and quantitative restrictions on items originating in the US; and it prohibited exchange control.

In return for the access to the Cuban market granted to US businesses in various agreements, Cuba was given a share of the US sugar market. Entrance to the US market on favourable terms did mitigate the impact on the Cuban economy of world market fluctuations. After rising steadily in the first quarter of the century, however, Cuba's sugar exports to the US were cut back or held constant by various US government adjustments; and the peak of the 1920s was never surpassed (see Table 2.4). Most important, the trade structure which resulted from the various agreements with the US assured the continued stagnation of Cuban industry, and the dominance of sugar.

TABLE 2.4 Cuban sugar exports to the US, 1906–13 to 1950–2 (millions of short tons)*

1906–13	1.7	1934–40	1.9
1914–18	2.1	1941–5	2.8
1919–29	3.2	1946–9	3.1
1930–3	2.2	1950–2	3.0

* Period averages.   SOURCE Seers (1964) p. 9.

It should be stressed that the domination of the Cuban economy by US business was imposed on Cuba by the US government, whose actions are highlighted by a series of direct interventions. To begin with, as Cuba's struggle for independence from Spain was nearing victory, the US intervened and occupied the country. As a condition for ending the occupation, the US government imposed, as part of the Cuban constitution, the infamous Platt Amendment, whereby the US was given the authority to intervene militarily in Cuba at its own discretion. (The Platt Amendment also placed limits on Cuba's freedom to determine its own foreign policy and contract debt.) The Platt Amendment was invoked three times: US troops were sent in 1906, 1912, and 1917. When the Platt Amendment was replaced by the 'good neighbour policy', US political authority over Cuban affairs had been firmly established. In 1933, when the Cuban people rebelled against the Machado dictatorship, the US government engineered a transfer of power to other friendly groups, without a direct military intervention. And in 1934 the Reciprocal Trade Agreement was established.

The US economic and political domination of Cuba was so thorough that Cuba did not share in the general wave of industrialisation that occurred in most of Latin America during the 1930s and early 1940s. In the late 1940s and 1950s, though the focus of foreign investment shifted slightly in favour of manufacturing (see Table 2.3), the general stagnation of the economy continued.

The cutback in US foreign investment brought about by the great depression and the Second World War did significantly reduce the role of US owners in sugar production. Moreover, with the rise in the role of Cuban owners, there was also a rise in the role of the smaller, independent cane growners (the *colonos*). Still the large estates, often connected to the sugar mills, continued to dominate Cuban agriculture in the post-Second World War period. In 1945, 8 per cent of Cuban farms constituted 70 per cent of the farm land. By the time of the revolution, there appears to have been no reduction in this degree of concentration. At the beginning of 1959, the 28 largest sugar companies owned 1437.3 thousand hectares; and they controlled another 617.3 thousand hectares through rental agreements, thus putting 28 companies in control of 20 per cent of the farm land. As another example of concentration at the beginning of 1959, the 40 largest cattle ranches owned 992.1 thousand hectares, or almost 10 per cent of the farm land.

Thus the system of large estates, a product of Cuba's long subordination in the international division of labour, continued to dominate the economy up to the time of the revolution. It is therefore necessary, especially in the context of understanding the role of agriculture in Cuba's development, to turn to the question of those estates.

3 Concentrated Land Holdings and Agricultural Stagnation

The structure of land holdings in pre-1959 Cuba was typical of much of Latin America. The great majority of the land was held in large estates. Small operators—peasant owners, sharecroppers, tenants and squatters—shared the remainder of the agricultural territory (see Table 6.1 for a detailed quantitative description of the distribution of land holdings prior to the revolution). The most important agricultural activities, sugar and cattle, were most thoroughly dominated by the large estates. Small farmers who did operate in sugar were dependent on contract relations with the mills. In cattle raising, where small operators played a significant role in breeding and raising calves, market power was in the hands of the large holders. The small farmers did play the main role in the production of food crops and secondary cash crops—tobacco and coffee. But the dynamic of Cuban agriculture was determined primarily by the activities of the large landowners.

The low productivity of Cuba's estates was severe. For example, in the 1950s, of 18 major sugar-producing nations, Cuba ranked 17th in terms of sugar-cane yields per hectare. And the general stagnation of sugar output and total agricultural output from the 1920s on has been noted in Chapter 1. The immediate causes of this low productivity and stagnation are to be found in the nature of Cuba's system of large estates.

The problem of production on the large estates was manifested in the low rate of land utilisation. In the 1940s and 1950s, only about one-fifth of Cuba's farm land was cultivated (see Table 3.1). Yet a World Bank mission reported in 1953 that nearly 60 per cent of the land was tillable. While some 40 per cent of farm land was utilised as pasture, a large portion was not used productively. Moreover, the land-utilisation rate decreased as farm size increased. With substantial land in reserve, the large estate owners, especially the sugar planters, followed a system of

17

TABLE 3.1 Cuban land in farms by use, 1945, and area under cane and cane area harvested in Cuba, 1950s (areas in '000s of hectares)

	Culti-vated	Cane	Pastures	Woods	Marabu*	Other uses†	Idle	Total
1945								
Total farm area	1970·4		3897·2	1265·7	268.1	1650.4	25·2	9077
Proportion of farmland	21·7		42·9	18·9	3·0	18·2	0·3	100
1952–8 average								
Area under cane		1434·8						
Cane area harvested		1073·6						

NOTES
* A thicket-like growth, one of the worst agricultural pests in Cuba.
† Includes roads, buildings, and unproductive lands.

SOURCE
Bianchi (1964) pp. 84–5, based on *Cuban Agricultural Census 1945* and *Anuarero Azucarero* (1959).

extensive farming rather than making efforts to raise yield through intensive cultivation.

STAGNATION AND PROFIT

The operation of Cuba's large farms would seem to be inconsistent with a system organised in pursuit of profit, and thus many analysts attempt to explain structures like Cuba's as a consequence of traditional, pre-capitalist modes of organisation. Especially in Cuba of the 1950s—with imports of food and agricultural raw materials that could be grown in the country and a high rate of unemployment—the low rate of land utilisation would appear to run contrary to a pursuit of profits. Nonetheless, there are several factors which together explain why profit-minded large-farm owners did not push towards the development of Cuba's agriculture. (The term 'latifundia' is often employed to charac-terise the large estates in pre-1959 Cuba and in Latin America generally. The term, however, often implies a pre-capitalist mode of organisation, and, as will be argued below, Cuba's large estates are best understood when seen as being within the capitalist system. Consequently, the term 'latifundia' will be avoided here.)

To begin with, from the point of view of the profit-minded estate owners, investment in agricultural expansion was often undesirable in comparison with available alternatives. The combination of a general capital shortage and opportunities for speculation in urban lands and commerce created a situation in much of Latin America in which any surplus generated in agriculture would be redirected to non-productive activity in the urban areas. Moreover, such investments could be undertaken as marginal propositions, without any need for complementary development or reshaping of the social and economic infrastructure.

Investment in agriculture, on the other hand, tended to be less attractive, in large part because of the lack of social and physical infrastructure. A labour force with the requisite technical skills for modern agriculture was lacking, for example. And, instead of a lack of capital, the missing ingredients in production expansion were often the organisational and control factors, or the availability of administrative personnel. In this context, an expansion of agricultural output would have required a major effort at social transformation, almost necessarily undertaken by the government rather than by the individual large landowner.

The particular conditions of the rural work force in Cuba made the pre-revolutionary situation there a stereotypical case of the general Latin American circumstance. Over 40 per cent of the rural population was illiterate. Less than 10 per cent of rural homes were electrified, and less than 3 per cent had any indoor plumbing. Throughout the rural areas there were only three general hospitals prior to 1959. These conditions of poverty and low socio-cultural development—for many a legacy of their slavery—reflected the fact that Cuba's rural workers were poorly equipped to provide the labour power required in the process of modernisation and mechanisation. Any substantial economic transformation of agriculture would have required a concomitant transformation of the rural work force.

Yet in Cuba, as throughout Latin America, steps to alter this status quo would have set in motion events that might threaten the power and profits of the landowners. Investments in economic infrastructure, education facilities, and so forth would have led to fuller employment and higher wages. Such changes would almost necessarily have been a threat to existing power relations. Consequently the low productivity and stagnation of agriculture in Cuba was, paradoxically, a condition for the continued prosperity of the large holders. They accordingly followed a strategy—affecting both their private-investment activity and the social policies which they pursued through the government—of avoiding policies which would upset the labour-supply structure.

MARKET STRATEGY AND IDLE LANDS

In addition, and of special importance in the Cuban situation, the expansion of agricultural output was inhibited by the limits of the market for sugar. During the early 1950s Cuba was the world's largest producer and exporter of sugar. The nation accounted for about 17 per cent of the world's sugar production and supplied more than 50 per cent of the sugar which entered the 'free' international markets. Moreover, considering only the US market, Cuban sugar accounted for 37 per cent of the total consumption in the 1950–3 period (and during the 1940s the figure had averaged over 42 per cent). In these circumstances, a sugar-supply strategy for Cuban sugar enterprises was a possibility.

As part of that strategy, the major sugar operators found it in their interest to maintain a sizable portion of their land in reserve, so that they could readily respond to changes in demand. It appears that sugar producers were sufficiently organised to limit production in an effort to avoid crises of overproduction and declining prices. At the same time, their mechanism for providing for years of favourable market conditions meant that large areas of cultivatable land, which might have been used for other crops, lay idle.

The policies of the large land holders explain the poor conditions of agriculture on their own large estates. In an agricultural economy like pre-revolutionary Cuba, with the high degree of concentration of landownership, stagnation on the large estates is almost the same as general stagnation. In addition, the policies of the landowners created a social environment that inhibited successful change by small farmers.

Small farmers in any poor economy are severely limited by such factors as lack of capital, an inability to take risks, and a lack of available modern inputs. Even if individual small farmers overcome these constraints, in an economy like Cuba's the large-estate owners' control of idle lands and their interest in maintaining control of those lands prevent small farmers from accumulating land to expand their success. There are, to be sure, exceptions, cases for example where small peasants attain some success through particularly intense cultivation. Tobacco production in Cuba was one such case. But the production success of some tobacco farms did not alter the general picture of stagnation in Cuban agriculture, nor did it bring substantial prosperity to the farmers themselves.

Agricultural expansion is not necessarily impossible in the type of situation which existed in pre-1959 Cuba. The causes of Cuba's agricultural stagnation discussed above may not be absolute in all cases, but they seem to have been dominant in Cuba and of importance throughout Latin America.

4 The Struggle for Political Power

The stagnation of Cuban agriculture, and of the Cuban economy generally, was an important factor giving rise to revolutionary movement within Cuban society. Without economic growth, there was no way the conflicting material demands of various social groups could be met. Moreover, in addition to stagnation, Cuba's heavy dependence on sugar created considerable instability, both on an annual basis and over the longer run. And economic instability piled insecurity on top of the economic deprivation of the Cuban masses.

As the twentieth century progressed, Cuba's upper classes were unable to establish and maintain political stability. In the colonial period the sugar oligarchy combined with Spanish authority to administer the nation's affairs. But in the twentieth century US capital undermined the position of the sugar operators, and urbanization and the rising political role of the Cuban working class created forces that the traditional élite could not contain. Nor did any national capitalist class emerge with sufficient strength to control the situation. Consequently the history of the nation since independence was characterised by frequent violence and changes in political authority. The historian Ramon Ruiz has noted that, 'On the political front, violence characterised almost a third of the Republic's history: the first decade of the twentieth century, the late twenties until 1936, and, again, after 1953.' No political party or group of parties was able to establish a stable existence, and authority was administered through political cliques, the *caudillos*. Yet. throughout the era of the Republic, the Cuban working class was growing in size and strength.

THE LONG HISTORY OF STRUGGLE

The rise of the Cuban working class was marked by a long history of political conflict. And the movement which Fidel Castro led to power in the 1950s had its roots in the long series of struggles beginning with the Ten Years' War against Spain, which commenced in 1868.

Prolonged struggle seems to have an important political impact on its participants. In revolutions, when formal victory is attained without a long period of combat, the changes are often not so far reaching. In such circumstances, the struggle for power usually does not extend to establish broad social foundations. Consequently, authority after the seizure of power is likely to be held by a relatively narrow social group without a well-developed political base. Long struggle, on the other hand, leads the revolutionary activists—if they are to be successful—to establish a firm base among the populace. Then, after the seizure of authority, the course of the revolution is in large part determined by the fact that it has a mass base. Furthermore, long struggle tends to undermine the ideological foundations of the old regime and to facilitate the actions of a revolutionary force in creating a new order; for in long struggle, revolutionary groups gain legitimacy and revolutionary leaders prove themselves. Although the 'one hundred years' struggle' in Cuba was not a continuous process, it nonetheless appears to have effected the sort of radicalisation associated with long revolutionary struggles.

The nature of the battle for independence in the nineteenth century set the stage for the later political struggle. From the beginnings of its military phase in the 1860s, the independence movement spread to include members of almost all segments of Cuban society—landowners, slaves, artisans, workers, small farmers. And, thus, the Ten Years' War began to establish the broad social character of revolutionary struggle in Cuba. In the 1890s, with José Martí playing an especially significant role, the ideological foundation of the independence struggle began to take on a radical and anti-imperialist character. When success was near, however, the US government intervened and was able to dominate the post-independence character of Cuban politics and economic organisation. Consequently the Cuban struggle for independence, while formally successful, was a frustrated revolution. The struggle still had a long road ahead.

In the first quarter of the twentieth century, the expansion of sugar, along with the growing concentration of sugar milling, increased the importance of the Cuban working class in Cuban politics. In this early period, the organisational achievements of Cuban labour unions were limited, but they began to play a significant educational role. Anarcho-syndicalists were particularly important, and this Spanish heritage combined with antipathy toward the growing role of US business to create a militant and relatively radical strain within the union movement. From the mid-1920s both labour unions and the Communist Party of Cuba played increasing roles. As the sugar boom gave out, many workers were more readily drawn into the unions, and the opportunities of the Communist Party expanded. In addition, the development of an international communist movement gave impetus to events in Cuba, as it did elsewhere.

In 1933, when the revolution against the dictator Machado took place, the labour movement played a major role in bringing down the government, and Communist participation, though not decisive, was significant. The events of 1933 were important in the radicalisation of the long struggle. To begin with, the political struggle of 1933 created the direct political antecedents of the movement which Fidel Castro would lead to power in the 1950s. For that early struggle had created a strong current of revolutionary ideology and action within the Cuban middle class, especially in the student movement. Also, the political disruption of 1933 and, again, the frustration of revolution engineered by the US government established a political context for the emergence of Communist strength in the late 1930s.

While Communists had not led the revolution of 1933, they were active and did make major organisational gains within the working class. The following quotation from Ramon Ruiz's history of the Cuban revolution captures the drama as well as the importance of the period:

> . . . in August 1933, urban workers in Havana, again with Communists participating, launched their own strike, which in less than a month forced Machado to flee. . . . Demanding better working conditions, higher wages and recognition of their unions, 200,000 sugar workers joined the protest. On August 21, 1933, the workers seized a sugar mill in Camaguey Province; in less than a month, thirty-five other mills had fallen into their hands, and by early September, 30 percent of the country's sugar production was under the workers' control. Meanwhile, rural Soviets made their appearance at Mabay, Jaronú, Senado, Santa Luciá and other centrales [sugar-mill complexes]. Mill managers were held prisoner; labor guards at the mills wore red armbands for uniforms; strikers fraternized with soldiers and police; and, at Antilla, a red flag fluttered over city hall, while Communist-led demonstrations in Santiago forced the mayor and the provincial governor to flee their offices. Never before had Cuba witnessed such labor unrest.

In 1934 the Communist-led 4th National Labour Congress claimed 400,000 members, and union activity was placed on an industrial (rather than craft) basis. By 1940, Communist Party membership stood at 43,000 and would grow to 150,000 by the end of the Second World War. And according to the 1951 report of the International Bank for Reconstruction and Development, the Communists had 'succeeded in attaining practically complete control of the Cuban labor movement' and had formed 'a relatively compact and disciplined proletariat'.

In the late 1940s and early 1950s, under the pressure of thorough government repression, the Cuban Communist Party was greatly weakened and membership dropped to 55,000 in 1952 and only 12,000 in 1958. Moreover, under attack and following the international communist line of peaceful coexistence, the Party's militance and revolutionary activity declined in this period.

In spite of the declining leadership role of the Communists, Cuban labour unions remained large and important in the 1950s. In 1954 the Cuban Federation of Workers claimed over 1 million members out of a total labour force of less than 2 million. (It should be noted that many agricultural sugar workers were unionised.) Moreover, in the 1950s the government and business were forced to make major concessions to organised labour on wage issues. However, organised labour greatly reduced its political role and became dominated by an ideology of 'business unionism'.

The rising role of 'business unionism' and an increasingly close relation between union officials and the government greatly reduced the unions' political and educational roles. Cuban unions primarily became institutions through which workers could obtain better wages. They became less a vehicle for political activism, and, further, they did not challenge management prerogatives on the control of production. Consequently they were not operating as institutions which could train workers for taking some greater part in economic organisation.

Nonetheless, the history of struggle had created a relatively cohesive and class-conscious proletariat. Skilled workers, for example, do not appear to have seen themselves as a separate and privileged group apart from the rest of working class, and the racial divisions within the working class were much less than in other former slave nations. Also, while formal organisation of the Cuban working class was concentrated in its industrial segment, the existence of unionisation within the major rural wage-labour force buttressed working-class strength. And, according to Maurice Zeitlin, in his important study of the Cuban working class, 'agricultural labourers were more likely [in comparison to traditional peasants] to compare their lot with that of other classes, to develop class consciousness and to organize, and to associate themselves with the struggles of the mill workers.'

The labour unions and the Communist Party would play little direct role in armed struggled leading up to the seizure of political power by the revolutionary forces at the beginning of 1959. Yet the influence of organised labour and of the Communists on the development of the revolution and on its course after 1959 had been well established by decades of activity and growth. As Ruiz sums up the situation, the urban proletariat was 'perhaps the one group in Cuban society acutely aware of its class interest—the result of decades of extremely effective popular education on the working of an economic system by communists and their predecessors, the anarcho-syndacalists'. Thus, the long struggle in Cuba was not simply a series of episodes of combat; in addition, the long struggle was the embodied political experience and organisation of the Cuban working class.

THE ARMED STRUGGLE

The armed struggle, which attained governmental authority at the beginning of 1959, started on 26 July 1953. On that date Fidel Castro led an armed group of 125 in an attack on the Moncada police barracks in Cuba's second city of Santiago. The attack was a failure, resulting in the death of many participants and the capture of the remainder. Viewed in isolation from the long history of political struggle in Cuba, the Moncada attack would appear as but an act of adventurism. Taking the entire armed struggle out of its historic context has, in fact, led to a great deal of misunderstanding of the Cuban revolution. Most particularly, Regis Debray's famous *Revolution in the Revolution: Armed Struggle and Political Struggle in Latin America* popularized internationally a view of the Cuban revolution which isolates the Moncada attack and the armed struggle of the 1950s from their historical antecedents. (Debray's view of the Cuban revolution in terms of a small band—a 'foco'—of armed men in the mountains was especially important because it was widely accepted that he was expressing Che Guevara's ideas as well as his own; also the Cuban government seemed to embrace Debray's views by lack of criticism and by publishing an initial edition of 200,000 copies of the book.)

However, in reality the Moncada attack had a rather profound impact because it took place as one further step in an extended history of organized political struggle. Moreover, the Cuban regime was extremely unpopular and lacked any substantial social base. Consequently, the Moncada attack was widely accepted as a legitimate revolutionary action, as another step in the long struggle. Indeed, so great was the popular support for the action that the government was forced to proceed cautiously with Castro and the other captured leaders. Except for those who were killed in and immediately after the attack, there were no executions; the leaders suffered only two years in jail and were than exiled.

In early December 1956, Castro returned to Cuba with a force of 82 to renew the combat against the regime. In three days most of the force. was wiped out, but the few survivors managed to establish a base of operations in Oriente Province from which they would move to take power in two years' time.

During 1957 and 1958, the Rebel Army grew, but it was never larger than 2000 persons. The success of such a small force resulted in part from the extreme weakness of the old regime. The dominant classes in Cuba had failed to consolidate their rule, and politics had degenerated to corruption and dictatorship in the 1950s. Even major segments of the upper classes were alienated from the regime. Furthermore, it would appear that the Cuban populace was 'ready for revolution'. The long struggle had established the general legitimacy of the revolutionary change. While other political groups—most particularly the Communist Party—did not support Castro's forces until near the end of the conflict, the political culture which had long been established within the Cuban working class and in other segments of the population was essential to the success of the armed combat.

And although various urban events of the struggle were not successes in themselves, they did contribute to the momentum of the revolution and help establish it as something more than the battles in the mountains. (These urban events included: a student attack on the presidential palace on 13 March 1957; a general strike set for August 1957; an uprising of naval officers on 5 September 1957; and another general strike set for 9 April 1958.)

Nevertheless, with no effective development of action in the cities, the revolution built itself in rural Cuba, most particularly in the remote, mountainous regions of Oriente Province. The peasants in this area, from whom the revolution gained important support, were not typical of the Cuban rural population. They were poorer and more isolated than their counterparts elsewhere in the nation. They, or their forebears, had established themselves in the remote areas to seek independence and refuge from the expansion of the large estates. Many were squatters, and continually in conflict with the government and large estate owners. They were poor and they wanted land. The social position of these Oriente peasants made them ready to support the revolution. Their isolation—that is, the weakness of the regime in these remote areas—made that support possible. Still, this support came slowly, only as the Rebel Army exhibited its staying power. According to Che Guevara:

> Little by little, as the peasants came to recognize the invincibility of the guerillas and the long duration of the struggle, they began responding more logically, joining our army as fighters. From that moment on, not only did they join our ranks but they provided supportive action. After that the guerilla army was strongly entrenched in the country-side, especially since it is usual for peasants to have relatives throughout the zone. This is what we call 'dressing the guerillas in palm leaves'.

During the final months of the campaign in the mountains, as the rebels began to establish a base area and a second front was opened, the Rebel Army began to implement social reforms. Some limited land reform was initiated and a few peasant schools were established. These reforms, however, were soon to be superseded by national programmes when the revolution gained power. They did not provide any great experience or training ground on which the revolution could later draw. But they did provide symbols and indications of the direction in which the revolution would move. These reform programmes and the support which the rebels gained from the peasants were factors encouraging the emphasis on rural change after 1959. There were many reasons why the revolution stressed the centrality of land reform and associated rural reforms (see Parts Two and Three), but the particular political experience of 1957 and 1958 gave a special strength to those programmes.

HISTORY AND SOCIALIST DEVELOPMENT

Thus, when the old regime finally collapsed and the rebel forces seized the government at the beginning of 1959, the Cuban revolution was widely perceived—and, indeed, in large perceived itself—as an agrarian or peasant revolution. The reality of history was a bit more complicated. The immediate struggle had been rural. But in its longer-run historical development the Cuban revolution was very much an urban and working-class phenomenon. Consequently the revolution might be characterised as having a double foundation: it was both a rural-peasant revolution and an urban-working-class revolution.

This double base and its particular character were major factors affecting the course of events after 1959. Much of post-1959 development in Cuba has revolved around the problem of finding an effective balance between the urban/industrial and rural/agricultural segments of the society. The nature of the revolutionary struggle—in its combined long-run and short-run aspects—established a social foundation for achieving such a balance. As we shall see in following chapters, solving the problem of rural–urban relations in Cuba has not been an easy task and continues to present difficulties in the 1970s. Yet if the revolutionary struggle had had a different character—if, for example, the armed conflict had been based in the working class—we could expect those problems to have developed in a rather different manner. Cuban revolutionary history has allowed socialist development to proceed on the basis of a relatively firm worker–peasant alliance. (A comparison with the Soviet Union might be noted in passing. In the Soviet Union, the peasants played a major role in the Revolution, but the role was independent of the Revolution's political leadership, the Bolsheviks. The Bolsheviks did not establish a base among the peasantry. Consequently the Soviets were unable to build on a firm worker–peasant alliance.)

The history of the Cuban revolution—the long revolutionary experience and the short military struggle—also had an important impact on the country's socialist development through creating a particular relationship between leaders and masses. On the one hand, the long organisational experience of the working class and its roles in the struggle over decades provided an important foundation for the reorganisation of the economy along socialist lines. Both the trade-union activity and the network of relationships developed by the Communist Party would be useful in this regard. On the other hand, no large segment of the working class, not even the active Communists, had played any significant role in the armed struggle itself. The Cuban revolution, in the immediate sense, was not made by the working class. Thus the working class had not been pulled in and transformed by the struggle. The combat did not bring forth working-class leaders nor did it contribute to the organisational strength of the working class. Moreover, the leaders of the revolution, in achieving success without building a mass movement, had not learned to rely on the masses for the articulation and execution of policy. (Both China and Vietnam, where the periods of armed struggle were so much longer and larger, provide examples of the way in which the period of combat can prepare the populace and the leadership for the organisational tasks of socialist development. In neither of those cases, however, was a modern working class anywhere near as large and important as in Cuba.)

In the following chapters, these points and their implications will receive considerable elaboration. Over and over again, we shall have occasion to refer back to these historical factors and the manner in which they have affected the organisational role of the working class in economic activity. Cuba's economic problems of the 1960s and its steps toward overcoming those problems in the 1970s are directly related to the political history of the revolution and its complex impact on the organisation of socialist development.

5 Prelude to Socialist Development: Successes and Setbacks

When the revolutionary government took power in Cuba, breaking the domination of imperialism and undertaking agrarian reform were high on its list of priorities. In particular, transforming the economic and social structure of rural Cuba was seen as an essential step in overcoming the stagnation of rural production. Also, rural transformation was seen as a basic factor in solving the country's unemployment problem, in developing income equality, and in beginning to wrest control of the economy from foreign interests.

A major land-reform programme (discussed in detail in the following chapter) was set in motion early in 1959. During the first three years of the new government's authority, the land reform, combined with other important actions of the government, went a long way towards destroying political, economic and social structures which had held Cuba in a condition of underdevelopment. Moreover, in the years 1959–61, a significant economic expansion accompanied the destruction of old institutions.

Destroying the old and creating the new, however, are not the same things. Indeed, in Cuba, the process of destroying the old contributed to the problems of agricultural production at the same time as it cleared the way for those problems to be solved. But the economic success of the 1959–61 period masked the nation's developing economic difficulties. And it was not until a severe crisis of production developed in the 1962–4 period, that a comprehensive development strategy—a strategy for creating the new—began to be formulated.

AN EARLY ILLUSION OF SUCCESS

Although the triumph of the revolution was the outcome of the military

31

struggle, there had been negligible physical destruction and a minimal disruption of economic activity. As it came to power, the revolutionary government had wide support among all classes. In spite of strong statements by Fidel Castro and other revolutionary leaders regarding their intentions to undertake major economic and social reform, their ascendency did not cause great alarm among Cuba's established dominant classes. The corruption of the old regime and nationalist sentiments put almost everyone in favour of some reforms. Consequently, as the Rebel Army rode into Havana, capital did not flee out the back door, and managers, technicians and professionals continued to perform their functions.

Moreover, in spite of the fact that the Cuban economy had been nearly stagnant in the preceding decade, the rate of new investment had been fairly high, and there was significant under-utilisation of capacity. Also, the investment in the mid-1950s appears to have been associated with a certain amount of import substitution. Thus, a potential existed for a short-run expansion of output without a great deal of new investment.

It is in this context, then—a revolutionary seizure of power without economic disruption and the existence of physical potential for expansion—that the early programmes of the new government had their impact. While data is sparse, the economic expansion of 1959–61 is clear. To begin with, sugar output in the three years was 5.9, 5.9, and 6.8 million tons, respectively. These harvests exceeded those of any other three-year period in Cuba's history. Other parts of agriculture also expanded in these years such that the index of agricultural production (1952–6 equals 100) rose from 108 in 1957 and 107 in 1958 to 112 in 1959, 114 in 1960, and 122 in 1961.

Information on industrial production is poor, but various estimates of overall economic growth for 1959 and 1960 range between 5 and 10 per cent per year, implying that growth rates for industry were substantially higher than those for agriculture. No comparable estimates seem to be available for 1961, but it appears that the large growth of the agricultural sector was counterbalanced by slowdown in the industrial sector.

A central explanation of the economic expansion of these early years is the major redistribution of income brought about by the many reforms of the new order (see Chapter 12 below). The consequent growth of consumer demand in the context of excess capacity in industry and under-utilised land in agriculture engendered a rapid expansion of output. Furthermore, the growth in the government's deficit between

1958 and 1961 more than offset the decline in private investment, marking an additional net contribution to demand.

The increased utilisation of land was also a direct consequence of the land reform of 1959. While in many cases renters, sharecroppers and squatters were simply given title to land they already operated, in many other instances, small operators obtained additional land and the state took over large estates. In both of these latter cases, it seems reasonable to assume that the intensity of land utilisation increased.

EMERGING PROBLEMS

However, the early production success of the Cuban revolution was largely illusory. In part it was the consequence of fortuitous circumstances—the earlier investment and existing excess capacity, for example. And in part, it was the result of the rapid expansion of demand. But Cuba's basic problems were not problems of insufficient aggregate demand. The basic problems were in the economic and social structures which had dominated Cuban life prior to 1959. And while the old structures had been destroyed in the 1959–61 period, new structures had not yet been created. Furthermore, the process of change in the early years contained its own contradictions: the same forces that generated the growth were also generating new problems. These problems, which will be analysed in the following chapters, included:

First, while the agrarian reform of 1959 was a far-reaching and radical restructuring of the rural sector, it was not complete. Hundreds of large and thousands of middle-sized farms still existed, and on these lands economic activity continued to be guided by a capitalist rationale. Threatened by the changes, these remaining large and middle farmers provided a class basis for political and economic resistance. The economic manifestations of this resistance were an excessive slaughter of livestock, over-harvesting of crops, poor upkeep and the cessation of investments. These actions constituted a *de facto* sabotage of the revolution, but it should be emphasised that for the most part they were probably economically rather than politically motivated: they were the reasonable response of profit-minded farmers to the uncertainty of their own future.

Second, the redistribution of income and the employment security created by the revolution disrupted the traditional system of labour incentives and supply in the rural areas. Yet no effective alternative system had been created. The consequences were a general agricultural labour shortage and a rise in the peasantry's own consumption of goods it produced.

Third, the rapid creation of state farms combined with the emigration of managers, administrators and skilled personnel created severe organisational problems. For example, of the 300 agronomists working in Cuba in 1959, approximately 270 left the country with the American enterprises in which they worked. The consequent organisational problems were exacerbated as the role of the market as an allocative mechanism was reduced and replaced by administrative processes.

Fourth, associated in part with the organisational problems of agriculture but having independent roots as well, the revolutionary process led to some serious economic-policy errors.

Class struggle and revolution in a particular nation can never be isolated phenomena, especially within the context of modern imperialism. The Cuban opponents of agrarian reform and of the revolution were able to mount only minimal internal resistance, but the US government in alliance with those opponents of change, did bring considerable pressure to bear on Cuba, which had serious economic consequences in the early 1960s.

To begin with, the US government sponsored military action against Cuba, highlighted by, but not confined to, the 1961 Bay of Pigs invasion. Speaking of the economic consequences of this situation, Che Guevara later wrote: 'For a while we did not even have time to think about the best means of economic action, for we were in combat, body to body, with the enemy, anxious not to lose an inch of our newly won terrain, and having constantly to defend ourselves against new threats from the enemy.'

The extent of economic sabotage undertaken by Cuban counter-revolutionaries and the CIA will probably never be known. Around the time of the Bay of Pigs invasion, such actions as the fire bombing of cane fields seemed to have become intense, but sabotage was not confined to the early 1960s. It has recently come to light that the CIA and its Cuban agents appear to have been responsible for the devastating tick fever that forced the slaughter of a substantial number of pigs in Cuba in 1971.

In 1960, the US government took away Cuba's share of the US sugar-import quota and, in 1961, imposed a trade embargo on Cuba. Having been dependent on the US for roughly 75 per cent of its foreign trade prior to 1959, Cuba suffered severe economic disruption from the embargo. Yet there is no way to measure the losses due to the embargo. Aside from the obvious difficulties, two particular problems are worth noting. First, close as it was to the US, the Cuban economy had been operated on the basis of quick supply and low inventories. The reorientation of trade towards the distant socialist-block countries required investment in considerable infrastructure, e.g., warehouses and expanded port facilities. Second, most machinery used in Cuba prior to 1959 was from the US and the spare-parts problem became especially serious. (On the other hand, by forcing self-sufficiency and the development of ingenuity to solve spare-parts problems, the embargo contributed to the people's solidarity and revolutionary élan—factors which undoubtedly had positive economic effects.)

Weather also contributed to Cuba's economic difficulties in the early 1960s. In 1961 and 1962, precipitation was 15 per cent and 28 per cent, respectively, below the historical average. And in 1963 Hurricane Flora criss-crossed Cuba's agricultural heartland, causing untold damage.

There is no way to untangle the various factors leading into Cuba's economic crisis of the 1960s. Perhaps the lion's share of blame should be placed at the doorstep of the US government and US business. Cuba's history of extreme foreign domination had made the revolution particularly vulnerable to the attacks of imperialism, and those attacks were undoubtedly sufficient in themselves to create some sort of economic crisis in the early 1960s. Nonetheless, while Cuba's vulnerability was extreme, the opposition and attacks of imperialism must be taken as one of the givens of any revolution. Likewise, bad weather may explain particular setbacks, but weather too must be taken as a fact of life—revolution or otherwise. It is the internal contradictions involved in the process of class struggle and agrarian reform which deserve primary attention.

Part Two

Agrarian Reform:
the Foundation for
Socialist Agriculture

6 The Initiation of Agrarian Reform

In May of 1959, less than five months after its seizure of power, the revolutionary government promulgated its first agrarian-reform law. The leadership of the revolution had made numerous statements as to its intentions, but, as one high official, Blas Roca, wrote in 1965:

> . . . the agrarian reform law was the first step revealing the true social and economic content of the revolution and the class character of the revolutionary government . . . it would not be confined to political changes alone, but would go ahead with a far reaching reconstruction of the socioeconomic structure of the country.

While the new law was not explicitly socialist in character—in the sense that it did not establish state-operated, planned agriculture—it did involve a wholesale restructuring of property relations in agriculture and a major alteration of class forces in the countryside. The main provisions of the law were as follows:

1. Properties in excess of 402.3 hectares—30 *caballerias*—were proscribed (1 hectare is 10,000 square metres and equivalent to 2.47 acres)
2. An exception to the upper limit on land holdings was established for especially productive land. (On sugar cane and rice lands, the upper limit was raised to 1342 hectares—100 *caballerias*—provided yields were 50 per cent greater than the national average.)
3. Large estates that had been worked as a single unit would not be divided up, but would be worked as cooperatives.
4. Every person—tenant, sharecropper, squatter—cultivating up to 67 hectares of land would be given ownership of that land.
5. Every person who worked the land was entitled to a vital minimum of 27 hectares.
6. The Instituto Nacional de Reforma Agraria (INRA) was established to implement the law.

By international standards, the upper limit on land holdings and the size definition of the 'vital minimum' would appear large, if not gigantic. Carlos Rafael Rodríguez, who served at the head of INRA, commented on this point as follows:

> Some comrades who examine the Cuban agrarian reform from the European [and Asian] standpoint find it difficult to understand why the maximum was set at 67 hectares—an area which in the conditions of intensive farming is quite a sizeable farm. The point is that in Cuba, owing to the extensive methods of farming, backwardness of agricultural techniques and lack of machinery, the bulk of those with 67-hectare holdings fall into the category of 'middle peasants.' It was necessary to find a criterion for defining the boundaries of the working peasantry, and the only possible yardstick was the maximum allowed one owner. We deliberately chanced the possibility that among the small peasants generally a few really rich peasants might slip through. Examples could be cited showing that the economic possibilities of peasants with less than 67 hectares of land depend in Cuba less on the size of the holding than on the quality of the land and the type of crop grown. For instance, in analyzing the income of 92,000 peasants with a total of 1,200,000 hectares it was established that the highest were the incomes of 18,600 peasants in Pinar del Rio province whose plots did not exceed seven hectares. All tobacco growers, their income averaged 350 pesos per hectare. At the same time the incomes of 1,551 owners with plots from 53 to 67 hectares averaged 90 pesos per hectare, since most of them went in for less intensive farming, besides which the bigger area created difficulties as regards labor power. . . .

Furthermore, it should be pointed out that the 67-hectare limit (and the other quantitative specifications is the law) applied to total land, arable and non-arable. On the private lands taken altogether, roughly 40 per cent of the land could be classified as arable, but on the larger peasant farms this percentage was probably smaller. After the second agrarian reform (see Chapter 10 below) 67 hectares would be the limit on all private farms. Then, for the private sector as a whole, the amount of arable land per worker would be a bit higher than in the state sector— about 3.5 hectares per worker as compared to roughly 3. But on the average private farm, with its 15 hectares, arable land per worker would be substantially less than in the state sector.

As a practical matter, the specific provisions for land expropriation and redistribution (1–5 above) were of less consequence than the establishment of INRA. INRA was given far-reaching authority. With its staff of functionaries drawn largely from the officer corps and ranks of the Rebel Army, INRA had power over the interpretation of the law's provisions, the determination of the actual ownership situation, the process of expropriation and redistribution, the organisation of cooperatives (and eventually state farms) on the large estates, and—perhaps most importantly—the speed at which everything was to be done.

DILEMMAS OF TRANSFORMING AGRICULTURE

With regard to the speed at which the law was implemented, INRA, at best, had to tread a narrow path, for it was continually faced with what seemed to be a serious dilemma. On the one hand, were INRA to move too slowly, the popular support of the rural poor which was a fundamental pillar of the revolution would be undermined. Moreover, moving slowly would offer the opposition the leeway to develop resistance. Too much land left in the hands of a rural bourgeoisie would mean too much power in the hands of potential opponents of the revolution.

On the other hand, were INRA to move too rapidly and fully implement the law, many middle-level landholders might be pushed into solidarity with the large holders. Also, rapid action could leave INRA itself in possession of lands which it had no effective way to administer. Without sufficient administrators and technicians, the result would be insufficient coordination of investment and marketing decisions.

The problem regarding the speed of revolutionary transformation has had its parallels in one form or another in other revolutionary situations. Comparison with both the Soviet and Chinese agricultural experiences is useful.

In the years following the seizure of political power in the Soviet Union, the government had neither the support nor the organisation in the countryside to move toward a socialist organisation of agriculture. The massive land reform that did take place resulted primarily from the spontaneous action of the peasantry (in the context, of course, of Soviet state power) and was directed toward the establishment of petit-bourgeois agriculture. Unable to place themselves in a leading role in agricultural transformation during the 1920s, the Soviet authorities then turned to the extremely rapid and brutal process of collectivisation. In the first period they moved slowly, never secured the support of the poor peasants, and allowed the emergence of opposition social groups in the countryside. In the latter period they moved rapidly, forced many middle peasants into opposition, and were left operating a collectivised agriculture without having developed an administrative foundation. As a result as much of historical circumstance as any 'errors' of judgement, the Soviets seem to have been unable to find some middle ground in the process of agricultural transformation. Lack of support and organisation led to too slow and then too rapid movement in the rural areas.

The Chinese experience, on the other hand, represents a rather different process of agricultural transformation. The Chinese Communists achieved state power on the basis of a long, rural-based struggle which gave them considerable support and organisation in the countryside as well as considerable administrative experience. Consequently, during the early 1950s, the Chinese had the political power to move step by step on agrarian reform, without fear of allowing any consolidation of an opposition, on the one hand, and without concern of alienating middle peasants, on the other hand. Moreover, their administrative experience put the Chinese authorities in a relatively good position to handle the new agricultural forms which they brought into being.

The Chinese, however, were unable to completely avoid the traps of too-slow or too-rapid a process of transformation. After a decade of relatively successful agrarian change the Chinese attempted the Great Leap Forward, and found that they were pushing the process of transformation well beyond their capacity to administer it.

FIRST STEPS IN IMPLEMENTING REFORM: DESTROYING THE OLD

In Cuba the revolutionary government did enjoy wide popularity in the rural areas. And this popularity gave INRA the authority to push the agrarian reform in a forceful manner without creating severe political problems. The lack of a thorough organisational foundation, however, meant that difficulties of administration and coordination were a continual threat.

The problem of administering agricultural production operations will be dealt with shortly. On the matter of handling the political conflict of the reform process—which of course had direct implications for production—INRA decisions, combined with the nature of the law itself, appear to have been rather effective. By proceeding sequentially against the most powerful groups and delaying implementation of any actions against the middle-level farmers, INRA kept the opposition weaker than it otherwise would have been. Nonetheless, INRA moved rapidly.

The cattle estates were the first against which INRA moved. James O'Connor summarises the process as follows:

By July 1959, 400 of Cuba's largest ranches, owned by forty US and Cuban companies, were seized. By the end of the year another 50 or so ranches had fallen under INRA's direction. One year later, the Institute's Cattle Administration occupied a total of 900 ranches, the vast majority of the over 1050 ranches comprising more than 500 head each . . . and covering well over 1 million hectares.

Although rapid, expropriation of the cattle ranches had met considerable political and economic resistance. The Cattlemen's Association protested the seizure and attempted to organise their opposition, though no actual physical resistance (military resistance to specific seizures) seems to have taken place. Of greater importance, under the threat of expropriation, ranchers simultaneously stepped up their slaughter rates and suspended their purchases of yearlings and calves. Based on figures for the early 1950s, it appears that less than one half of yearlings and calves were owned by large ranchers themselves. The majority of calves were bred by small farmers, purchased and raised to yearlings by medium farmers, and then sold to the large ranchers. Consequently, when the large ranchers stopped buying, the shock had far-reaching implications.   The ensuing market crisis led INRA to speed up the expropriation process and push it beyond the actual provisions of the law.

The problem of livestock slaughter in response to agrarian reform was parallel to, but nowhere near as extreme as, the situation in the USSR during collectivisation of the early 1930s. In both cases, the important point to recognise is that livestock slaughter is the spontaneous and natural response of farmers whose future is under threat. It results in serious sabotage of revolutionary change even though it is primarily economically motivated. In the USSR, the ownership of livestock was less concentrated than in Cuba, and in the former case livestock was slaughtered and eaten as well as sold. Also, given the far greater opposition to collectivisation, as compared with the Cuban agrarian reform, in the USSR the livestock slaughter was so much greater as to take on a qualitatively different significance.

In comparison to its actions with the cattle ranches, INRA proceeded less rapidly against the more important category of large farms, the sugar estates. In July 1959, it was announced that INRA would not take over sugar properties until 1960, after that year's harvest. Although the explanation for the delay was lack of sufficient money and personnel rather than lack of intent, it had the effect of inhibiting opposition from the National Association of Sugar Mill Owners. (The mill owners were also the largest landowners and controlled through contract a large extent of land which they did not own.) Thus a possible alliance between the cattleman and mill owners was effectively undermined. Some economic resistance did take place, in that many sugar producers failed to plant new seedlings and cultivated the cane more poorly. But when INRA did move against the sugar estates in 1960 and 1961, the political and economic foundations had been more firmly established.

A major factor which minimised political resistance to the Agrarian Reform Law and its implementation was that only a small percentage of landowners actually had land taken from them. The high concentration of landownership meant that this was possible while at the same time a very large percentage of land was affected. It was most important that INRA did not attack many medium-sized and smaller land holdings— those between 67 and 400 hectares—which would become subject to expropriation in the Second Agrarian Reform (1963). While the 1959 law did not proscribe farms in this category simply on the basis of size, INRA could have moved against a substantial number whose owners did not operate them. Also, by the exception made for productive lands, INRA left some 400,000 hectares of large holdings in private hands. These limits helped INRA avoid both political problems and a more severe administrative burden. By mid-1961, the private-land situation had been altered as shown in Table 6.1. Table 6.2 shows how the land was distributed in 1963, on the eve of the second agrarian reform.

Carlos Rafael Rodríguez, an important figure in the revolutionary government, described the process as follows:

> There could be no question of remedying the state of affairs at once by nationalizing all holdings over 67 hectares. Had this been done in 1960 and 1961, economic consequences would have been disastrous, for the revolution still lacked the organizational wherewithal and the managerial and technical personnel to organize production over the nearly 7 million hectares which would have come into its possession.

It was therefore necessary to co-exist for a time with these class adversaries, in the meantime laying the organizational groundwork for state-conducted agriculture. . . .

[On the other hand] mistakes were made . . . for one thing, some local bodies were unable to correctly differentiate between the rural bourgeoisie and former landlords, the organizers and chief protagonists of the counterrevolution, and the small peasants, who, under the influence of the propaganda conducted by the former, collaborated with the enemy to one or another extent.

TABLE 6.1 Changes in private land holdings by the First Agrarian Reform

A   Land expropriation and redistribution (000s hectares)

Total private agricultural land at the beginning of 1959	10070
Total expropriated land as of July 1963	6073
Land redistributed to:	
A Small peasants	883
B To public sector	3768
C To state ownership with operation in hands of former private managers	1422
Land not expropriated	3997

B   Private land holdings at the beginning of 1959, prior to the Agrarian Reform

I   Land potentially affected by the First Agrarian Reform Law

	Area (000s hectares)		Number of farms (000s)		Number of owners (000s)	
Less than 67 hectares	628.7	(7.4%)	28.7	(68.3%)	20.2	(66.1%)
67–402 hectares	1641.4	(19.3%)	9.7	(23.2%)	7.5	(24.5%)
More than 402 hectares	6252.1	(73.3%)	3.6	(8.5%)	2.8	(9.4%)
Total	8522.2		42.0		30.5	

II   Land not affected by the Law 1,448,000 hectares

This includes farm less than 402 hectares operated by their owners and not subject to special provisions of the Law, e.g., those provisions proscribing foreign ownership or lands taken from criminals. The number of farms and owners in this category is not available. A very rough estimate of the number of owners would be 16,500—the difference between the total number of owners in the 1946 census—reported by Bianchi (1964)—and the 30,500 owners accounted for in Part I of this table.

C   Private land ownership, 1961–2

	Area (000s hectares)		Number of farms (000s)	
Less than 67 hectares	2348	(52.8 %)	154.7	(93.2 %)
67–402 hectares	1726	(38.8 %)	10.6	(6.4 %)
More than 402 hectares	377	(8.5 %)	0.6	(0.4 %)
Total	4451		165.9	

NOTE
Land included in this table does not include land owned by the state but privately managed. Also, whereas Part C shows the total land in the private sector as 4451 thousand hectares, Part A shows 4880 thousand. The discrepancy could be explained by the different times the data were collected and by the incompleteness of the data in this part (see source note), but the discrepancy should be taken as an indication of the crudeness of the data.

SOURCES
A – The total land figure is from Bianchi (1964) p. 129 and is almost identical to O'Connor's (1970) figure. The remaining data are from O'Connor, pp. 320, 322, and 319. The exact values of lands publicly owned but privately managed and of lands not expropriated have been obtained as residuals.
B – Bianchi (1964) p. 102. Land not subject to expropriation has been taken as the residual.
C – O'Connor (1970) p. 325. The data were compiled from the 1961 cattle census, which was incomplete, and from data gathered during the 1962 sugar harvest.

TABLE 6.2 Distribution of land holdings, 1963, prior to the Second Agrarian Reform (000s hectares)

Public sector		3768	37.4 %
Cane farms	904		9.0 %
People's farms	2844		28.2 %
Henequin cooperatives	20		0.2 %
ANAP		2348	23.3 %
Other private sector		3954	39.3 %
Privately owned	2532		25.2 %
Privately managed, state owned	1422		14.1 %
Total		10070	

SOURCE
O'Connor (1970) p. 320 and Table 6.1.

In spite of the relative success which was attained during the process of implementing the reform, land reform and the resistance against it—however unavoidable—were economically disruptive. Whatever the land reform's positive social and long-run economic implications were, in the short run it helped bring about the severe production crisis of 1962–4. The particular ways in which the land reform and other factors led toward the crisis will be taken up in the following chapters.

7 Establishing a Public Sector in Agriculture

From the initiation of the 1959 agrarian reform, the revolutionary government instructed INRA to avoid breaking up the large agricultural production units. INRA was charged with the the task of maintaining the estates as single production units and creating cooperatives whenever possible.

The government's desire to maintain the large production units was motivated by several factors. One of these was an interest in taking advantage of economies (often only potential) of large-scale cultivation. Also, in its programmes to provide social services to the rural masses, large-scale farms provided the organisational context in which medicine, schools, day-care programmes, etc. could be developed.

In a speech on 18 August 1962, Fidel Castro set forth the reasons for not dividing up the land. While the economies-of-scale argument is well known, the point regarding the provision of social services in the countryside is less often raised. As Castro put it:

'If the latifundias had been divided, each [person] would have built his own [hut] on his own piece of land; the school would have remained several kilometers from where the children live; the possibilities of electricity, suitable roads, sewage, recreation sites, and shopping centers would not have been realized . . . none of the many towns that have appeared . . . could have been built either. Bringing the comforts of city life to the countryside would have been impossible.'

Given the role which social services have played in Cuba's overall strategy of rural development—a matter discussed in Chapter 11 below—this statement deserves emphasis.

Furthermore, the fact that the estates had been worked in large part by an agricultural proletariat meant that there would have been little basis to break them into separate plots even if the government had

48

wanted to do so. As Sidney Mintz points out in speaking of the Cuban situation:

> A rural proletariat working on modern plantations inevitably becomes culturally and behaviorally distinct from the peasantry. Its members neither have, nor (eventually) want land. Their special economic and social circumstances lead them in another direction. They prefer standardized wage minimums, maximum work weeks, adequate medical and educational services, increased buying power, and similar benefits and protections.

Mintz's statement probably is an oversimplification of the consciousness of both Cuban rural proletariat and peasants. Moreover, there is good reason to believe that the rural work force was not so proletarianised as Mintz—and many others—believed. Still, by way of comparison with the rural situation in many other poor nations, Mintz's statement is a useful characterisation of the Cuban context. Whatever the exact quantitative make-up of the Cuban rural work force—how many proletarians, how many semi-proletarians, etc.—there is little reason to believe that Cuban workers on the typical plantation wanted and were able to transform the estate into separate, private plots. Consequently INRA had no opposition or problems in the formal task of maintaining large production units.

FROM COOPERATIVES TO STATE FARMS

More complexities, however, surrounded the question of how these estates would be operated. At no time did INRA establish true cooperatives, in the sense of self-administered units in which the producers were renumerated by sharing the cooperatives' proceeds.

During the first 18 months of the agrarian reform, a form of cooperative was widely organised. These cooperatives, however, operated on the basis of a wage system and their managers were appointed by INRA. To be sure, managers were often appointed from among the cooperative members, and members were to elect their own councils to play a role in administration. Also, revenues above wages were supposed to be distributed at the end of the year, but such a distribution never took place. Actual procedures varied from cooperative to cooperative with regard to particulars of administration and authority simply because of lack of technical experience in INRA and anti-bureaucratic attitudes in government. In any case, by the middle of 1961, before any unified system of organisation had been developed for the cooperatives, they were abandoned in favour of state farms. The same factors explain both why the cooperatives did not move toward becoming true cooperatives and why the cooperatives were abandoned in favour of state farms.

First, in the years leading up to the seizure of power, the revolution had not involved any mass activity on the part of rural workers—peasants or wage workers. The Cuban experience was very unlike the Soviet where, as the Bolsheviks with the urban working class seized political authority in the urban centres, peasants were rising throughout the countryside, seizing estates on their initiative, and dividing the land among themselves. Also, Cuba was very different from China, where the rural masses had provided an organisational base for the revolution, and the peasants themselves consequently took a major role in the process of land reform.

In Cuba, the actions and involvement of the rural workers in the revolutionary struggle had not been extensive. The support of the peasantry in particular areas had been crucial to the success of the revolution. But the duration and extent of the struggle limited the translation of that support into any widespread organisation or action. Moreover, although Cuba's rural population was no more quiescent than its counterparts in most other nations, the years leading up to 1959 were not characterised by any widespread acts of violence against landlords or land take-overs by peasants. Consequently the rural population was not in the role of initiator. INRA's actions had wide support, but effective participation by the rural population would only have come via its own initiative.

A second factor explaining the move from cooperatives to state farms was that the large estates, as noted above, had been worked in large part by landless wage labourers. Unlike the situation in some nations, where the estates were worked by small holders whose view of the world is dominated by their desire to expand their holdings and become independent, the central concerns of the Cuban rural proletariat were security, employment, and a higher standard of living. (Here again the difference from the Soviet and Chinese situation is worth noting, and was discussed in Chapter 1.)

Moreover, there is little reason to believe that Cuba's rural proletariat was equipped with the skills necessary to independently operate the estates. The conditions of their labour, unlike those of a peasantry, excluded them from the acquisition of any administrative or land-utilisation experience on which they could have successfuly built the cooperatives. Consequently there was little pressure from the working masses for full development of the cooperative form. Indeed, when during the first year of their operation the cooperatives in fact remained under INRA's control, there were some pressures from below to bring the form in line with the structure. O'Connor notes that: 'Regular lines of communication were never established in many units, and no systematic attempt to integrate the workers into the administration of the cooperatives was undertaken. Meanwhile, the workers—as cooperativistas—had been derpived of their unions.'

Thus, at the Cane Cooperatives Congress of August 1962, local delegates voted almost unanimously to reorganise the cooperatives as state farms.

Still a third factor pushing INRA toward centralised control was the emergence of certain administrative problems. One of these was the lack of experienced administrators and technicians at the local level. In the absence of an effectively operating market system, and in the context of the developing problems of production in 1960 and 1961, there appeared to be little choice but to make more and more decisions about production at the higher levels. The other, and related, administrative matter that encouraged the move toward state farms was the desire of the government to maintain control of the food supply. The rapid rise in the purchasing power of working people throughout the country meant a sharp expansion of demand for food at the same time as the independence of the small farmers led towards a rise in their own consumption. Thus, aware of the food problems that would in fact arise very soon, the government did not want to give up what control it had over the food supply.

Finally, the cooperative system was undermined because it threatened to run counter to the revolutionary government's fundamental commitment to equality. Part of the problem was the potential inequality between cooperatives which, either because of their land or other particulars of their pre-1959 history, were especially productive and those which were less productive. In addition, a potential conflict existed between the interests of the regular labourers who were the original cooperative members and the seasonal or part-time workers. Were the cooperative system allowed to develop, the regular members would have had an interest in maximising returns per member, which would have meant restricting cooperative membership as well as failing to maximise the total output.

RAPID TRANSFORMATION

Actually, INRA had been developing state farms from the initiation of the agrarian reform. INRA, it will be recalled, moved first against the cattle ranches, yet the high land–labour ratio of cattle ranching led INRA to conclude that cooperatives created on the ranches would become privileged groups, both in terms of income and potential political power. Thus, primarily on the cattle ranches and on some large rice plantations, INRA established directly managed state farms as soon as the land was expropriated.

When the large sugar estates began to be expropriated in 1960, they were transformed into a special type of enterprise called 'cane cooperatives'. However, these were cooperatives in little more than name and differed little from the enterprises on the former cattle lands. The cane cooperatives did have elected boards to aid and advise the INRA-appointed manager; and INRA was to appoint managers only 'until the cooperatives were perfectly organized and their members had acquired the necessary administrative experience'. But the same factors that led to transforming the other cooperatives to state farms also prevented the cane cooperatives from ever moving effectively in the direction of cooperative organisation.

In the first year of its operation, INRA had established some 881 regular cooperatives (550 of which were devoted solely to crops, 10 to livestock, 220 to mixed crop–cattle farming, and the rest to poultry and the exploitation of timber and coal). By the end of the second year of agrarian reform, however, with the exception of a few henequin farms, all the cooperatives had been moved into the state sector. At that point, the structure of public land organisation (cooperatives and state farms) stood as shown in Table 7.1. Thus, although the cane cooperatives

TABLE 7.1 Public-sector units, May 1961

		Area (hectares)	Average size (hectares)
Cane cooperatives	622	809448	1301
Peoples' farms	266	2433449	9149
Henequin cooperatives	11	20000	1730
Total	899	3262897	3629
All agricultural land		10070000	

SOURCE
O'Connor (1970) p. 326.

remained cooperatives in name, in fact, by the second anniversary of the agrarian reform, 32 per cent of agricultural land was administered in the state sector, forming the basis for the development of a socialist agriculture. (It is interesting to note that April 1961 marks the date of the US-sponsored invasion of Cuba by counter-revolutionary forces and the formal proclamation by Fidel Castro of the Cuban revolution as a socialist revolution.)

EMERGENCE OF A LABOUR SHORTAGE

This extremely rapid organisation of state agriculture would present some severe administrative or planning problems that will be discussed in Chapter 9. Most immediately, the rapid creation of state agriculture contributed to the development of a labour shortage, and was one of the forces presenting the revolution with the incentive problem which would loom so large in the next few years.

While no precise figures are available regarding the overall extent of the labour shortage, it appears to have been substantial. A census, taken by local cane commissions, estimated for 1963 a total demand for 352,000 labourers and a total supply of only 260,000. In 1959, there were roughly 350,000 cane cutters, but by 1967 there were only 79,986 regular cane cutters.

The labour shortage, which began to appear in Cuba in the early 1960s, was in part of a result of the Cuban revolution's success in achieving two of its principle goals: the establishment of employment security and the reduction of inequality. Prior to 1959, Cuban agriculture, especially cane cutting, had relied upon an impoverished rural proletariat, bereft of alternative means of subsistence, and suffering from severe unemployment during the non-harvest months (*el tiempo muerto*). The agrarian reform, combined with the other early reforms of the revolution, had a dramatic impact on the position of the rural masses.

To begin with, by as early as 1960, a reduction in seasonal unemployment began to appear, although the overall unemployment situation remained severe. The improvement in the unemployment situation appears to have continued steadily, and it can be traced in part to the growth of regular employment, (though not necessarily productive employment) in the state farms. Whereas, prior to 1959, employment on the lands destined to become state farms probably did not exceed 50,000, it grew in subsequent years as follows: May 1961—

96,000; August 1961—103,000; August 1962—150,000. (A small part of the increase resulted from the expansion of lands in the state farms.)

The new job security for agricultural labourers is only a partial explanation of labour-supply problem. In addition, the payment for cane cutting declined in 1962 and 1963 because cane cutters' wages were tied to yields, and for a variety of reasons yields were declining in these years. In particular, much of the higher-yield cane had been harvested in 1961; and weather conditions were unfavourable in 1962 and 1963. Also, the situation was self-exacerbating: once the labour shortage began to develop, the fields were insufficiently cultivated, yields suffered, and the labour shortage worsened.

The labour shortage was not a consequence only of events within the agricultural sector. Other programmes of the revolution provided employment alternatives. Early on, for example, the revolutionary government invested heavily in housing, schools, and medical clinics, creating a minor construction boom. The general rapid economic expansion of the 1959–61 period drew workers out of agriculture into the urban centres.

Finally, the development of the armed forces and the rapid expansion of education undoubtedly put strains on the overall labour supply. (Emigration too played a role in the overall labour-supply problem; but in this regard the impact was greatest in higher-level types of employment—e.g., doctors and other professionals—and probably had little direct effect on the agricultural labor supply.)

The labour shortage of the early 1960s, however, was more than a deficiency in the number of workers. There was also a decline in the intensity and hours of work on the state farms. The evidence is summarised by Carmelo Mesa-Lago as follows:

> Salaried workers in state farms no longer feared unemployment, were not under strict labor discipline, and felt they were government employees; thus, they did not work too hard, and absenteeism began to grow. René Dumont (1964, p. 64, 85), the French agronomist, reported that malingering among workers and managerial disorganization in state farms led to underutilization of equipment: 'tractor drivers were without work from 9 to 11 days per month; agricultural machinery remained idle during the whole day, or only operated half of the work day'. An investigation conducted on 136 state farms in 1963 showed that employees only worked from 4.5 to 5 hours daily but were paid for 8 hours (Palavera and Herrera, 1965). Later, a report of the Cuban government to ECLA stated that such a vice was

typical in a majority of rural tasks. (Cuba Socialista, 1966, p. 162). A Chilean economist, working for JUCEPLAN (Romeo, 1965, p. 19) stated: 'The destruction of the capitalist organization in almost all economic sectors...in agriculture, productivity fell due to a decrease in labour intensity', and Ernesto Guevara (1963, p. 26) said: 'the absence of basic discipline violently changed the general attitude of the workers. And so there is the paradox that we still have unemployment (in the cities) but a manpower deficit in agriculture.' The slackened labor effort reinforced over-staffing in state farms, as the vice-chairman of INRA acknowledged: 'the explanation of the labor shortage in agriculture is very easy, if a worker does not work 8 hours, and, in addition, his productivity is very low, then 2 or 3 men must be employed instead of 1.' (Curbelo, 1966, p. 6)" [The references have been adjusted in line with my own system—A. M.]

These data are what one would expect, at least with hindsight, given the circumstances. By 1963, relatively little organised effort had been made in Cuba to develop a new incentive structure. Yet by providing rural labour with security and a rising standard of living, the old incentive structure—based on poverty and insecurity—had been destroyed. Shorter hours and less strenuous efforts would seem the most natural manner for rural workers to take advantage of their improved situation. As the production crisis of the early 1960s limited the continued growth of personal income, and combined with the trade embargo to create a variety of commodity shortages, it was small wonder that the labour shortage became serious.

8 Transformation of the Private Sector

The creation of an important state sector, with the associated problems of production on the state farms, was one part of the story of Cuba's first agrarian reform. In addition, while the state sector was being created, the private sector was being transformed. Tables 6.1 and 6.2 have provided a picture of both aspects of the reform's impact.

At the beginning of 1959, there were 40,000 to 45,000 small peasants owning farms of less than 67 hectares. (This number may appear rather small, and the available data may in fact lead to an understimate—e.g., by not fully including the private plots of the semi-proletariat. Nonetheless, the figure is probably roughly correct and indicates the extent to which the concentration of land ownership—and the concomitant alienation of working people from the land—had proceeded in Cuba.) The agrarian reform of 1959 added roughly 110,000 peasants in the small-holder category by giving title on the lands they worked to renters, sharecroppers, and squatters. The lands for these new small holders and the lands for the state sector came primarily from the very large farmers. The number of farmers holding more than 402 hectares was decreased from 3,597 to 592, and the land they held from 5.8 million hectares to 380,000 hectares. The high concentration of land meant—as has been noted above—that a large amount of land could be expropriated from a relatively small number of individuals.

Middle-level farmers—those with between 67 and 400 hectares—were much less affected by the redistribution of land. Their number was increased (by the addition of former large farmers who had lost a portion of their land) from 9,752 to 10,623, and their holdings from 1,655,000 to 1,702,000 hectares. These middle farms, along with the 592 remaining farms of more than 400 hectares accounted for almost half of the private agricultural lands. Thus a class of rural capitalists, farmers holding enough land to require the hiring of labour for its cultivation, continued to exist in Cuba after the first agrarian reform.

It should also be noted that the majority of those peasants holding less than 67 hectares of land were operating on very small plots. The average of their land holdings was only 16 hectares, substantially less than the 'vital minimum' of 27 hectares established by the Agrarian Reform Law. (It should not be forgotton that on the private lands taken altogether, *arable* land per worker would be about 3.5 hectares—see page 40 above.)

The vital minimum was not reached by many small farmers partly because of technical considerations. In tobacco production, a particularly labour-intensive process, the optimal size of farms was often less than 27 hectares. Also, in many cases, there was no available land contiguous to properties of small farmers; many of Cuba's 20,000 coffee farms were in isolated mountainous regions, for example. However, technical considerations were only a part of the story. In many cases, the goal of giving peasants a vital minimum came into conflict with the goal of maintaining the large estates as unified production units. It appears that the latter goal dominated.

THE FORMATION OF ANAP

As with the state sector, the formal process of restructuring land ownership in the private sector was only the beginning of the reform process. Having created a class of small holders, the revolutionary government turned its attention to organising their role in the economy. In this task, it was not necessary to start from scratch; almost all of Cuba's independent farmers had been involved in a variety of agricultural organisations prior to 1959. The largest of these was the Colonos Association (the association of independent sugar producers). In late 1960, a crisis developed in the Colonos Association when the old leadership, made of larger growers, refused to cooperate in making preparations for the first 'people's *zafra*'. In cooperation with the government, small growers took over the organisation.

Pre-empting such crises in the other associations, the government moved rapidly to emerge all the agricultural associations into the National Association of Small Farmers (ANAP), which held its first national congress in May 1961 on the second anniversary of the agrarian reform law. Membership in ANAP was restricted to those holding less than 67 hectares of land (with exemptions made for individuals with active revolutionary backgrounds). It was headed by a general administrator appointed by INRA, with elected bodies of provincial, regional and local delegations.

The mandate of ANAP was broad. It had the task of organising the small peasants in the process of agrarian reform, and of guiding the small peasants to attain national goals. In addition, as with all mass organisations being developed in Cuba, ANAP was given a set of political tasks: raising the political consciousness of farmers, defending national sovereignty, defending Cuba's socialist revolution, etc.

ANAP's principal tools for organising peasant activity were its roles in credit policy, the purchase of agricultural products, the supply of agricultural input through the people's stores, and the organisation of various forms of cooperative associations among the peasantry. When ANAP came into being, the process of organising cooperatives among the peasants was viewed as the route to move towards more effective modes of agricultural production. However, the government continually emphasised that these cooperatives would be based on the principle of voluntary association.

As the redistribution of land took place, the government began to take steps to provide a system of credit for small farmers. The agrarian reform law included provisions for INRA to establish a department of credit. It did so, first by incorporating the pre-existing Agricultural and Industrial Investment Bank. But, in 1961, the role of administering credit to the small farmers passed into the hands of ANAP, with the National Bank assuming the role of credit provider. (The bank provided credit directly for the rest of agriculture.)

ANAP's primary task was to make credit available to the small farmers so that their production activity would remain viable. In doing so, of course, it gained a powerful leverage over the future pattern of production, and over the forms of peasant organisation. In this latter respect, the credit policy was structured so as to encourage the formation of peasant credit and service cooperatives. For peasants participating in such groupings, interest charges were as low as 3 per cent. Otherwise, ANAP charged 4 per cent on loans up to $5000 and 6 per cent on larger amounts.

Data on credit provision in the early years is incomplete. However, by May 1963 (just prior to the second agrarian reform) loans outstanding amounted to $180 million—$136 million as short-term production loans and $44 million as investment loans. The number beneficiaries of these loans is listed as 208,000 While many peasants were the recipients of more than one loan, it would appear from these data that the credit programme of ANAP was spread widely.

SMALL-FARM PRODUCTION PROBLEMS

The provision of land to 150,000 small peasants, the incorporation of these peasants into a new organisation, and the development of a widespread credit programme were major accomplishments. But these actions did not forestall the development of production and supply problems after the initial (1959–61) expansion of output.

The data in Table 8.1 shows figures on 'production' for several important food products and for coffee and tobacco, all items in which the private sector played a significant role. In almost all cases, the initial period of expanding output is evident, only to be followed by a pronounced decline, beginning in different years for different products, but generally becoming serious by 1963 and 1964.

However, these data may be misleading. From at least 1962 onward (and probably from 1960 or 1961) official Cuban production data for agricultural goods include all production in the state sector but only that part of private production collected by the state collection centres. Part of the apparent decline in production is therefore simply a statistical artefact resulting from a change in the meaning of the statistics. Also, and of continuing importance, part of the decline could be explained by a rise in consumption by the private farmers, by a rise in the use of commodities (e.g., feed grains) within the private sector, and by a rise in sales outside the government collection system.

There is little doubt that a rise in the peasants' consumption of their own products did take place. An increase in their own consumption would be the most reasonable response of peasants relieved of rent (or sharecropping payments). Especially as shortages of manufactured goods developed—becoming especially severe by 1962 as the US trade embargo became effective—the tendency to increase consumption would have been intensified. (There seems to be a clear parallel to the situation in the Soviet Union during the early 1920s—though in the Soviet context the role of peasant proprietors was much greater and the problem more severe.)

Of course, the decline shown in the production data can only be partially explained by rising peasant consumption, and with tobacco and coffee the explanation has little if any relevance. Nor do sales outside the market explain the figures. There was certainly a production problem of serious proportion in Cuba's agriculture during the early 1960s.

In any case, from the government's point of view in its effort to

TABLE 8.1 'Production' of selected agricultural commodities, 1957–64 (see text for explanation and qualification of 'production' figures) (000s tons)

	Malanga	Maize	Rice	Potatoes	Boniato	Ñame	Beans	Tomatoes	Tobacco	Coffee
1957	91.2	246.9	167.3	94.3	161.3	23.0	35.7	43.9	41.7	36.6
1958	225.7	148.1	207.2	70.6	159.8	26.2	10.0	55.2	50.6	31.0
1959	239.8	193.9	282.2	82.9	183.3	30.7	13.8	65.0	35.6	55.1
1960	256.7	213.9	306.5	101.2	230.5	41.3	37.1	116.3	45.3	37.0
1961	77.0	197.8	212.8	89.6	117.0	25.0	54.5	109.2	57.6	46.5
1962	60.2	158.7	229.8	100.2	181.0	20.2	55.7	140.4	53.4	55.0
1963	45.0	88.2	204.3	85.7	81.7	8.8	17.5	92.5	47.6	34.7
1964	43.2	35.5	123.5	75.3	89.3	8.4	14.3	111.6	43.8	32.0

SOURCE
Ritter (1974) pp. 188–90.

reorganise the economy and develop a system of planning, both declines in production and rising consumption, and distribution outside the government network presented difficulties. A sizable potential economic surplus remained out of the government's control and could not be directed toward economic transformation. A solution to the problem would require some combination of extending government control of agriculture and providing stronger incentives to the private farmers. However, in pursuing those courses of action, the government was faced with the existence of 10,000 middle farmers, rural capitalists who generally remained antagonistic to the revolution. Thus, a second agrarian reform, which we shall deal with in Chapter 10, would be instituted.

9 Agrarian Reform and Problems of Planning

The immense transformation of the land-tenure structure in agriculture presented the Cuban government with a high degree of control over production decisions. On the state farms, INRA's control of production was direct. Control of production in the private sector could be implemented through credit and pricing policies.

The Cuban government did not begin comprehensive national economic planning in a formal sense until the socialist political character of the revolution had been firmly established. Nonetheless, the process of reform in agriculture and the nationalisations in the rest of the economy necessitated the articulation of general production strategies. In the agricultural sector, production policy was dominated by what Guevara has termed 'a fetishistic idea [by which we] connected sugar with our dependence on imperialism and with the misery in the rural areas.'

The 'fetish' with which Guevara was concerned was in mistaking the manifestation or mechanism of Cuba's underdevelopment for the cause. Surely, Cuban underdevelopment had had its most dramatic manifestation in the domination of the economy by sugar. Sugar represented both the orientation of the nation's economic structure towards the world market (rather than towards its internal needs) and the domination of the land (and consequently the nation) by a small number of foreigners and rich Cubans. In Cuba, as elsewhere in the Caribbean, sugar had come to dominance in a dual process of forcing out other crops and forcing the work force into a position of dependence on sugar production and the interests of sugar magnates. It was the mechanism through which the economy was tied firmly to imperialism and thereby to underdevelopment.

THE ANTI-SUGAR POLICY

Thus it is not surprising that Cuban economic policy during the first years after the revolution can be characterised as 'anti-sugar'. The guiding principle of agricultural production policy was diversification. In the way it was carried out, however, diversification was a costly policy. Guevara described the erroneous aspects of the policy in terms of two errors:

> Our first error was the way in which we carried out diversification. Instead of embarking on diversification by degrees we attempted too much at once. The sugar cane areas were reduced and the land thus made available was used for the cultivation of new crops. But this meant a general decline in agricultural production. The entire history of Cuba had demonstrated that no other agricultural activity would give such returns as those yielded by the cultivation of the sugar cane. . . .
>
> The second mistake made was, in our opinion, that of dispersing our resources over a great number of agricultural products, all in the name of diversification. This dispersal was made not only on a national scale, but also within each of the agricultural productive units.

The policy of diversification had led by 1961 to taking 200,000 hectares—roughly 15 per cent of the area cultivated with cane—out of sugar with the intent of devoting it to other crops. Yet, INRA took no steps to increase cane yields, and for some of these other crops, the sufficient experience and technical skills were lacking.

Moreover, the 'anti-sugar' policy led to errors of omission as well as errors of commission. For example, the agricultural labour shortage discussed above can be interpreted in this light; by giving emphasis to other sectors of the economy and other problems, while neglecting sugar, the labour shortage in cane production was automatically created.

Other sorts of errors in production policy were closely tied to political problems which arose in the agrarian reform. One such problem resulted from the natural response of small proprietors to the rapid rise in consumer demand. A vendors' market arose along with speculation and an evasion of the official commercial avenues. In combating these phenomena, state functionaries sometimes took actions which had a negative impact on production. Also, in the context of combating active counter-revolutionary activity, sanctions were taken indiscriminantely against poor and rich peasants, and illegal expropriations were carried out.

The policy deficiencies of this early period are traceable to several sources. Two relatively obvious factors were the dominance of an ideology which saw the nation's problems in terms of sugar, and a revolutionary situation which required rapid decisions and actions on the basis of minimal preparation.

THE ORGANIZATION PROBLEM

There is a third, and perhaps more fundamental factor which, as shall be seen below, provides a recurring theme in any explanations of Cuba's development problems. Put simply, the revolutionary government lacked the organisational foundations necessary to develop and implement policy in a smooth and effective manner. The rapidity with which the state placed itself in control of the economy meant that individuals with little experience in matters of production and administration were making decisions of national import. Again, Guevara provides a useful statement of the problem:

> The change made from monoculture to the development of a great number of agricultural products implied a drastic transformation within a relatively few months. Only a very solid productive organization could have resisted such rapid change. In an underdeveloped country, the structure of agriculture remains very inflexible, and its organization rests on extremely weak and subjective foundations. Consequently, the change in the agricultural structure and diversification, coming simultaneously, produced a greater weakness in the agricultural productive organization.

The Cuban revolutionary government had been confronted with a central dilemma of agrarian reform: move too slowly, and the political opposition may beat back the reform; move too rapidly, and the reform may lead to widespread disorder (see Chapter 6, pp. 41–2 for a more thorough statement and discussion of the dilemma). In order to avoid impalement on the first horn of the dilemma, INRA appears to have grabbed hold of the other horn. The ensuing ride was rather rough.

The emerging problem of organisation was more than that of an insufficient planning apparatus and a shortage of administrators, accountants, etc. In addition, there was insufficient organisational experience and structures among the masses; and the level of political development of the population was far from sufficient for the implementation of new, socialist forms of organisation (see especially Chapter 17 for an elaboration).

In subsequent years, the 'problem of organisation' continued to underlie both agricultural and general development in Cuba. It lay at the heart of early policy difficulties; it begins to provide an explanation to the difficulties of the late 1960s; and its solution, at least partial, was closely related to the emergence of success in the 1970s.

THE CRISIS OF THE EARLY 1960s

The great transformation of Cuban agriculture immediately after the seizure of power by the revolutionary government had cleared the way for new forms of economic organisation, but in the short run at least, the process of transformation, combined with the economic aggression by the US and the extremely unfavourable weather of 1961–3, created a severe crisis of production. (Again, it is worth noting, that while focusing my analysis on internal contradictions, I do not wish to imply that they, rather than the US actions or the weather, were necessarily most important in bringing about the crisis.)

Sugar production is a key indicator of the overall condition of the economy. For the three years, 1962–4, sugar output averaged 4·3 million tons (4·8, 3·4, and 4·4 million tons respectively), lower than for any other three-year period since 1945–8. The declines in the collection of several other types of agricultural produce are shown in Table 8.1 above. Overall, the index of agricultural output (1952–6 equals 100) declined from 122 in 1961 to 100 in 1962, 86 in 1963 and 93 in 1964.

In the industrial sector performance was mixed, but in addition to industries (like sugar) directly related to agriculture some key sectors showed badly. For example, the output of electrical power, which had increased by over 15 per cent between 1958 and 1961, stagnated in 1962 and 1963; and cement production peaked in 1961 and ran at levels 10 per cent below the peak in the next three years.

The crisis placed a severe squeeze on consumption, and led the government to introduce rationing on a wide basis in 1962. However, the imposition of rationing was as much a reflection of the government's commitment to equality as an indication of the severity of the crisis.

The government responded further to the crisis by undertaking a thorough re-evaluation of its economic policies. As the crisis had developed, the government had established its political commitment to socialism, and now it became necessary to determine what that commitment meant for the economy. The answer, which we shall examine in Chapters 13 and 14, was a new growth strategy in which agriculture would play a fundamental role. While that strategy was being formulated, however, various actions were being taken which would prove to be important preconditions for the new strategy.

Part Three

Social Transformation: Steps towards a Development Strategy

10 The Second Agrarian Reform

Cuba's agricultural problems of the early 1960s were but one aspect of the nation's change, conflict and crisis during the years following the triumph of the revolution. Both internal and external events were carrying Cuba towards a more radical political stance and a more thorough restructuring of its economic affairs.

In the industrial and commercial sectors of the Cuban economy, the process of nationalisation was not guided by a comprehensive programme such as the agrarian reform law. Nonetheless, the process was extremely rapid. Nationalisation commenced with the take-over of assets owned by persons closely involved in the old regime. Then, as the government pushed forward on its social programmes, including the agrarian reform, it incurred the hostility and non-cooperation of both Cuban and foreign business. In response to such general opposition, and stimulated by particular problems such as labour conflict, financial difficulties, and supply problems, the government took over numerous enterprises. In addition, the government took over certain key industries in order to ensure its control over production, investment and prices. By the end of 1961, measured in terms of value of production, 85 per cent of Cuba's industry was in the state sector; by 1963, the state's share had risen to 95 per cent. The data in Table 10.1 describe the extent of the nationalisation process by sector.

SOCIALISM BECOMES EXPLICIT

The manner in which the nationalisation of industry had been pushed forward revealed a basic contradiction in Cuba's immediate post-1959 situation. On the one hand, the revolutionary government was committed to a set of far-reaching socio-economic reforms that attacked the income inequalities and system of privileges and power which Cuba's economic structure had created. On the other hand, it did not, at the outset, have a comprehensive programme for reorganising the economic structure. The government either had to back off from its reform or take on the task of creating a new economic structure. Refusing to do the former, but proceeding only on a piecemeal basis with the latter, the Cuban government found itself in 1961 needing a new mode of economic organisation.

The choices that were in fact made were prompted as much by external as by internal contradictions. As the internal reforms of the Cuban revolution were in conflict with the existing economic structure, so were they in conflict with any favourable relation with the US government and US business. Thus, while the Cuban government pushed ahead on reforms and began to dismantle the existing economic structure in both agriculture and industry, the US government took both economic and political—including military—actions against Cuba.

TABLE 10.1 The extent of nationalisation by sector, 1961, 1963 and 1968

	1961	1963	1968
Agriculture	37	70	70
Industry	85	95	100
Construction	80	98	100
Transport	92	95	100
Commerce, local	52	75	100
Commerce, large and foreign	100	100	100
Banking	100	100	100
Education	100	100	100

SOURCE
Acosta (1974) p. 79.

The combined weight of these internal and external contradictions, as well as the continuing struggle in the agricultural sector, pushed the Cuban revolution toward the explicit adoption of a socialist outlook. On 1 May 1961, two weeks after Cuba's victory over the US-sponsored counter-revolutionary invasion, Fidel Castro proclaimed,

'We must talk of a new constitution . . . a constitution contributing to a new social system without the exploitation of man by man. That new social system is called Socialism, and, this constitution . . . will therefore be a socialist constitution. . . . The general assembly of the Cuban people . . . proclaims the following: the right to work, education, the dignity of man, civil rights for women, secure old age, artistic freedom, nationalization of monopolies, and the necessities of life. This is the program of our socialist revolution.'

From the point of view of the development of socialism in Cuba, certain aspects of the agrarian situation as it stood in 1961 were unsatisfactory. In particular, from an ideological point of view, it simply did not make sense to have a large portion of agriculture organised under conditions of capitalism, while 90 per cent of the non-agriculture sector had passed into state hands. The crux of the problem, however, was not an ideological one. Between 1961 and 1963, the contradiction between the socialist transformation of the economy generally and the continued existence of an important capitalist sector in agriculture had concrete manifestations.

LIMITS OF THE FIRST AGRARIAN REFORM

The agrarian reform law of 1959 had maintained the existence of roughly 10,000 capitalist farmers who controlled 20 per cent of the agricultural land (see Table 6.1). These were the farmers who each controlled more than 67 hectates of land and who, in general, needed to employ workers in order to cultivate their land. The role of the capitalist farmers in production was proportionately greater than the amount of land they controlled.

Economically, the middle farmers were not cooperating with the government's economic programs. Explaining the implementation of the Second Agrarian Reform, Fidel Castro stated: 'The better part of these lands were badly attended and badly cared for. They [the rural capitalists] speculated with the products. They distributed milk according to privilege . . . they did not have the spirit of collaboration.' This non-cooperation was not simply a result of explicit intentions of economic sabotage, though such intentions were surely present to some degree. More importantly, the combination of uncertainty over their situation, the elimination of financial investment opportunities, and the declining availability of consumer goods, especially from 1962 on, gave the rural capitalists little incentive to invest or to maximise production.

Moreover, the large farmers acted in a way which aggravated the developing labour shortage. Because conflicts with labour were often the immediate reason for government take-over of an enterprise, these farmers offered little resistance when workers pushed for higher wages. Also, the absence of either investment motivation or the availability of consumer luxuries reduced the importance of profits and further weakened the farmers' resistance to wage increases. Yet, regardless of the fact that they may have been partly motivated by a desire to avoid conflict, the large farmers' action in raising wages aggravated the labour-supply problem in the state sector and underscored the difficulties which their continued operation created for agricultural planning.

In order to formulate an economic plan for agriculture, those peasants who held private lands would have to be organised—through ANAP—so as to cooperate with the state. Yet as long as a sizable group of middle farmers (rural capitalists) remained in existence, effective organisation of the small farmers was inhibited. For the hostility between the capitalist farmers and the government was an open affair, and the consequent aura of uncertainty over future policies affected the outlook of the small farmers as well. In addition, the lack of incentives for private agriculture, which held back production by the capitalist farmers, also held down production by small peasants; and it would have been difficult to provide incentives to the latter without ultimately favouring the former. (The problem was similar to that faced by the Soviet government in the mid-1920s. As a basis for industrialisation, the Soviet government desired to find ways to expand agricultural production. However, were they to rely on a private agricultural sector, there was no way they could accomplish expansion without also increasing the power and wealth of the upper peasantry (the kulaks). This was a matter of central concern in the famous Industrialisation Debate.)

Finally, effective agricultural planning, in addition to requiring an integration of the peasants, would be greatly facilitated by an expansion of lands in the state sector. In the agrarian reform of 1959, the maintenance of large agricultural units had been justified on the basis of productivity. As that reform proceeded, the establishment of state farms had been pushed on the basis of furthering the social goals of the revolution, especially the goal of equality. But as the economy began to be organised along socialist lines, the issue of state control of agriculture constituted an argument for pushing the process of socialisation of agriculture one large step further.

THE SECOND AGRARIAN REFORM

In October 1963, the Second Agrarian Reform was promulgated. It expropriated the land of farmers holding more than 67 hectares, and these lands were consolidated into the state-farm system. Also at this time, those lands which had been expropriated at an earlier date but which had remained under private management were brought into the state-farm system. As a consequence of the Second Agrarian Reform, the state held 76 per cent of the nation's total lands, and roughly 63 per cent of the cultivated land. (Confiscated lands were paid for on the basis of 15 pesos per expropriated *caballeria* per month—with a 100 peso minimum and a 250 peso maximum—payable for ten years. Lands which were not being worked, however, were paid for on the basis of 10 pesos per month per *caballeria*.)

The Second Agrarian Reform appears to have been implemented without significant disruption or conflict. By this date, counter-revolutionary forces had been decisively defeated, and the capitalist farmers had no basis on which to resist.

The Second Agrarian Reform was accompanied with a firm assurance to the small peasants that this was the final step in the process of expropriation. They were promised that their property would be respected and that they would be allowed to operate within a context of cooperation with the state agricultural system. (It will be recalled that farmers holding 67 hectares or more had been treated as a separate group since the First Agrarian Reform; for example, they were not allowed to join ANAP.)

Thus, by the end of 1963, the Second Agrarian Reform had established a foundation for the development of socialist organisation in Cuban agriculture. In addition, through ANAP, the state had begun to create the political conditions for the integration of the small peasants into a comprehensive economic programme. The structure of land tenure had been radically transformed in the five years since the triumph of the revolution, and a major element in the nation's history of agricultural stagnation had thus been dealt with. The new structure established by 1963 would provide the basis of agricultural developments in Cuba through at least the late 1970s.

11 Social Foundations for Agricultural Development: the Literacy Campaign and other Reforms

The radical alteration of the structure of land holdings in Cuba was one—but only one—aspect of establishing the context for the development of a socialist agriculture. Another important accomplishment of the early years of the Cuban revolution was the establishment of extensive social programmes in the countryside. Building up medical programmes and educational facilities for the rural population, taking steps to change the position of women, and in general providing the services of modern society to the countryside were also part of the process of transforming Cuban agriculture. In addition, various special production campaigns were organized during the 'big push' of the 1960s. While these will be discussed below, Chapter 15, it should be noted here that they served some of the same ends as the social programmes.

The social programmes simultaneously served two functions: they improved the rural economic infrastructure; and they contributed to the transformation of the way individuals viewed their position in society and their relation to the government. In this latter regard, the various social programmes were major incentives encouraging the people to take an active part in economic affairs.

THE LITERACY CAMPAIGN

The most dramatic programme of the early years, which served this dual function of altering both infrastructure and ideology, was the literacy campaign of 1961. Throughout the period of revolutionary struggle,

Fidel Castro had made it clear that education in general and literacy in particular would be given highest priority by the new government. In 1960, it was announced that 1961 would be the 'Year of Education' with the goal of wiping out illiteracy. The task would be undertaken through a mass mobilisation of those capable of teaching others to read and write.

At the beginning of 1961, there were roughly 1 million illiterates in Cuba—that is, about 25 per cent of the adult population. As of 21 December 1961, the formal end of the campaign, the number of illiterates had been cut to 250,000 and would decline further in the subsequent months. Even this figure, which is a conservative estimate of the final consequences of the campaign, would represent a considerable success and place Cuba on a par with most of the so-called advanced nations. Furthermore, since illiteracy had been concentrated in the rural areas—at least three-quarters of Cuba's illiterates had lived in the countryside—it was there that the literacy campaign had its major impact.

The explicit accomplishment of the literacy campaign, however, represented only part of its significance. Other accomplishments of the programme included: the provision of a catalyst for the rapid continuing development of educational programmes; integration of the masses into solving the socio-economic problems of the nation; the training of large numbers of people, not only in the tasks of education, but in the tasks of organisation and leadership as well; and the direct and indirect extension of political education.

The explicit accomplishments of the literacy campaign might have been eroded over the years had the campaign not contributed to establishing the primacy of educational development in Cuba. In the following years, hundreds of thousands of individuals were involved in adult education programmes, allowing them to build on the literacy they had gained in 1961. The 'campaign atmosphere' of the literacy drive was maintained in factories, offices and farms, where regular classes were established to raise the education of all workers to the sixth-grade level. Regular education grew by leaps and bounds with enrolment in the Cuban educational system approximately doubling between 1956 and 1966, from 800,000 to 1.6 million. Included in the expansion was the creation of a massive scholarship programme to bring rural children to boarding schools where they could share the advantages of a modern education. The literacy campaign was the impetus to the development of a pedagogical establishment that could carry out this programme. The continuing growth of the pedagogical establishment was provided for by the rapid extension of teacher-training programmes. The number of students in teacher-training programmes almost tripled between 1956 and 1966, growing from 8.8 to 25.5 thousand.

When visiting Cuba, I have been confronted by numerous examples of the impact of the literacy campaign and its aftermath. For example, driving in the Escambray Mountains in 1968, I (along with two Cuban companions) picked up a peasant woman who was hitchhiking into town with her ten-year-old daughter. On the short trip she responded to my questions with the details of her own experiences: yes, she had learned to read in the literacy campaign. Now she had gone on to achieve a third-grade level of education, and planned to continue further. She could read the newspapers, and she could correspond with her teenage son who was in a boarding school in Havana. She had been married but was ill-treated by her husband. The employment opportunities created by the expansion of a state farm and her education meant that she could now provide for herself and her children on her own.

On another visit in 1969, I went to the San Andreas Project in Pinar del Rio Province. Here, in what had been an extremely poor area, the government was engaged in a special rural-development programme. The centrepiece of this programme was a collection of boarding schools in the valley where peasant children from the surrounding area were provided with all the facilities of a modern educational system. The San Andreas Project was a good example of the government's effort to bring peasants into modern communities in order that they might be provided with social services. The schools were the central element in this process.

The significance of the literacy campaign resulted not only from its outcomes but also from the way in which it was organised. Mass involvement was the central feature. In the cities, over 100,000 people were organised to teach in their spare time at work centres and evening classes; these were the *alfabetadores populares*.

But the focus of the mobilisation had to be rural Cuba: sending teachers to the countryside became the greatest task of 1961 and 100,000 secondary school students were organised in brigades to go to the rural areas, to live and work with the peasants, and to teach them to read and write.

In addition to the *alfabetadores populares*, who taught in their spare time, and the young *brigadistas*, for whom subsistence living was viewed as a positive part of the experience, over 30,000 school teachers and 15,000 other workers were released from their regular duties to take part in the literacy campaign. These latter groups continued to receive their regular salaries. In total, then, roughly a quarter of a million people were directly involved as teachers during 1961. When the figure is added to the nearly 1 million students, it would seem that there were few families in Cuba not touched by the mobilisation.

As a consequence of this mass-mobilisation character, the literacy campaign contributed to the rise of self-reliance, the identification of the individual with the government and society at large, and the creation of a sense of *esprit de corps* which have been foundation stones for subsequent development in Cuba. In addition, the campaign was focused on the rural areas and thus contributed to a reduction in their traditional separation from the mainstream of Cuban progress.

Beyond its explicit literacy accomplishments and beyond these attitudinal or ideological functions, the illiteracy campaign served training functions. In addition to teaching people how to read, the literacy campaign taught people how to teach and how to teach people how to teach. And perhaps of greatest importance, the literacy campaign was a training ground for organisational and leadership abilities. In a process of learning by doing, the participants in the literacy campaign learned how to mobilise themselves. People who were able to lead and direct were brought to the fore; and others were provided with strong motivation to participate in organised group activity.

It would be difficult to exaggerate this leadership and organisational training function of Cuba's literacy campaign (and of the other special programmes). The leaders, administrators and organisational forms of pre-1959 Cuba were products of the old system and were hardly suitable as the foundation for a socialist development strategy. While the revolutionary struggle for power had provided the embryo of new leadership, that struggle had been a relatively limited affair (see Chapter 4). It had only begun to involve the masses in a manner which would prepare them for active roles in the process of socialist development. Consequently, special programmes implemented after the seizure of power—of which the literacy campaign is the most outstanding example—had to be relied upon. Such programmes brought forth the large numbers of people needed for the operation of the new system. (This aspect of the Cuban revolution is better understood by comparison with the Chinese experience. The Chinese Communists were engaged in a much longer and more widespread military struggle prior to the seizure of power. The long period of struggle in China appears to have served the functions of developing organisers and organisation and of creating socialist consciousness. In the absence of such a struggle, Cuba's special programmes, such as the literacy campaign may have provided a mechanism which served the same function.)

Today in Cuba, one often meets people in responsible positions who began their development as revolutionaries in the literacy campaign of 1961. Almost as much as those who participated in the military struggle, the veterans of 1961 are viewed as models for emulation by Cuba's youth. In 1969, for example, when I was visiting the above-mentioned project in Pinar del Rio, I met and talked with a young Communist Party cadre at the office of a rural-development project. Later, my Cuban friend with whom I was travelling was expressing his admiration for this man, and first on his list of noteworthy accomplishments was his experience as a *brigadista* in the literacy campaign. There his abilities and dedication had been revealed, and he had gone on to hold several important posts. Too young to have participated in the pre-1959 revolutionary struggle, this cadre had come forth in a subsequent struggle against illiteracy.

Its consciousness-creating and organisational functions were probably the most important political education of the literacy campaign. But in addition the literacy campaign was an explicit exercise in political education as well as in reading and writing. The explicit political education was embodied in the texts used in the campaign. A new primer and a new instructor's manual had been developed by the Ministry of Education. Both were highly political, organised around 'themes of revolutionary orientation' and included such subjects as nationalisation, racial discrimination, and revolutionary struggle. Those who had not been previously involved in the political struggles of the revolution learned of them in 1961. (Part of Theme One of the *Instructor's Manual* runs as follows: 'People need revolution in order to develop and advance. When a nation is dominated by another, more powerful nation, only through revolution can it end foreign domination and establish its own government free from such domination.' And so on. While in Cuba at the beginning of the campaign, I was told that in preparing the text the Ministry of Education had carried out a study to determine what people were talking about and what words they were using. The result was to increase the book's orientation toward revolutionary politics.)

But perhaps of more lasting importance was the implicit politics of the literacy programme embodied in its form or process. Much of the politics of the process has been described above in terms of the politics of mass participation and the development of organisation and organisers. Furthermore, in its entire conception and execution, the campaign exhibited a fundamental aspect of the Cuban approach to socialist development: throughout, political and economic considerations were inseparable. The gains of a rapid mass-literacy programme were seen to be both the economic gains from general literacy and the political gains of consciousness development through mass involvement. And, of course, the political gains provided a basis for further economic progress.

While the literacy campaign was a national programme, it had, as has been noted above, its principal impact in the rural areas. It was the rural population whose educational level was most remarkably altered. Thus, the literacy campaign began a transformation of the rural work force that could be expected to have profound impacts. The same rural focus of education would be continued in the late 1960s as school groups were sent to work in the countryside as part of their education (*escuelas al campo*), and then increased in the 1970s with the extensive establishment of boarding schools in the rural areas (*escuelas en el campo*) (see Chapter 23 below). Further, the literacy campaign and the spread of education which followed it were dramatic pay-offs of the revolution to the rural population. As such, this advancement of education was a central component in the social transformation of rural Cuba.

INITIATING OTHER REFORMS: HEALTH AND WOMEN

There were other programmes, perhaps less dramatic than the literacy campaign, which had similar implications for rural Cuba. The expansion of medical services and their redirection towards the rural areas is a case in point. While in 1958 there were only three general hospitals in the rural area, in 1963 there were 38. (In the urban areas, the number of general hospitals was increased from 67 to 72, but many of the older ones were also expanded.)

However, roughly 40 per cent of Cuba's 6300 physicians emigrated after the revolution, and in the early 1960s there appears to have been a deterioration in health conditions. (The infant mortality rate, for example, rose substantially in the early 1960s, though by the early 1970s it was below the pre-1959 level.) Programmes instituted by the revolutionary government in the early period thoroughly altered that situation. By the beginning of the 1970s, there were over 7000 physicians in Cuba. Between 1959 and 1967, nearly 18,000 persons were trained as medical technicians and paramedics. And major preventive-medicine programmes and inoculation campaigns were carried out resulting in the practical elimination of polio, diphtheria and malaria, as well as the substantial reduction of other diseases.

Still another programme of social reform affecting the context of production activities in Cuba was the initiation of steps to integrate women into production activity outside the home. At the time of the triumph of the revolution roughly 15 per cent of Cuban women worked outside the home, and more than 25 per cent of these were domestic servants. In 1960, the Federation of Cuban Women (FMC) was established and initiated its activity by involving 90,000 women in the drive against illiteracy. (It should also be mentioned that 56 per cent of those who became literate in the campaign were women.) The FMC also devoted itself to encouraging women to participate in the labour force and to creating the conditions—e.g., day-care centres—which would allow them to do so. In the late 1960s, the FMC would play a role in bringing women into the labour mobilisations for the sugar harvest.

Progress in involving women in work outside the home was not rapid. Even by 1973 the percentage of women who were in the labour force had grown to only 24 per cent. In rural Cuba, where traditional attitudes were especially powerful, change was particularly slow. By the early 1970s women made up less than 10 per cent of the agricultural labour force.

The poor progress integrating women into the work force is directly related to the major economic events of the 1960s, which will be taken up in subsequent sections. The heavy emphasis on non-material rewards in production, combined with the general shortage of consumer goods, served to limit the incentive for women to work outside the home. Indeed, it is likely that in the context of the late 1960s, were a women to enter the work force outside the home, she and her family would suffer a material loss. Her additional income would be little if any use with goods' shortages and rationing. And the loss of her labour within the home and in such tasks as standing in line to obtain goods would have been rather costly. Also, the major effort to attain high levels of productive investment probably discouraged the expansion of rural day-care facilities. (But it should be emphasised that there was no *necessary* connection between a heavy emphasis on productive investment and a lack of expansion of rural day-care facilities. Given the rural labour shortage, investment in rural child-care facilities might well have been a high pay-off type of investment. Yet in the context of traditional attitudes about women and child care, the emphasis on productive investment easily became a factor restricting social change.)

In spite of the slow progress in bringing women into the labour force, the foundations had been established to carry the process of change much further. By 1970, 49 per cent of Cuba's elementary-school students, 55 per cent of high-school students and 40 per cent of students in higher education were women. Also, Cuba's new Family Code (established in the early 1970s) created a thorough foundation for women's economic participation. The quantitative limitations of these processes notwithstanding, when measured against the weight of Cuban tradition, the changes in the position of women, which were set in motion by the reforms of the early years, had profound social implications which could be expected to affect economic activity in the coming years.

These various aspects of social transformation of Cuban life—in education, in health care, in the position of women—ranked alongside the transformation of land tenure as providing the foundations for Cuba's agricultural-development strategy. To appreciate the extent of the social transformation, it is useful to examine what happened to income distribution in Cuba during the years following the triumph of the revolution.

12 The Distribution of Income in Cuba

In the period following the triumph of the Cuban revolution, a major redistribution of income took place. Not only was the redistribution of great magnitude, it was also extremely rapid, coming in most part as a consequence of the reforms implemented by the revolutionary government during its first years in power. Consequently the redistribution of income became a central factor influencing the course of the economy and the formulation of economic policy in subsequent years.

THE IMPORTANCE OF INCOME DISTRIBUTION

Income equality, or inequality, plays a major role in the organisation of incentives and the structure of work in any society. Indeed, the distribution of income intertwines with almost all aspects of social organisation. In pre-1959 Cuba, for example, great inequality assured the availability of cheap labour for society's harshest tasks—most particularly for cane cutting. In addition, income inequality was both cause and effect of the extreme social and political inequality that existed in Cuba. A society with exclusive clubs and private beaches, with extensive dependence on domestic servants, with more than 1 per cent of women engaged in prostitution is unthinkable in the absence of great inequality of income. Politics was a mechanism by which the wealthy simultaneously protected and enhanced their own position.

During its initial period in power, the Cuban revolutionary government instituted a series of reforms and programmes (the agrarian reform, housing reform, an employment programme, etc.) which, in altering the distribution of income, broke a key link in the system of work organisation and in the social structure. When it began to develop a comprehensive economic strategy in the early 1960s, the government had to take the income equalisation as a *fait accompli*. It has to find an incentive structure, forms of work organisations, and social structures which would not conflict with the equalisation already accomplished. Without a recognition of this constraint on Cuban planning, it is easy to misinterpret various policy choices of the mid-1960s. In particular, some choices may appear as 'idealistic' errors, when they are more accurately interpreted as necessary results of the existing reality (see below, Chapters 14 and 25).

The primary reason for discussing the redistribution of income here is to gain an understanding of its relation to economic change and policy formulation. It should be pointed out, however, that there are other reasons why it is useful to examine income redistribution: its accomplishment, something valued in and of itself by many people, is an indicator of successful social transformation in Cuba; also, the distribution of income is a useful indicator—albeit a crude one—of the distribution of social and political power. For example, if an élite group or class controls political and social authority, it would use that authority to bring about a distribution of income in its own favour. Thus, lasting income equality may be taken as an indication of wide participation in social and political affairs and of a dispersal of authority. This reasoning and the facts of Cuba's redistribution are useful inputs to interpreting the course of economic events, especially in the 1970s (see below, Chapter 25).

In light of the important role of changing income distribution in the Cuban economy, it is especially unfortunate that no comprehensive studies of income distribution exist for either the pre-1959 or post-1959 period. Nonetheless, it is possible to piece together a picture of what has happened and of the degree of change.

REFORMS AND REDISTRIBUTION

Prior to 1959, Cuba was among the richer nations in Latin America, with a per capita income of about $350. (The figure is in 1959 dollars.) Yet in terms of income distribution, there is no reason to believe that Cuba was atypical. Fragmentary evidence indicates a highly unequal distribution of income. In spite of the lack of studies of pre-1959 income distribution, there is widespread agreement as to the great inequality. In light of the data that do exist, particularly on land distribution, any other hypothesis would be highly suspect.

The two reforms which probably had the greatest impact on income distribution were the land reform instituted in 1959 and the government's general employment policy. The land reform eliminated rent payments for the tens of thousands of renters and sharecroppers producing an immediate rise in their net income. Also, many small farmers were given land, and squatters obtained title to the land they worked.

The land reform and employment policies worked together on the state farms, where workers were assured regular employment. As noted above (Chapter 7) employment on the areas covered by the state farms grew from 50,000 prior to 1959 to 150,000 by August 1962. The general employment policy was one of proscribing lay-offs, absorbing the unemployed in new programmes, raising minimum salaries, and placing upper limits on salaries for new appointments. In his early study of the Cuban revolution, Dudley Seers, referring to the period up to 1962, notes: 'Very few appointments are made at more than $300 a month' which can be compared with the $60 minimum agricultural wage ($69 on state farms) and the $85 minimum urban wage.'

On an economy-wide basis, unemployment, by conservative estimates, ran at annual rates of 12–16 per cent of the labour force during the 1950s. It had dropped to 9 per cent of the labour force by 1962, 8 per cent by 1963, and continued downwards thereafter. Moreover, the harsh seasonal fluctuation in unemployment was substantially reduced as early as 1961.

The cumulative impact of the various early reforms was huge. Felipe Pazos, a director of the Banco Nacional de Cuba in the pre-1959 period, has estimated that the urban rent reduction alone transferred 50 million pesos to lower-income groups. Also, Pazos has written that: 'In its first months the revolution realized the redistribution of great magnitude of the national income in favor of workers and employees, in the countryside and in the city, whose real income grew about 25 per cent to 30 per cent.' Pazos then estimates that the changes during the first months amounted to a 'redistribution of national income from the property classes to the working classes of probably 15 per cent or more of national income'.

These large changes are corroborated by Seers who writes:

According to estimates given me by JUCEPLAN (Central Planning Board) wages and profits of the self-employed rose by 40 per cent between 1958 and 1961, attributable about equally to the increase in the average income and to the reduction in unemployment (including seasonal unemployment). There were more gains in employment in the following year though little further changes in average wages. This suggests that the total wages rose about 50 per cent between 1958 and 1962.

Seers goes on to note that deductions for all purposes from employment income rose from about 6 per cent before the revolution to nearly 12 per cent in 1962, for incomes less than 250 pesos. Moreover, Seers estimates that prices rose by about 10 per cent between 1958 and 1962. So his data lead to the conclusion that real spendable income of the working population rose from 25 per cent to 30 per cent between 1958 and 1962.

Reporting on the position of the poorest group in Cuba, agricultural labourers, Nelson Amaro and Carmelo Mesa-Lago have noted an even greater magnitude of change: 'In 1957 the monthly income of the average family of six members, of which all those of working age had an agricultural job 23 hours a week, was $46, including the food produced by themselves in their plot or vegetable garden. The average monthly wage of the agricultural worker (not of his family) was $80 in 1962, and increased to $88 in 1966.' Real national income in Cuba in 1962 was roughly the same as in 1958. Thus, the increases in incomes in that period for the poor categories of the population were the result of redistribution.

The losers in the process were primarily rural and urban property owners, businesses and those private individuals who earned their income from profits. In addition, high-salaried business personnel, professionals, and individuals involved in gambling and related activities undoubtedly lost heavily.

In addition to the various programmes which brought about a quantifiable change in the distribution of income, the numerous social reforms—particularly in education and health care—contributed to a substantial real redistribution which does not appear in the data. Moreover, the social reforms have probably had a profound long run income equalising impact.

The pattern of relative income equality established in the early years of the Cuban revolution appears to have been maintained at least through the late 1960s and early 1970s. In October 1967, in the context of explaining the details of making wage calculations, the Cuban government printed the table of salaries reproduced here as Table 12.1. These data are of rather limited usefulness, since they tell nothing of the distribution of individuals among various groups. They do indicate the nature of the wage structure, however, and in that regard indicate a relatively narrow wage spread.

TABLE 12.1 Salary structure, 1967

	Groups		Gross rates		Net rates†		Monthly salaries		
General	Agricultural workers	Industrial workers	Hourly	Monthly*	Hourly	Monthly*	Administrators, Gross	Technicians, Net	Officials
I	I	—	0.37	70.52	0.33	62.90	65.00	57.00	
II	II	—	0.42	80.05	0.37	70.52	74.00	65.00	
III	III	I	0.48	91.49	0.43	81.96	85.00	75.00	
IV	IV	II	0.56	106.74	0.50	95.30	98.00	86.00	
V	V	III	0.65	123.89	0.58	110.55	114.00	100.00	
VI	VI	IV	0.76	144.86	0.67	127.70	134.00	118.00	
VII	VII	V	0.89	169.63	0.79	150.57	157.00	138.00	
VIII		VI	1.05	200.13	0.93	177.26	185.00	163.00	
IX		VII	1.23	234.44	1.09	207.75	218.00	192.00	
X		VIII	1.37	261.12	1.21	230.63	240.00	211.00	
XI			1.49	283.99	1.31	249.69	263.00	231.00	
XII			1.64	312.58	1.44	274.46	285.00	250.00	
XIII		—	—	—	—	—	314.00	275.00	
XIV		—	—	—	—	—	344.00	300.00	

NOTES
* The original table also includes daily rates, based on an eight hour day. The monthly rates are the hourly rates times 190.6. This implies an average of 23.8 working days per month.
† The difference between gross and net is accounted for by various taxes, including, presumably, pension contributions.

SOURCE
Cuba (1968) p. 48.

During interviews in 1972, I gathered some data on the wages and salaries which reinforce the same picture. Interestingly, in 1972, the minimum wage seems to have been substantially higher than in 1967, while upper limits appear unchanged. (It was often difficult to ascertain whether the figures I was given were before or after taxes; however, either way, the spread is the same.) I have reported these data as follows:

A cement factory near Santiago seemed to be typical of the industrial sector. There the lowest salary rate was 100 pesos a month, the highest 300, and the average around 170. On a state farm in Pinar del Rio, I found the minimum salary to be 90 pesos a month, the top 250, and the average around 140. In the Institute of Economics at the University of Havana (where I spent a good deal of time), I was told that a professor begins with a salary of 225 pesos a month; the top of the regular scale is around 300 pesos; and a department head receives 325. A secretary working in the university would receive about 150 pesos a month. There are some higher salaries—some doctors and government officials receive well over 350 pesos a month; some persons receive 'historical wages' above the official scale; some private, small farmers earn relatively high incomes. But for the vast majority of the people in Cuba, the salary range seems to run within a ratio of 1–3.5.

The 'historical wages' that I refer to are wages received by persons who, in the past, received a wage greater than the current one that is designated for their position. These people are allowed to maintain the higher wage, although all new persons entering the position and those who in the past received a lower wage than the one currently designated receive the official wage. While there are some cases in which people have chosen to take the lower wage rather than maintain their historical wage, that does not seem to be the general case. It is hard to judge how important these historical wages are, but my impression is that they are not significant enough to alter the general picture. For example, in the cement factory mentioned above, where there are about 600 workers and where, because the factory has existed since 1954 and the average age of the workers is 39, one might expect historical wages to be relatively important, only 30 workers received historical wages. Of these, only five or six received more than the 300 pesos quoted to be the top salary in the factory.

Bonachea and Valdés have compiled bits of data from a variety of sources on income distribution at the beginning of the 1970s. In their text they attempt to paint a picture of much greater inequality than the one I have portrayed. The actual data they present, however, does not justify their case. The only category for which they give salaries above the range I have described are judges, cabinet ministers and university professors. In the last category, my more recent data would seem more reliable. Perhaps they place a greater weight on historical wages than I do, but they are not explicit on this issue.

THE PRIVATE FARMERS

These data for the more recent period exclude one significant group, however—the private farmers. Leo Huberman and Paul Sweezy, in the context of discussing possible political pitfalls of the revolution, suggest that in the mid-1960s many of the remaining private farmers were able to earn substantial incomes. They report 'Private farmers with incomes of ten, fifteen, even twenty thousand pesos a year are not uncommon . . . [and] apart from a few remaining physicians still in private practice, the richest people in Cuba today are private farmers.'

Since the Second Agrarian Reform, farmers have not been allowed to operate more than 67 hectares. But as Huberman and Sweezy point out, by standards of most parts of the world, this is a considerable amount of land. With the favourable treatment offered to farmers, incomes such as those reported by Huberman and Sweezy would seem possible.

Their data, however, is subject to question. Carlos Rafael Rodríguez has stated that in 1964 the average payment to small farmers by INRA (not counting the some 40,000 who produced no surplus) was 1500 pesos, and he estimates that other sales on average amounted to 500 pesos. Rodríguez's data are based on a survey taken among farmers. The survey also showed tobacco producers to be receiving the highest payment from the state: 350 pesos per hectare (with a maximum of 7 hectares) for an annual payment of 2450 pesos. Even with a substantial allowance for non-state trade, the incomes of farmers in the best-paid category would still be far below those reported by Huberman and Sweezy. Huberman and Sweezy's figures may refer to exceptional farmers. But the existence of a small group of wealthy farmers would not seriously alter the aggregate income distributions situation.

The political issues raised by Huberman and Sweezy as their chief concern may be a different matter. In raising the issue of rich farmers, they do not question the equality of income in Cuba, but do suggest that the policies allowing a few peasants to enrich themselves may have perverse political implications in the long run. Such a group, through its economic importance, could conceivably gain political power, and, of course, its interests would run counter to the general development of socialism. Huberman and Sweezy are not alone in expressing such concerns, and others have raised an analogy to the position of the kulaks in the USSR during the 1920s. To this argument, Rodríguez has responded as follows:

> As we have seen, in Cuba the small peasants are an island in a Socialist ocean. Further, by fixing just prices for the produce of the small peasant the Cuban revolution is far from being guided by the 'get rich!' slogan of Bukharin addressed to the Kulak. These are purchasing prices which would stimulate the most efficient farming methods but do not result in either excessive accumulation or indolence. More, the peasant cannot use his income to acquire machines, for their sale to private individuals is prohibited, or more land, since the state has the priority to buy land put up for sale, and, moreover can forbid sales, making for excessive individual holdings.

Developments in the 1970s seem to support Rodríguez's position, but the issue is one which cannot be ignored.

NON-MARKET DISTRIBUTION

In any case, even while confining our attention to the current distribution of income in Cuba, it is necessary to look beyond money income; for money income provides only a first approximation of real income distribution in Cuba. Many important items in Cuba are distributed outside of the market, and with other goods market distribution is severely limited. To begin with, medical services and education are free in Cuba and have been rapidly extended since 1959; while there are many nations in the world with extensive free health and education, the contrast with pre-1959 Cuba in this regard is extreme. Moreover, in capitalist nations, when public health and education are provided, there usually, if not always, exists private systems as well. Thus these areas still provide a basis for inequality.

In relation to the role of education in creating equality in Cuba, it should be noted that, while education is free for all, some inequalities have developed in the system. In particular, there is a tendency for the sons and daughters of the highly educated to advance most in the system. Exacerbating this tendency is the persistent tendency in rural areas for the drop-out problem to be quite serious. I received the impression during interviews in 1972, however, that while these problems had been severe in the 1960s, they were being confronted and significant progress has been made. There is a similar problem that may affect the provision of health care. Taking advantage of the free facilities is a habit that can only be developed over time. A Cuban peasant is likely to suffer through a minor illiness, whereas the urban professional would quickly go to the free clinic. Therefore, although health care may be equally available, it is not necessarily equally used. But these sorts of problems are vestiges of the past, and they are likely to be overcome with time.

In addition to education and medical care, housing is another extremely important area in which distribution takes place outside the market. Housing is free to most people and costs no more than 10 per cent of income to anyone. Also, with the provision of food, basic commodities are rationed and kept at low prices, and many people receive a portion of their food in schools and work centres. In a speech of 13 March 1968, Fidel Castro commented that 'the number of persons served meals daily outside their homes has increased from 626,300 in 1965 to 1,529,000 as of today'.

The distribution of several consumer durables also takes place partially outside the market in such a way as to reduce the importance of income differentials. Refrigerators, for example—still quite unusual in Cuban homes—are distributed to various work centres. Then within the work centre the workers decide, primarily on the basis of work record, which of them will have the privilege of purchasing the refrigerators. (Such decisions are usually handled by a committee of the union, but they could come before a general workers' meeting.) It is quite likely that an unskilled production worker who puts in extra volunteer hours, and who is an example and leader for other workers, will have an opportunity to purchase the refrigerator before a highly paid but less hard-working technician. The most important instance of this type of distribution procedure is undoubtedly its application to the allocation of new housing. The same process applies to vacation houses at the beach, reservations to some of the nicer restaurants, TV sets, and some other items. In these latter cases, provisions are made for low time payments without interest, otherwise a low-paid worker could hardly take advantage of the opportunity to buy.

In all probability, the non-market nature of consumption items is subject to some abuses. For example, cases have been reported by foreign visitors, in which persons in authority used their position to obtain automobiles for their personal use. Furthermore, as with expense accounts in capitalist nations, the distinction between official use and personal consumption is not always clear. Also, at various times, a black market has played a role in Cuba, reducing the equalising role of rationing. However, there appears to be no evidence that either abuses of privilege or the role of the black market is or has been so extensive in post-1959 Cuba as to seriously distort the general picture of income distribution given above. And the non-market distribution of goods can only be taken on net as increasing equality.

When non-market distribution is considered along with the relative equality of money incomes, it becomes clear that—either by international standards or by comparison with pre-revolutionary Cuba—income in Cuba is distributed relatively equally. The rural urban differences have been substantially reduced. The income spread within particular enterprises is small, and the ownership of capital is not a source of income in Cuba. It seems clear that, in a very short period, Cuba moved from among those countries with relatively unequal distributions of income to being among the world's most equal societies. This major change would be a principal foundation of economic policy and growth in subsequent years. (In Appendix 1 an attempt is made at crude quantification of the changes in income distribution during the 1958–62 period.)

wages are fairly even — ranging from 1. – 3.5

most services are also supplied: housing, education, medical care

Part Four

Cuban Development Strategy in the 1960s

13 The Formation of an Agriculture-Based Development Strategy

In the period immediately following the triumph of the revolution, the Cuban government did not have a development strategy. The government had a set of goals regarding social reform, and it put into effect a number of programmes to implement those reforms.

In the process of reform, however, the Cuban government found itself in control of a larger and larger segment of the economy. Consequently, some form of economic planning became necessary. Yet, the economic planning of the early period was of an *ad hoc* nature. It was guided by a collection of ideas about what should happen. The Cuban leaders wanted, for example, to diversify the economy and reduce its dependence on sugar. Also, they wanted to industrialise. But they did not have a comprehensive development strategy which could carry them toward these goals.

Because the economy was expanding in the 1959–61 period, the lack of a strategy did not appear to be a problem. Indeed, the disorganisation of economic affairs in that early era was sometimes seen as a virtue rather than as a fault; it was taken to represent a lack of regimentation and a willingness to experiment. Economic planning came to be described by the term '*por la libre*'—doing things in a free way. The accomplishments of the new government created a sense of revolutionary excitement that pervaded economic as well as political affairs, and self-criticism was submerged (if not drowned) in the sea of enthusiasm.

With the development of economic crisis in 1962, however, self-criticism became the order of the day. Most importantly, the Cuban leadership acknowledged the excessive de-emphasis of sugar (see Chapter 9 above) and the need to go about industrialisation in a more organised manner. The production crisis, the self-criticism, and the consequent effort to formulate a new economic policy came at the time when the general political direction of Cuban socialism was being

95

established. The working-out of an economic development strategy in the early 1960s thus became a key element in giving substance to the Cuban brand of socialism.

THE RETURN TO SUGAR

The Cuban brand of socialism in the 1960s appeared to diverge from traditional concepts of socialist development in two ways. First, the Cuban strategy gave agriculture the leading role; this aspect of the strategy will be taken up here. Second, the Cuban strategy gave a heavy emphasis to non-traditional forms of planning organisation and work incentives; these matters will be the subject of the following chapter.

In giving agriculture the leading role in their development strategy, the Cuban leaders were departing both from ideas they themselves had had regarding the importance of industrialisation and from traditional socialist attitudes regarding the primacy of industrialisation. The departure from tradition, however, was much less than it might seem. Because Cuban agriculture was in large part a proletarian-based agriculture, the decision to build on a rural base did not mean that the working class and its organisation were relegated to secondary roles. The operation of state enterprises and the organisation of work would be basically the same in both the rural and urban areas; these matters will be taken up in later chapters.

The immediate reasons for the general emphasis given to agriculture and the particular emphasis given to sugar in the 1960s were both practical and ideological. On a practical level, any programme of general economic modernisation was going to require a great deal of foreign exchange to purchase machinery, fuel and other basic commodities. And the costly effort to diversify out of sugar had indicated that, in the short run at least, sugar was the only viable source of substantial foreign-exchange earnings. As Guevara stated in 1964:

> The entire economic history of Cuba had demonstrated that no other agricultural activity gives such returns as those yielded by the cultivation of the sugar cane . . . hard facts have shown us, both the errors and the road toward their correction, which is the road the Cuban revolution is at present following in the agricultural sector. Sugar now has first priority in the distribution of resources and in the assessment of those factors which contribute to the most efficient use of those resources.

Sugar, then, was to be the mechanism through which Cuba was to take advantage of its particular geographic–climatic and historically created conditions, and sugar would thus provide the foreign exchange for the advancement of the rest of the economy.

Geographic–climatic and historical conditions, however, only provide part of the rationale for the Cuban government's decision to place sugar at the centre of its development strategy. Another important practical factor was the willingness of the Soviet Union to enter into long-term trade agreements, by which it would purchase Cuba's sugar on favourable terms. In explaining the process by which sugar-production goals had been established in the 1960s, Fidel Castro later stated:

> The original development plans of the Revolution called for exporting 3 million tons of sugar to the Soviet Union at a price of 4 cents a pound . . . it would mean sugar exports of 264 million pesos. . . . When our import needs were studied, we saw that the gap between our imports and exports would widen with every passing year. . . . We therefore proposed a long term agreement with the Soviet Union based on our possibility for increasing sugar production. . . . As a result of the acceptance by the Soviet government of the proposal made by Cuba, it was decided to gradually increase exports [to the USSR] until the figure of 5 million tons of sugar was reached. The price was also upped, from 4 to 6·11 cents a pound.
>
> With exports of 5 million tons at 6·11 cents a pound, the value of our exports [to the USSR] would be increased by 408 million pesos.

This 6·11 cents per pound sugar price was roughly double the world market price in the 1964–70 period though it was below the world price for 1963. (However, Cuba's receipts from the USSR in the sugar trade have not been in hard currency. To fully determine the meaning of the 6·11 cents price, it would be necessary to know the prices paid by Cuba for Soviet goods; but such information is not available.) The long-term agreement with the USSR reduced one of the central problems associated with dependence on exports of a single primary commodity, namely, the uncertainty of price fluctuations on the international market. The necessary stability therefore existed to undertake long-term economic planning.

The return to sugar, however, was not based solely on such practical considerations. The Cuban revolution had always had the self-image of a rural movement. Although urban support was not unimportant, the military struggle had taken place in the countryside; and the direct and indirect support of the rural population had been very significant (see Chapter 4). In spite of the centrality that had been attached to industrialisation as a goal, the particular reforms of the early years had had a rural emphasis. The agrarian reform had been, of course, the most notable of these. But the literacy campaign, the general development of education, the expansion of health care had all had a decidedly rural character. Moreover, the early years had seen several symbolic returns to *el campo* by Fidel Castro and other leaders of the revolution.

Thus the explicit emphasis that was given to agriculture—and to sugar as the most important part of agriculture—in the Cuban strategy of the 1960s may have come into conflict with certain ideas about the negative historical role of sugar and the urgent need for industrialis- ation. Nevertheless, that emphasis was in line with a deep ideological commitment of the Cuban revolution. Furthermore, in retrospect, it seems that only an agriculture-based strategy could have been consistent with the incentive programmes and mass mobilisations which were also important parts of the Cuban strategy in the 1960s (see Chapters 14 and 15). The heavy stress that was placed on wide participation in and general understanding of the central economic tasks of the nation would have been thoroughly frustrated had the sectoral focus of the strategy been industry. As we shall see, the Cuban economic plan for the 1960s had sufficient difficulties as it was.

THE CONTENT OF THE PLAN

The Cuban economic plan for the 1960s was dominated by the emphasis on sugar production. In particular, the overriding goal was the production of 10 million tons of sugar in 1970. Achievement of the goal would mean increasing sugar output by almost 40 per cent over the pre- vious peak (the 7.2 million tons produced in 1952; the 6.8 million tons produced in 1961 was Cuba's second biggest sugar output). From the 4.5 million tons produced in 1964, the plan called for an expansion of sugar output as follows.

Year	Planned number of tons in millions
1965	6
1966	6.5
1967	7.5
1968	8.0
1969	9.0
1970	10.0

After 1970, sugar output was to remain at 10 million tons, or increase only gradually, and foreign-exchange earnings from sugar were to provide the basis for switching the focus of development efforts toward other sectors.

While sugar would be the linchpin of Cuba's development in the 1960s, the entire agricultural sector would be given emphasis. Specific objectives for 1970 included:

raising coffee production to 90,000 metric tons from its 1959 peak of 55,000;

cultivation of 65,000 hectares under beans and 200,000 hectares under rice;

meeting all internal needs for vegetables and fruits and beginning to export these products;

providing all the raw materials necessary for the textile industry;

cultivating 100,000 hectares under citrus fruits;

developing thousands of new hectares of tobacco cultivation;

establishing an export capacity in the cattle industry.

In addition to goals for agricultural output, the plan called for the rationalisation and modernisation of agriculture. In particular, in sugar cane, mechanisation was to be given high priority as the principal means of relieving the labour shortage. Mechanisation was also to be pushed in rice cultivation and in dairies.

Along with mechanisation, other aspects of scientific agriculture were called for. New seed varieties would be introduced in sugar cane and rice, not only for their higher yields but also, in sugar cane, to lengthen the duration of the *zafra* and thereby relieve the pressure on labour supply. The use of pesticides and fertilisers was to be greatly expanded throughout agriculture. Efforts would be made to upgrade the genetic quality of cattle herds through development of cross-breeding. And mathematical techniques would be applied to rationalise transportation of agricultural products (particularly sugar cane to the sugar mills) and to determine optimal cane-cutting schedules.

The various steps to be taken in agriculture were, as far as possible, planned so as to take advantage of potential linkages among various activities. For example, the cattle ranches would use molasses to upgrade the diets of their herds, and khinaf (a fibre producing plant) would be cultivated to supply material for bags in which sugar could be shipped.

Also, extensive infrastructure expansion was planned in connection with the development of agriculture. Most important, the Cuban strategy placed heavy emphasis on the construction of water-storage and irrigation facilities. While the Cuban climate is such as to supply sufficient water naturally, the timing of that supply is seldom as needed when left to natural forces. Thus, a water-control programme, based in large part on numerous small dams, was an important aspect of growth strategy for the late 1960s. The extension and improvement of the rural transportation network was another matter of high priority. While a transportation network is a major part of any agricultural development programme, it is especially important in a sugar-cane-dominated agriculture because the sugar yield of cane is so sensitive to the quickness with which the cane is milled after it is cut.

The concern for linkages in the Cuban strategy was not confined only to connections among agricultural activities and to agriculture's dependence on infrastructure extension. In placing agriculture at the base of their development strategy, the Cubans meant to expand industry in connection with that base. Of course, in large part the connection between industry and agriculture would be through the foreign exchange earned with agricultural exports. But, in addition, the Cuban plan was sensitive to the direct linkages which could be exploited. In this regard, for example, food-processing industries were to be expanded; fruit canning would be built on both the increased output of fruit and on the availability of sugar; and plants would be constructed for the processing of meat and meat by-products (e.g., shoe factories) and of dairy products (e.g., yoghurt plants). Also, as an extension of the sugar network, large-scale shipping and loading facilities would be constructed. Inputs to agriculture would likewise be given emphasis. There would be investments in fertiliser factories and, to a limited extent, in farm equipment.

The development of industry would not be wholly confined to agriculture-related activities. Industries for which Cuba had a natural-resource base would also receive attention. These included, most importantly, nickel production (a significant source of foreign exchange) and cement production (for which a large demand was anticipated in infrastructure development and future housing construction).

Nonetheless, any general expansion of industry independent of the agricultural base was not seen as part of the development strategy for the

1960s. General industrial development was projected for the future—when, according to anticipations, the strategy for the 1960s would have placed the economy on a firm footing.

A PRELIMINARY APPRAISAL OF THE 1960s STRATEGY

Whether or not the Cuban development strategy for the 1960s would, in fact, put the economy on a firm footing is a matter that can only be appraised on the basis of the events as they unfolded. It is useful, however, to make a preliminary appraisal and note some of the *a priori* merits and weaknesses of the plan.

To begin with, the Cuban strategy had some significant appealing aspects. Perhaps most noteworthy, it was based on a recognition of the nation's existing comparative advantage in agriculture and yet the plan also incorporated a recognition of Cuba's dynamic or changing comparative advantage. The strategy of moving more and more into industrial activities (especially those using highly modern; educated-labour intensive techniques) after 1970 was based on two aspects of dynamic, or changing, comparative advantage. First, if the strategy of the 1960s was successful in exploiting the country's existing comparative advantage, the foreign-exchange constraint on economic growth would be alleviated; a redirection of expansion into more foreign-exchange-intensive activities would then be possible. Second, the strategy for the 1960s included a heavy emphasis on the growth of education; consequently by the 1970s Cuba would be in a position to undertake more skill-intensive activities.

A second positive aspect of the Cuban strategy in this period was its emphasis on linkages. The Cubans were in a position to use central planning in the manner whereby it can be most effective. Being able to anticipate changes in one sector, they could plan to meet the demands and use the supplies of that sector by making changes elsewhere.

Finally, among these broad positive attributes of the 1960s' strategy, there is the general employment policy of ensuring jobs for all those willing to work and the necessary corollary of reducing the tie between productivity and remuneration. This policy provided a direct solution to the nation's most pressing problem of unemployment. It also contributed to the expansion of output by eliminating the waste resulting from unemployment. (It should be noted, nonetheless, that the employment policy also was associated with problems of labour incentives, a matter which will be taken up shortly in Chapter 14.)

These various positive aspects of the Cuban strategy for the 1960s should not be ignored. They were, however, to be overshadowed by problems which would develop in the coming years. These various problems will receive considerable attention in following chapters, but it will serve to note them here.

First, while existing comparative advantage may well have justified an emphasis on agriculture in general and sugar in particular, the degree of emphasis appears to have been far too great. Instead of constituting a reasonable programme of unbalanced growth, the Cuban strategy was one of lop-sided growth.

Second, the lop-sidedness was bound up with a severe over-optimism regarding what could be accomplished. The over-optimism applied to the 10 million ton goal for sugar output in 1970. It also applied to expectations of the rate at which new investments could become effective, particularly investments directed toward mechanisation of the sugar harvest.

Third, the new strategy involved not only overcoming the unfounded prejudices about relying on sugar and agriculture. It also involved ignoring the real weaknesses of an agriculture-based strategy. Cuba would remain tied to the unpredictability of the weather. In spite of Soviet purchase agreements, Cuba would still be affected by world-market-price fluctuations. And Cuba would still be relying on traditional economic activities, activities in which backwardness was most severely entrenched and activities which hardly provide the foundation for the transformation (modernisation) of the labour force.

These problems, as noted, will be taken up below as the experience of Cuban development is examined. There is, however, another side to the Cuban strategy which must be given attention. An economic plan must specify what is to be done, and that has been the topic of this chapter. A plan must also specify how things are to be done: how production will be organised, how labour will be motivated. This is the topic of the following chapter.

14 Labour Supply and Incentives in the Plan for the 1960s

The decision to place agriculture at the centre of the Cuban plan had involved relatively little controversy once the errors of the initial period had become apparent. On the other hand, considerable debate, both within Cuba and internationally, surrounded the questions of how the plan would be organised, how economic affairs would be coordinated, and how labour would be motivated. The debate received wide attention because of its focus on fundamental theoretical problems of socialist economic organisations such as: the role of the law of value in the transition to socialism; the relation between the transformation of productive forces and the transformation of social relations; and the question of incentives in a socialist society.

While this debate and the attention it was given focused on fundamental issues of economic theory, the issue at hand was a very practical one: was it possible to do away with inequality and insecurity, as the Cuban revolution had begun to do, and still get people to work hard? Once personal gain was reduced as a motivation for work and as a guide to allocation decisions, would people work effectively for the collective welfare?

These were questions which had been forced to the fore by the experience of the early reforms. We have described above (Chapters 7–9) how the rise in incomes of the rural poor, the creation of job security, and the increase of job opportunities in the urban centres had contributed to the production crisis in agriculture through the creation of a labour shortage. If the economy were to be organised around an agricultural-based development strategy, some means would have to be found to overcome the labour shortage.

THE CUBAN APPROACH TO WORKER MOTIVATION

The outcome of the debate which took place in the early 1960s was the official adoption of the position that the Cuban economy should develop with a heavy emphasis on 'moral' incentives as a basis for worker motivation. For the Cuban leaders, this meant that, as far as possible, people should be motivated to work by their commitment to the welfare of society at large, rather than by their desire for personal gain. Consequently this incentive system tied work and politics together, since it could only be through political development that such commitment could become widespread and effective. Furthermore, if personal gain were to be given a secondary role in motivation, income differentials would necessarily be small. (The concept of a 'moral' incentive is usually counterposed to a 'material' incentive, the traditional situation where an individual works for personal material gain. These terms, however, can be misleading. What is meant by a 'moral' incentive often involves material gain for the collective, e.g., when people work without individual remuneration to build a new school in their community. It might be more useful to categorise incentives as 'collective' or 'personal', for it is this distinction which is often paramount in discussions of the issue.)

The official Cuban position on incentives did not mean that wage differentials should be abolished, but it did mean a strong stress should be placed on movement toward equality. Moreover, the central issue in the long run would be how pay differentials were viewed. Castro argued that wages should be viewed as giving 'a man participation in more collective wealth, because he does his duty and produces more and creates more for society' and not as a mechanism to get 'a man to do more than his duty'. The goal of economic expansion was by no means abandoned: 'As we said before, communism, certainly, cannot be established if we do not create abundant wealth. But the way to do this, in our opinion, is not by creating political awareness with money or with wealth, but by creating wealth with political awareness, and more and more collective wealth with more collective political awareness.'

This approach to work motivation was based on the principle that when given the opportunity to work, and the knowledge that their labour is serving a serious social need, people will work hard regardless of the immediate personal gain. To a large degree, then, the success of Cuba's incentive system would depend on the development of political consciousness, a sense of identity by the individual with the collective.

The task was seen as one of transforming the way in which people viewed their work. Consequently the ideology which surrounded the work process would be as important as the process itself: material (personal) incentives would be used, but they would be officially viewed as a necessary evil. It was believed that over the long run, as people's view of the work process was altered, it would be possible to alter the work process itself.

In fact, dramatic changes in the work process in Cuba had already taken place, and the official position was in large part the acceptance of, and attempt to improve upon, a reality that already existed. For in redistributing income and providing social security (both through guaranteed employment and through education, health and other reforms) the Cuban revolution had already altered the work process a great deal. Consequently the choice which confronted Cuban leaders in the early mid-1960s, was not whether to change the work process, but how to deal with the changes that had already taken place. Within this framework, alternatives were surely possible, but, barring a reversal of the basic programmes of the revolution, all alternatives would have accepted a large element of moral (or collective) incentives.

The Cuban position on incentives and the work process provided a guide for dealing with the labour shortage in agriculture. The labour-supply problem in agriculture was most acute in the sugar harvest because cane cutting did not provide regular employment, had traditionally relied upon labour that was in large part unemployed during the non-harvest season, and was considered the most onerous sort of work. Moreover, the new programme to expand sugar production to 10 million tons required a sizable expansion in harvesting capacity. The central elements of the Cuban solution were, first, an effort to mechanise the cane harvest, and, second, a mobilisation of labour from other sectors of the economy in the period prior to the implementation of mechanisation. Little, if any, effort would be focused on structuring direct personal, material incentives to maintain the traditional cane-cutting labour force; the movement of the majority of its members to other sectors of the economy—including more secure agricultural activity—would be accepted. While a sizable labour force was needed, it would be brought to the agricultural sector from other occupations and motivated on a political (moral) basis. The sugar harvest would be transformed to a national activity in which everyone would be encouraged to participate for the good of the nation.

The particulars of this programme for solving the labour-supply problem in agriculture were but one part, albeit a central part, of an overall economic strategy. Raising political consciousness and building motivation through moral incentives were features of the entire economy. It should be emphasised that the process of developing this programme, of developing new attitudes towards work, was not simply, or even primarily, one of political exhortation and appeals to sacrifice and moral principles. The foundations of the process were the collective pay-offs which had been achieved by the Cuban people through the revolution. Most importantly, the development of social services and the establishment of relative equality provided the context for such a development strategy (see Chapters 11 and 12 above).

Furthermore, work attitudes would be affected by new forms of collective action. The labour mobilisations which would be so important in the sugar harvest, but which were also employed in other sectors, were seen by Cuban leaders as one mechanism for creating new attitudes towards work. Numerous special programmes, of which the literacy campaign had been the prime model, would serve the same function. Special youth brigades for work in agriculture, volunteer labour mobilisations for a variety of special projects, neighbourhood organisation for urban repair, and special housing-construction brigades are all examples of special programmes which would simultaneously rely upon collective commitment to work and further create and spread that commitment. These special programmes would not be typical work activities; most work in Cuba would continue to take place during regular hours in traditional sorts of work centres. Nonetheless, these special programmes would play a central role in the attempt to reshape economic organisation and the structure of incentives.

THE STRUCTURE OF PLANNING

The attempt to develop a new structure of incentives in Cuba had its counterpart in the nature of the economic planning system which was being shaped at the same time. As with incentives, the rationale behind decisions on the structure of planning was a complex mixture of ideological and practical factors.

The Cuban leadership believed that the principles which lay behind the adoption of moral incentives would be violated by a system of economic coordination which relied on prices as a guide and which measured the success of enterprises in terms of their own profits. Using prices and profits was seen as necessarily bound up with both individual motivation and the dominance of market relations. Individual motivation and market relations, in turn, were seen as necessarily connected to inequality.

This reasoning was used to justify the Cuban government's adoption of a highly centralised system of economic planning and accounting in the 1960s. Individual enterprises would be guided by quantitative production targets established in coordination with the central planning authority. This general procedure would be followed both in industry and in agriculture.

The most thorough statement of the Cuban position on this question of centralised accounting and planning in relation to incentives was articulated by Guevara in 1964. Explaining the difference between the Cuban system of 'budgetary finance' and the alternative of 'economic calculus' or 'self-management' he stated:

> The most immediate difference arises with regard to the enterprise. For us an enterprise is a conglomerate of factories or production units that use similar technology, possess a common market for their output, or are located, in some cases, in the same geographical area. The economic calculus system views an enterprise as a production unit with its own legal personality. A sugar mill is an enterprise under the latter system, while under our system all sugar mills as a whole, together with the other production connected with the sugar industry, constitute the Empresa Consolidada del Azucar. . . .
>
> Another difference is the way money is used. Under our system, it functions only as a means of measurement, as a price reflection of enterprise performance that is analyzed by central administrative bodies so as to be able to control such performance. Under economic calculus, money serves not only this purpose but also acts as a means of payment, an indirect instrument of control. . . .
>
> On the basis that under both systems the general state plan is the supreme authority, adherence to which is compulsory, operational analogies and differences can be summed up by saying that self-management is based on overall centralized control and more exaggerated decentralization. The bank exercises indirect control by means of 'the rouble', and the monetary results of the enterprise's operation provide a measure for premiums. Material interest is the great lever that moves workers both individually and collectively.
>
> The budgetary finance system is based on centralized control of the enterprise's activity. Its plan and economic activity are directly controlled by central administrative bodies; it has no funds of its own nor does it receive bank credits. And it uses material incentives on an

individual basis or, in other words, individual monetary premiums and penalties. At the proper time, it will also institute collective incentives. Direct material incentives, however, are limited by the method of wage payment.

On their face value, Guevara's assertions and the official Cuban position that a necessary connection existed between the structure of planning and the structure of incentives are difficult to maintain. There is no reason, in theory, why it is not possible to have decentralisation combined with political or collective motivation. Also, in theory, profits may be used as accounting devices without being a motivating factor. Consequently, when the Cuban position on planning structure is examined on a theoretical level, it is difficult to understand. (The assertion of a necessary connection between the form of economic planning and the substance of social relations is a common one in much Marxist literature. The issue is most usefully joined in a debate between Paul Sweezy and Charles Bettelheim. The conclusion of that debate seems to me to be extremely useful in that it emphasises that the fundamental issue is who – which class – ultimately controls the econ-omic process. The mechanism of control—the nature of the planning system—is a secondary issue.)

It is useful, however, to look beyond theory *per se* and take cognisance of the particular historical circumstances. To begin with, it may be possible to combine decentralisation with political motivation, but in the Cuba of the early 1960s the collective consciousness needed for such a system to work had not been created. Given this reality, de-centralisation almost surely would have led to a pre-eminence of personal motivation, or material incentives. Centralisation, on the other hand, could provide a degree of control which would allow personal incentives to be given minimal emphasis while the foundation for an alternative might be created.

Furthermore, there were immediate practical difficulties which pushed the Cubans toward highly centralised economic control. The combined impact of the various reforms, the nationalisations, the US trade embargo, and the imposition of rationing had thoroughly upset the structure of prices, and limited the usefulness of the market as a meaningful coordinator of economic activity. In the economic environ-ment of the mid-1960s, had the market been allowed to operate, prices might have fluctuated sharply. Had firms been evaluated on their short run profitability, many would not have made the grade. The general disruption of the period could have been aggravated, and the drive to eliminate unemployment could have been inhibited. Moreover, with the exodus of managers, technicians and administrators, the planning process had to operate with a shortage of skilled personnel. The personnel shortage provided a further rationale for handling decision-making and accounting on a centralised basis. (It should be noted, however, that the personnel shortage could equally as logically be used to justify the alternative conclusion; and, indeed, advocates of de-centralisation have often argued that a market system of coordination requires less administrative skill.)

In subsequent chapters, when the experience of the 1970s is discussed, the issues lying at the foundation of Cuban incentives and planning structures will be re-examined. That context should help clarify the alternative relationships which can exist between the structure of planning and the substance of social relations. For now, it suffices to emphasise the importance of the practical considerations which shaped the nature of Cuban strategy—both in terms of incentives and planning structures—during the 1960s. Taken at face value, the statements of Cuban leaders would imply that basic decisions were determined primarily on the basis of certain ideological principles. Then, when examining the difficulties that arose in later years, it would be all too easy to identify their source as 'wrong decisions'. Ideological principles were important and 'wrong decisions' might well have been made. But in understanding the various phases of the Cuban experience it is extremely useful to recognise the material circumstances which led into each phase, which created difficulties, and which, as they changed, pushed the economy into a subsequent phase.

15 The Big Push of the 1960s

In addition to the basic role of agriculture and the stress given to reshaping work incentives, Cuba's economic development strategy for the 1960s incorporated a third defining element, a very high rate of investment. The highly centralised planning system, whatever its other merits or shortcomings, would give the government far-reaching control over the nation's economic surplus and would allow the direction of that surplus towards capital accumulation.

DIMENSIONS OF THE BIG PUSH

The implementation of Cuba's new development strategy in the mid-1960s appears in the aggregate investment data of that period. Investment as a percentage of gross material product (GMP) rose from 16.4 per cent in 1962 to 20 per cent in 1965 and to 31 per cent in 1968 (see Table 15.1).

The rise in investment was primarily a result of increased domestic savings. Savings as a percentage of GMP rose from 8.9 per cent in 1962 to 19.7 per cent in 1968. Foreign finance did cover a substantial share of the investment (36.4 per cent in 1968); but its relative importance shows no trend after 1964, and its relative importance had declined substantially compared to 1962 and 1963. Accordingly it seems reasonable to attribute the rising rate of investment to successful control over the nation's surplus by the planning authorities.

Along with the rise in investment, there was a substantial shift in the distribution of state investment (see Table 15.2). The share of investment going to agriculture fell from 29.4 per cent in 1962 to 24.3 per cent in 1963, reflecting the continued emphasis on non-agricultural development up through that period. (It is also possible that the severe weather of Hurricane Flora kept investment in agriculture lower than it would otherwise have been in late 1963.) However, after 1963, investment in

TABLE 15.1 Investment and related aggregates, 1962–8 (million pesos)

Year	Gross material product*	Gross invest- ment**	'Aid'†	Saving‡	I/GMP	S/GMP	A/I
1962	3689.2	607.6	277.0	330.6	.164	.089	.455
1963	3736.7	716.8	322.2	394.6	.192	.106	.449
1964	4074.6	794.9	304.5	490.4	.195	.120	.383
1965	4136.5	827.1	175.6	651.5	.200	.158	.212
1966	3985.5	909.8	327.7	582.1	.228	.146	.320
1967	3612.5	979.0	294.1	684.9	.271	.189	.300
1968	4000.0	1240.0	450.9	789.1	.310	.197	.364

NOTES
* Note that these data taken from Ritter (1974) are reported by him as Gross Domestic Product figures and differ somewhat from the Gross Material Product figures developed in Appendix 2 and used elsewhere in this book. ** State sector investment. † Aid equals the trade deficit. ‡ Savings equals investment less aid.

SOURCE
'Aid' figures from *Anuario Estadistico de Cuba* (1973) p. 186; other data from Ritter (1974) p. 140.

TABLE 15.2 Distribution of state investment, 1962–6 (% break-down)

	1962	1963	1964	1965	1966
Agriculture	29.4	24.3	30.5	40.5	40.4
Industry	23.1	31.6	29.1	18.1	16.7
Transport and Communications	9.5	9.6	9.1	11.7	14.3
Housing and social services	13.5	11.5	11.4	9.4	9.6
Education and culture	8.1	7.0	5.3	5.0	4.4
Construction	4.3	5.8	4.6	3.8	2.2
Other	12.1	10.2	10.0	11.5	12.4

SOURCE
Auroi (1975) p. 90, based on Cuba, Junta Central de Planificacion, *Boletín Estadístico, 1966* (Havana: 1966).

agriculture as a share of the total rose rapidly, reaching 40.5 per cent in 1965, and remaining at that level in 1966 (data for later periods do not seem to be available).

The rise in the share of investment going to agriculture came largely at the expense of investment in the industrial sector. Indeed, between 1963 and 1966, not only did industry's share of investment fall, but the absolute volume of investment in industry fell from 227 million pesos to

152 million pesos. In the mid-1960s period, there was also a relative rise in the importance of investment in transport and communications (reflecting the development of agricultural infrastructure) and a relative decline in the importance of investment in housing, social services, education and culture (reflecting a readjustment after the early heavy emphasis on these sectors).

TABLE 15.3 Tractor imports 1962–70

	Traction tractors	Tractors with tyres	Total
1962	350	1600	1950
1963	921	2874	3795
1964	770	3483	4253
1965	1470	3898	5368
1966	789	2910	3699
1967	1445	4390	5835
1968	1098	5677	6775
1969	1208	7774	8982
1970	402	6873	7275
Total	8453	39479	47932

SOURCE
Cuba (1972a) p. 185.

The plan's emphasis on development of the agricultural sector is seen in several other statistical series. Tractor imports (see Table 15.3) rose from 1950 in 1962 to 7275 in 1970 and totalled almost 50,000 for the nine-year period. In 1960, there had been fewer than 10,000 tractors operating in

TABLE 15.4 Availability of fertiliser, 1963–8 (in 000s metric tons)

1963	444.1
1964	650.2
1965	500.6
1966	581.5
1967	980.6
1968	1487.8

SOURCE
Cuba (1970a) p. 59.

the country. The annual supply of fertiliser was increased from 444.1 thousand metric tons in 1963 to 1487.8 thousand metric tons in 1968 (see Table 15.4). And the use of pesticides and herbicides rose similarly; for example, in 1966 4.3 million pesos of pesticides were used, and in 1968 the figure was 7.8 million. (In the entire 1954–8 period, Cuba had imported only 7.9 million pesos of pesticides.)

Between 1963 and 1968, 600 million pesos were invested in expanding water-control facilities. Water-storage capacity, which had been 28 million cubic metres in 1958, stood at 324.7 in 1966 and it jumped to 1762 by 1970. Corresponding to the increase in water-storage facilities, the area under irrigation was expanded from 160 thousand hectares in 1958 to 587.5 thousand in 1971. Also in the mid-1960s, 6000 kilometres of roads and highways were constructed; 10,000 kilometres of roads had existed in 1958. (By 1975, total water-storage capacity would be further increased to 4400 million cubic metres. And the road network would be increased to a total of 27,000 kilometres.)

In addition to expanding the supply of modern agricultural inputs and equipment and extending the agricultural infrastructure, consider-able effort was devoted to establishing a scientific foundation for the development of agriculture. On the one hand, this effort involved the development of modern cattle-breeding techniques and the introduction of new seed varieties for various crops. On the other hand, the educational system was being structured so as to supply the trained personnel to develop and operate a modern agriculture.

As far as the particular emphasis on sugar was concerned, Castro later described the actions taken as follows:

The first plan for the development of the sugar industry was put into practice in the five year period, from 1966 to 1970. The objectives were those of increasing installed capacity, replacing the industry's ob-solete equipment, massively introducing advanced techniques in cane planting and cultivation, and solving the problem of mechanizing the harvesting. In those years, 334 million went into reconstruction and 235 million into enlargement. The lands earmarked for cane growing increased by 35 per cent, new varieties of cane were introduced, and the extension of irrigation and the use of herbicides was begun. The use of fertilizer was considerably increased. In this period, new machines were designed to mechanize the harvesting. In 1970, Cuba grew its biggest sugar harvest ever and the world's biggest cane-sugar harvest. The progress made in agricultural yield and the use of technical means was considerable. Cultivation was mechanized and the mechanization of harvesting was started. The bulk-sugar shipping system wa$^.$ enlarged.

THE LABOUR MOBILISATION

In addition to a heavy investment programme, the 'big push' in the agricultural sector involved a huge labour mobilisation. The role of sugar cane in the strategy of the 1960s meant a continuation of the seasonal fluctuation in the demand for labour. And this fluctuation would be severe until mechanisation could reduce the demand for labour during the harvest season. In an effort to solve the problems associated with the seasonality of sugar production as well as the problem of continuing general labour shortage in agriculture, labour regularly employed in other sectors of the economy was brought to the countryside for the cane harvests. The extent of the general problem can be seen from the fact that prior to 1959 there had been roughly 350,000 regular cane cutters, but by 1967 there were only 80,000; this latter figure does not include persons employed full time on state farms.

The labor mobilisations of the late 1960s, involving several categories of workers, were tied to the general programme of developing a system of workers motivation based on moral incentives. Workers regularly employed in other occupations (including other parts of agriculture) volunteered to leave their regular jobs for extended periods and cut cane; such workers were paid their regular salaries while in the cane fields. Special brigades were formed in which young people enlisted for a period of two or three years to work in agriculture. Students from secondary schools and colleges spent considerable time working in the cane fields. And thousands of women were organised to the mobilisations through the Committees for the Defence of the Revolution (CDRs)—the basic neighbourhood organisations of the Cuban people—and the Federation of Cuban Women (FMC).

Aside from those regularly employed in other sectors and brigade members who received a minimal payment, the participants in the mobilisation were not paid. They were encouraged to donate their labour to further the national welfare; in other words, they were motivated on the principle of political commitment, or a moral incentive. The operation of the special brigades, the minimal salaries notwithstanding, was also based primarily on political consciousness. And even workers receiving their regular salary were encouraged to take part in the mobilisations on the basis of an appeal to the collective welfare and thus received no special remuneration for doing so.

Partial figures on the labour mobilisations of 1966–8 are presented in Table 15.5. These data indicate that in 1967, for example, 25,000 workers from other sectors were mobilised for the entire harvest; 10,000 were involved in the Giron Brigade; and another 28.5 thousand were mobilised in various other programmes. In addition, 140,000 students participated in the harevest and 29,000 people were mobilised through the CDRs and the FMC.

TABLE 15.5 Sugar-harvest mobilisations, 1966–8 (000s)

	1966	1967	1968
Workers from other sectors	25.0	25.0	30.0
Giron Brigade	8.0	10.0	21.0
Other mobilisations of employed persons	28.0	28.5	56.0
Students	20.0	140.0	160.0
CDR and FMC mobilisations	25.0	29.0	35.0

SOURCE
Cuba (1970a) p. 136.

NOTE
These data are incomplete and do not include all labour mobilised for these harvests.

For 1967, the data from Table 15.5, combined with the 80,000 figure for regular cane cutters involved in the harvest, would indicate a total of 312.5 thousand people working in the cane cutting. These data, however, are partial figures. They do not include, for example, persons who were employed full time on state farms, who cut the cane on their own farms. Moreover, there is no indication of the average time that each member of the mobilisations actually worked in the harvest.

In the harvest of 1970, the labour mobilisation appears to have been substantially greater. Some 1.2 million persons were mobilised. At the peak of the harvest, roughly 200,000 of these were employed daily. (These figures are not directly comparable to those given above for the preceding years, since the 1970 harvest was spread over a longer period; and, in any case, the data in Table 15.5 are only partial.)

This synopsis of the figures on investment and labour mobilisation in the late 1960s gives a crude picture of Cuba's 'big push' in agriculture. The results of the 'big push' need to be appraised from the standpoint of both immediate production gains and longer-run social and economic development. In the following chapter, we shall report the immediate production gains (and losses) of the 1960s; from this standpoint, the 'big push' and the general strategy of the 1960s show rather poorly. When we turn to longer-run considerations and offer an explanation of the 1960s—beginning in Chapter 17—a more positive picture will emerge.

16 The Frustration of Cuban Development in the 1960s

Cuba's agriculture-based development strategy of the 1960s ran into difficulties early on. Except for the first year of the new strategy's implementation, 1965, the targets for sugar production were not attained (see Table 16.1). Indeed, 1966 and 1969 were poor sugar-production years by historical standards, let alone the standards of the plan. The 1970 harvest was in fact a record harvest of 8.5 million tons— 18 per cent higher than the previous peak—but it was far short of the targeted 10 million.

TABLE 16.1 Plan targets and sugar production, 1965–70 (000s tons)

	Plan target	Actual production	Deficit	% deficit
1965	6.0	6.2	+ 0.2	+ 3
1966	6.5	4.5	− 2.0	− 31
1967	7.5	6.2	− 1.3	− 17
1968	8.0	5.2	− 2.8	− 35
1969	9.0	4.5	− 4.5	− 50
1970	10.0	8.5	− 1.5	− 15

SOURCE
Cuba (1973) p. 124, and p. 98, above.

The significance of the failure to harvest the 10 million tons of sugar in 1970 appeared all the greater because of the importance which had been attributed to that goal by the Cuban leaders. In a speech of 13 March, 1968, for example, Fidel Castro had stated: 'The question of a sugar harvest of 10 million tons has been something more than an economic goal; it is something that has been converted into a point of honor for this Revolution; it has become a yardstick by which to judge the

capability of the Revolution . . . and, if a yardstick is put up to th
Revolution, there is no doubt about the Revolution's meeting the mark.

Speaking of economic goals in this way was part of the process o
attempting to establish a political basis for economic motivation. B
raising the 10 million ton harvest to the level of 'a yardstick of th
Revolution' Castro was attempting to create a campaign atmospher
and strengthen political-based incentives. But when the sugar target wa
not obtained, aside from the immediate economic implications, th
political foundations of the incentives system were threatened.

In other parts of the agricultural sector, the plan also fell short. In th
cultivation of rice, for example, the plan had called for the cultivation o
200,000 hectares by 1970, but only 187,000 were cultivated in that year
and, in the preceding five years, the figure had been far lower. The targe
for citrus fruits had been the cultivation of 100,000 hectares; but in 197(
only 46,000 hectares were in citrus fruits. For beans, instead o
expanding to the 65,000 hectares targeted, the area cultivated decrease
to 11,000 hectares. Performance in coffee, tobacco, fruits and vegetables, and milk and meat production also fell far short of the planned
targets. There were areas of success within agriculture—egg production
for example, increased from 309 million in 1964 to 1.4 billion in 1970—
but these were small and exceptional.

The agricultural sector did poorly in the late 1960s, not only in
comparison with planned targets, but also by comparison with previous
years. The index of agricultural production did not surpass its 1961 peak
until the huge sugar harvest of 1970. Even in that year, agricultural
production per capita was less than 1 per cent above the 1961 level.
Throughout the 1962–9 period, agricultural production per capita was
substantially below the level of the mid-1950s (see Table 16.2).

It is worth noting that these data probably portray the situation as
somewhat worse than it actually was. As noted above (Chapter 8),
Cuban agricultural data only include that portion of private production
actually collected by the state purchasing agencies. In so far as the
peasants' own consumption grew, or in so far as sales outside the state
agencies took place, the official figures understate growth or overstate
decline. (It is, of course, very difficult to obtain any reliable appraisal of
the extent of private sales in Cuba, i.e., of the black market. Various
indirect evidence suggests that in the late 1960s private sales were not
trivial.)

The economy as a whole did somewhat better than agriculture in the
mid-1960s but did not grow rapidly. While the agricultural sector of
gross material product (GMP) grew by 9.5 per cent between 1962 and

TABLE 16.2 Agricultural production in the 1960s

	Total agricultural production (1952–6 = 100)	Agricultural production per capita (1952–6 = 100)	Sugar harvest (million tons)
1960	114	101	5.9
1961	122	106	6.8
1962	100	85	4.8
1963	86	72	3.8
1964	93	75	4.4
1965	112	89	6.1
1966	94	72	4.5
1967	116	88	6.1
1968	106	79	5.3
1969	99*	73	4.4
1970	151*	107	8.5

NOTE
* The huge jump in the index between 1969 and 1970 is explained by the fact that sugar output almost doubled between these years—see text.

SOURCE
Ritter (1974) p. 113, based on various UN sources. Ritter notes that the data on which the indices are based are 'fragmentary and incomplete'. Many important products are excluded from the calculations, and very crude estimates for other products are included.

1969, GMP increased by 16 per cent, a bit better than 2 per cent per year, and industry grew at roughly the same rate. (It will be recalled that 1962 was a rather poor year; but then so was 1969.) Some of the non-agricultural growth was directly tied to the sugar push. The major expansion of the transport sector, which (in current prices) more than doubled its output in the 1962–9 period, and the 3 per cent growth rate of construction are at least in part tied to sugar—not to mention the expansion of industrial-sugar activities. Still, it is worth noting that while growing slowly, non-agriculture did better than agriculture, even though the latter was receiving the major emphasis.

It is also worth noting that the economy did very well in 1970. The large sugar harvest led a major spurt in the economy, even though the target of 10 million tons was not achieved. Total GMP rose by 20 per cent between 1969 and 1970; industry (including the sugar industry) grew by 25 per cent. Non-cane agriculture output did decline between 1969 and 1970—by 5 per cent—but the output of the livestock sector rose by 16 per cent. With the exception of a 3 per cent drop in construction, all other major sectors of the economy showed increases.

The large mobilisation for the sugar harvest and consequent general disruption could have had a serious negative impact on non-agricultural (and non-cane agricultural) production. But this does not seem to have been the case. Whatever negative spin-off there was from the 10 million ton campaign seems to have appeared in earlier years.

Regardless of events in 1970 itself, however, the 1960s were a poor period for the Cuban economy. Yet this had also been a time of great expectations. In the following chapters we shall attempt to explain why those expectations were frustrated. In doing so, we hope to obtain some useful insights on the operation and contradictions of the Cuban economy.

Part Five

Organisation,
Socialist Development
and Class Power

17 Organisation, Socialist Development and Class Power

The poor performance of the Cuban economy during the 1960s has given impetus to a wide set of explanations and serious criticisms of the Cuban strategy, its theory and practice. Some analysts have taken the experience of those years as evidence for the impossibility of combining economic growth and economic equality. From this perspective, the Cuban leaders are viewed as being too idealistic and unrealistic in their attempt to achieve economic expansion through an emphasis on moral incentives. Other critics explain the poor performance in the 1960s as a consequence of bureaucratic control and argue that the Cuban leadership had been remiss in centralising authority so thoroughly. This argument sees the labour mobilisations, the role of the army in production campaigns and the general military or campaign atmosphere of the late 1960s as the vain efforts to overcome the deficiencies of bureaucratic misorganisation.

These various analyses seem to be deficient in several respects. First, they tend to see the Cuban experience primarily in terms of decisions—usually viewed as wrong decisions—taken by the leadership. There is relatively little effort to examine the historical context which led to those decisions and shaped their outcome. Second, few if any critics of the Cuban experience place their analyses in the context of a theory of socialist development. Without a theory, they are reduced to explanations based on particular events and 'erroneous' decisions. Third, most critics of the Cuban experience in the 1960s did not take account of events in the early 1970s. Eager to offer indictments of the Cuban strategy, they developed their analyses quickly and would later find themselves contradicted by the next phase of Cuban develpopment.

For in the early 1970s, the Cuban economy grew extremely rapidly. In the five years from 1969 to 1974, Cuba's gross material product expanded at a rate of over 10 per cent a year. The agricultural sector did not do nearly so well as the rest of the economy, but grew at about 4.5 per cent a year. In the mid-1970s, the growth of the Cuban economy has not been so rapid. Yet, overall, the contrast between the 1960s and 1970s is very sharp. The experience of the 1970s will be described and analysed in subsequent chapters. It must, however, be kept in mind while considering the problems of the 1960s.

In this chapter, it will be useful to focus on 'the problem of organisation' and build upon comments which have been made in earlier chapters. It will be possible to develop some components of a theory of socialist development which will enhance our understanding of the 1960s and place those years in the context of Cuba's historical development. Moreover, a focus on organisation and its relation to class power will allow several issues dealt with in subsequent chapters to be usefully tied together.

THE SOCIALISATION OF PRODUCTION

A central component in the advancement of economic activity is the creation of patterns of social relations in which people interact with one another in an effective and disciplined manner. Such patterns of social relations are often seen in terms of 'modernisation', and they are in fact usefully counterposed to 'traditional' modes of social relations.

In traditional modes of social relations, one factor which stands out particularly vividly is the independence or isolation of various economic activities. Traditional peasant or craft activities are carried on by individual producers or very small groups (often families). Also, a large share of production activity is oriented toward the consumption needs of the producers, and contact with other producers through some form of exchange relationship is minimal.

The independence of economic activities in the traditional situation is associated with stagnation and lack of economic innovation. Production activity is ruled by long standing practices, and an ideology of traditionalism—in which things are done a certain way because they have always been done that way—becomes a powerful force. This is not to say that the ideology of traditionalism is in some sense 'irrational'. Often, sticking to well-established production practices is the most effective manner of assuring economic survival, given the general social context in which the individual producer operates. Nonetheless, ir-rational or not, traditionalism reinforces the stagnation of the system.

Traditional economic practices and ideology can persist in an environment even after many of the basic foundations—most particularly the isolation of production activity—have been altered. This can be the case especially in a capitalist underdeveloped nation such as Cuba was prior to 1959. Integrated in the world system of production with large-scale production units playing a major role, traditional modes of economic activity persisted in pre-revolutionary Cuba. The operation of international capitalism had kept Cuban production activity from being isolated activity in a truly traditional sense. But at the same time—as argued in Chapter 2—the force of international capitalism prevented the development of a strong and independent capitalist class from emerging in Cuba. Consequently basic traditional practices had not been thoroughly altered and stagnation persisted.

In understanding how the process of economic development can proceed, how traditional patterns of social relations can be replaced by patterns in which people interact in an economically effective and disciplined manner, it is useful to employ Marx's discussion of these sorts of issues as a reference point. Marx wrote about the changing patterns of social relations in terms of the 'socialisation' of the production process. He saw this as one of the principal features of capitalist development. The socialisation of the production process can be viewed as involving two components.

On the one hand, socialisation of production is external to the enterprise, involving the increasing interdependence *among different economic units* and the successful coordination of their mutual activity. In capitalist society, this interdependence and coordination is mediated through the market, but it nevertheless involves the formation of human abilities and behavioural patterns. The market as a dominant form of economic organisation is peculiar to capitalist society, but the importance of the organisational function which it serves should be seen as transcending any particular type of society.

On the other hand, socialisation of production is internal to the economic unit, involving the increasing interdependence *among the individual workers* and successful coordination of their mutual activity. Again, in capitalist society, the market plays a role in this second aspect of socialisation, but its role is more limited. The direct exercise of authority in the capitalist work place—the exercise of power by the owners of capital and their agents—is the primary direct mechanism of socialisation internal to the enterprise. The market, most particularly the labour market, operating as a mechanism through which workers obtain their livelihood, lies behind this direct exercise of authority, and makes it possible. Moreover, the capitalist state stands ready to enforce the authority of the owners of capital. (The state, of course, also stands behind the effective operation of markets, enforcing contracts, controlling the monetary system, and developing an infrastructure.) As with the effective coordination of the activity of different enterprises, socialisation internal to the enterprise involves the formation of human abilities and behavioural patterns. And while the particular mode of socialisation—the exercise of authority by bosses—may be peculiar to capitalist society, the internal organisation of work activity is a general problem in the process of economic development.

CAPITALIST UNDERDEVELOPMENT AND SOCIALIST DEVELOPMENT

From a classical Marxist point of view, the task of the socialisation of production activity was, or would be, accomplished by capitalism. Indeed, creating an organisational structure which allowed rapid accumulation of capital and the revolutionising of the forces of production was the great historical feat of capitalism. From the point of view of classical Marxism, the task of socialist societies would be one of building on this accomplishment of capitalism, of using the modern productive forces as a basis on which to transform social relations—that is, to replace competitive organisation of production and inequality with cooperative organisation, equality, and associated humane relationships.

For Marx, it was the contradiction between the concentration of ownership and the increasingly private nature of appropriation, on the one hand, and the increasingly social nature of production, on the other hand, which was central to the destruction of capitalism. The development of this contradiction is a consequence of capitalist success—that is, success in its own terms of expansion, accumulation and transforming the production process.

Yet the reality of socialist forces coming to power—in Cuba and elsewhere—has been different than as envisioned by Marx. Socialist groups have not successfully seized power in the centre of the capitalist system, where its success (and the contradictions associated with that success) are most manifest. Instead, they have taken power in those areas of the world where capitalism has not been successful, where it has not accomplished its historic task of socialising the production process. (In an important sense, these areas of failure are manifestations of a central contradiction in capitalist society, namely, the contradition of inequal development. The success manifested in the centre of the capitalist system is dependent upon and creates the failure in the periphery.)

The problem faced by Cuba, and by other nations attempting to build socialism in the context of capitalist underdevelopment, has been how to accomplish the task of both transforming the productive forces of society *and* transforming social relations. More particularly, the problem is one of creating the forms of organisation—human abilities and behavioural patterns—that allow economic development without preventing or perverting the movement towards socialist social relations. For example, in Cuba, a central component of socialist social relations is economic equality. Accordingly the use of a system of material, personal incentives as a mechanism to enforce worker discipline and create effective work organisation needs to be limited, because an unlimited system of personal incentives is inconsistent with equality.

ORGANISATION AND CLASS POWER

Many analysts have recognised the importance of organisation as a central feature in economic development, though there is often a tendency to identify the peculiar modes of organisation of capitalist development as universal phenomena. In particular, organisation is often seen as a top-down process, involving two sorts of complementary human abilities. One of these abilities is identified as the capacity of an elite to impose organisation on workers and to operate in a market setting. This capacity is often identified as 'entrepreneurial ability'. In addition, in this view of development and organisation, workers need to be able to follow orders and respect authority, to be disciplined in a hierarchical mode. Moreover, the central factor which both provides motivation to the entrepreneur and maintains discipline of the worker is seen as individual self-interest.

There is no doubt that a top-down system of organisation, based on a personal-gain incentive structure, can be an effective form of economic transformation. But whether or not it is the only effective form of economic transformation is another matter.

It is essential to recognise that the process of organisation and development is not just the collection of a number of particular traits or abilities. More fundamentally, the problem of organisation can be seen as a problem of class power. In capitalist development, successful organisation is tied in with the successful dominance of the bourgeoisie in economic and political affairs. The ability of the bourgeoisie to organise society in pursuit of its own interests—accumulation of capital in particular—is the epitome of the exercise of its power as a class.

In the transition towards socialism, successful organisation is, similarly, tied in with the effective exercise of power by the proletariat. And the extent to which successful economic organisation is achieved in a transitional society, may be taken as an indicator of the extent to which the proletariat has been able to organise society in its own interests.

In any revolution, but particularly in the Cuban revolution, the seizure of political power is only one step in the process of class transformation. In Cuba, there was minimal immediate and direct participation of an organised working-class movement in that political step. A state came into being which took actions in the interests of the working class and actions which can be interpreted as leading towards the rise of working-class power (both the agrarian reform and the literary campaign would be examples of such actions). But the Cuban state did not immediately become a state based on a thorough political organisation of the working class.

In the final analysis, while there are several features of Cuba's economic weakness in the 1960s, the underlying weakness can be interpreted as the inhibition on the exercise of power by the working class. Likewise, an important component of the changes in the 1970s has been the development of political forms which can facilitate working-class power in Cuba. These points will be substantiated in what follows, here and in later chapters (especially in the general argument of Chapter 21).

ORIGINS OF THE ORGANISATION PROBLEM

The role of the Cuban working class in the country's socialist development has its roots in the pre-1959 period. The organisational foundations among the populace, on which the revolution could build, were not strong. For all practical purposes, there was no effective organisational infrastructure of workers in the various enterprises that could take a role in the development and implementation of planning. The problem was especially severe in agriculture, where the proletariat had been so thoroughly alienated from authority in production.

Here, in the lack of preparation of the Cuban masses for the administration of a socialist economy, lies a conundrum for the Marxist analysis of the revolutionary transition to socialism.

In the process of successful capitalist expansion, the production process is increasingly socialised—workers become interdependent both within and between enterprises—and ownership becomes increasingly concentrated and detached from production. As noted above, this process is what Marx saw as the central contradiction of capitalist expansion, the contradiction which would lead to socialism. The contradiction was at work in pre-1959 Cuba, where the sugar complex carried the socialisation process much further than in many otherwise more advanced nations. And domination by foreign interests exacerbated concentration and the separation of ownership from operation.

Marxist analysis, however, recognises another facet of the capitalist expansion process. It is a process which degrades workers, deprives them of general skills and knowledge of the work process, and subordinates them to the control and authority of capitalists and their agents. This degradation, deprivation and subordination of workers is what Marx described as alienation. The alienation of workers from the work process in which they were engaged was, for Marx, the mechanism by which they were deprived of the product of their labour, i.e., by which they were exploited. Again, pre-1959 Cuba, especially in cane agriculture, exemplifies this process: cane cutters provided an extreme case of workers involved in a specific and limited aspect of the production process, extremely exploited and bereft of overall knowledge of the production in which they were engaged. With other Cuban workers, the situation may have been less extreme, but its general character was the same.

For Marxists, the revolutionary process, brought about directly and indirectly by the operation by capitalism's central contradiction, is a revolution against alienation and exploitation. And socialism should constitute a negation of those processes. Yet—and here lies the conundrum—how are people so thoroughly degraded, without experience in or knowledge of the organisation of production, going to be able to administer socialist production? Capitalism may automatically create conditions which lead toward its own demise, but it certainly does not prepare people for the creative act of building and running a new society. Indeed, it appears to do just the opposite.

How, then, do the conditions for the organisation of socialist development get created? The suggestion of an answer to this question can be inferred from certain aspects of Marxist historical analysis. The operation of the central contradition of capitalist expansion—increased socialisation versus increased concentration of ownership—creates the condition for an historically new type of political struggle. It is the collective struggle of an exploited class, brought together in large numbers by the very success of capitalist development. *The struggle itself* creates and requires the development of the organisational capacities of the working masses. Moreover, a socialist revolution is not an event; the struggle does not end with the capture of state power. In the period after the seizure of state power (what Marx called 'the dictatorship of the proletariat') the struggle continues on numerous levels—political, economic and cultural. and the success of that struggle can be measured in terms of how thoroughly it creates the institutions which further the ability and authority of the working people to administer the new society.

In the Cuban revolution, the immediate struggle for power provided little foundation for the organisation of socialist development. The old order had fallen before there had been any thorough involvement of the masses in the military phase of the struggle. Furthermore, the early reforms, while extremely popular, were decreed and carried out from above. INRA did not, for example, organise rural workers and peasants to carry out land reform themselves. Nonetheless, there was in Cuba a long history of working-class struggle and organisation. Unions had risen to an important position in the pre-1959 period, and the Communist Party had been relatively large. The experience of the Cuban working class did provide a basis on which the Cuban revolution might build. (Chapter 4 contains an elaboration of the points in this paragraph.)

Cuban experience in the late 1960s can be interpreted in relation to the broad issue of how new class relations and associated forms of organisation can be constructed as a foundation for socialist development. And the weakness of the Cuban economy during this period indicates the inherent problems encountered and the explicit errors committed in the effort to transform class relations and solve the 'organisation problem'.

Various particular difficulties—which will be examined in more detail below—indicate the significance of organisational problems in Cuba during the 1960s. While tractors, for example, were imported at record levels, they often lay idle, either delayed in reaching the farms or poorly maintained when they did reach the farms. Worker absenteeism became a severe problem, even at the peak of the major national labour mobilisation. Production processes were often carried out in a wasteful and inefficient manner. Consumer services deteriorated. A reliance on central decision-making often created delays in deliveries of raw materials and consequent work stoppages. Such particular difficulties an be analysed in terms of investment, problems of the design of development strategy, and problems of incentives. Each will be taken up in due course.

In the following chapters, as these categories of problems are examined, the concept of 'organisation' will be given more substance. It should become evident that the development of organisation involves formation of several subsidiary human traits and social relations. Among these are effective work habits and discipline, technical skills, administrative and coordinative relationships, and systems of incentives and motivation.

18 Investment and Organisation in the 1960s

One of the major achievements of the Cuban planning authorities in the 1960s was their success in mobilising the nation's economic surplus to attain high rates of investment. The large investments, however, do not appear to have been effective, at least in the short run, in leading to a growth of output. Some examples from the period will indicate the way in which the ineffectiveness of investment was tied to organisational deficiencies.

THE INEFFECTIVENESS OF INVESTMENT

In the agricultural sector, an example of ineffective investment was the rapid increase in the supply of tractors (see Table 15.3 above). Data shown in Table 18.1 for 1970 indicate that, on a national level, only a quarter of tractor capacity was actually in use. Tractor time loss was accounted for partly by rainfall, but almost half of the time loss was due to 'breakdowns, repairs and maintenance'. More than a quarter of the

TABLE 18.1 Utilisation of the work day by tractors at the national level, 1970

	%
Work time	25.2
Time lost	74.8
Rainfall	9.9
Break-downs	31.7
Repair and maintenance	4.6
Administrative	20.7
Other	7.9

SOURCE
Pensamiento Critico (October 1970) p. 183, as reported by Ritter (1974).

132

ost time was the result of problems of 'administration'; presumably this explanation refers to organisation factors such as failing to get tractors where they were needed.

Other cases of ineffective investment appear in the efforts to mechanise the cutting of sugar cane. For example, by 1967 a total of 000 combines had been imported from the Soviet Union for the sugar harvest. But it was then found that the combines were too heavy, complicated, and fragile for Cuban conditions. They had to be discarded.

Other examples are contained in Fidel Castro's speech of 26 July 970, in which he provides an extensive discussion of the failure to harvest 10 million tons of sugar and of the general problems of the Cuban economy up to that point. Investment in the expansion of Cuba's dairy herd was rendered ineffective because insufficient complementary investment was devoted to dairy and milk-processing equipment. Investment in beef production was hurt by, among other things, poor transportation; delays meant that cattle lost weight excessively on the way to slaughter. Poorly coordinated investment in transportation, especially the failure to supply sufficient spare parts, created numerous problems in agriculture and elsewhere. New trucks and rail equipment sat idle, and investments in the sectors which they could therefore not service were less productive.

Not only were investments ineffective but, in addition, investments were made with little attention to cost. For example, in a description of his visit to Cuba in 1970, Wassily Leontief cites a cattle barn air-conditioned with expensive imported equipment. And the entire investment programme directed at obtaining the 10 million ton harvest seems to have been undertaken with little consideration for the relationships between costs and yields (see below, Chapter 19).

Moreover, the structure of the programme to produce the 10 million tons exhibited a severe imbalance of investment. According to Castro, the failure to obtain the harvest goal resulted from problems in the mills, not from problems in the fields. The bottle-neck at the mills rendered much of the investment in the fields ineffective. Furthermore, the problem in the mills was in large part one of making the newly installed equipment operate effectively. The equipment was there; the investment per se was accomplished; but its use and productiveness was another matter.

These cases of ineffective investment, cited here, are confined to the agriculture and the sugar industry, but the same sort of problems existed throughout the Cuban economy.

ORGANISATION AND EXPANSION

The widespread ineffectiveness of investment in the 1960s provides very powerful illustration of the organisation problem. Moreover, i brings out the fact that organisational factors become of specia importance in the process of economic expansion.

Any production activity involves labour working with capital equip ment. And, in general, as the amount of capital equipment is increased labour can produce more. Yet increasing the amount of capita equipment—that is, investing—necessarily changes the nature of th production process. New activities take place; or, what amounts to th same thing, old activities are done in new ways. In other words expansion is change.

Changing the way things are done, however, is a complex process First, experience *per se*, for the worker or the enterprise, becomes a les useful guide in a period of economic expansion. Second, in the process o expansion, people's activities generally become—directly or indirectly— interconnected and interdependent with a larger number of othe workers. In this context, processes such as the learning of new skills an coordination of economic activity become increasingly significant.

The role of organisational factors rises, or their absence becomes ver clear. More new tractors cannot harvest the crop unless they are at th right place at the right time. Nor can a mass mobilisation of labour b effective unless those involved acquire needed skills, work together, an are transported to the places where they are needed. A larger diary her cannot bottle and deliver milk to consumers on its own. And truck without ball-bearings cannot roll.

The sorts of organisational deficiencies which appeared in Cub during the 1960s are present to one degree or another in all underde veloped countries. They appeared especially vividly in Cuba, however because of two particular aspects of the expansion effort. First investments were not directed by cost and yield calculations undertaker at the local level, but by centralised analyses of the need for capacity t meet certain aggregate goals. In a capitalist underdeveloped economy operated on profit principles, the constraint of organisational capacity affects local-level profit calculations, and investments do not get made The result is often misanalysed as being the consequence of insufficien capital when the capital is not forthcoming because an inability to effectively organise production limits profitability. In Cuba, investment was not inhibited by profitability considerations, but the organisational constraint on development was revealed most clearly.

Second, the organisational limits appeared sharply in Cuba because the big push was so concentrated in a single sector of the economy. The experience and skills—relating both to technical operations and group activity—which constitute organisational capacity are not readily transferable from one activity to another. Thus the big push that was undertaken in sugar ran up against the organisational limits of the sugar industry.

The last point calls into question one of the basic aspects of the design of Cuban strategy in the 1960s, namely its extreme reliance on an unbalanced development programme. Indeed, the entire discussion of effectiveness of investment raises questions about the design of strategy.

19 Weaknesses in the Design of Development Strategy

In designing and implementing their development strategy for the 1960s, the Cuban leaders operated as though a high level of investment, especially investment in modern equipment, was the key to economic expansion. This view of the development process probably had origins in a limited diagnosis of Cuba's failure to develop in the capitalist era, a diagnosis which confused manifestations with causes. Cuba's subordination within the imperialist system was, to be sure, the central factor in the diagnosis. But, in particular, the diagnosis focused on the fact that domination of Cuban society by imperialism had meant an alienation of the country's economic surplus and, consequently, low rates of investment. Moreover, the structures imposed by imperialism had also led to high rates of unemployment and relatively limited use of modern technology.

It was easy to infer from this diagnosis of Cuban history that once the old system was destroyed, once the shackles of imperialism were broken, the impediments to investment, full employment, and modernisation would be eliminated. So, it would seem development of the economy could then proceed apace.

Such a view of underdevelopment tends to give insufficient attention to the impact of imperialism on social organisation. As we have argued in Chapter 2, imperialism inhibited Cuban development primarily through its impact on the socialisation process. It simultaneously prevented the development of a nationally oriented capitalist class that could organise production in its own interest, and created an economic structure dominated by agriculture, which limited the preparation of the working class for a role as organiser of production. The quantitative or technical deficiencies of the Cuban economy—underinvestment, unemployment, backward technology—may be most usefully interpreted as manifestations of this particular social structure. To overcome these deficiencies within the context of socialism, it would be necessary to create a working class which could accomplish organisational tasks.

Some efforts were being made in this direction during the 1960s—see below, Chapter 23—but at best, their fruition was far off.

There is little evidence that the Cuban leaders viewed the expansion of society's capacity for organisation as a central factor in determining the design of a development strategy. Their views, dominated by their diagnosis of Cuban history, placed technical factors—primarily more modern capital equipment—at the centre of their strategy. This view of economic development is reflected in various documents of the Cuban government and various statements delivered by its officials. There is a continual emphasis on what is seen as the technological base of development—new tractors, fertiliser, new equipment in the sugar mills, new cattle-breeding techniques, educated technicians, and new seed varieties. In so far as attention was devoted to people's behaviour in the Cuban development strategy, the focus was almost entirely on motivation. Nowhere, it seems, did the Cuban leaders directly address the matter of how they could accomplish the socialisation of the production process.

SUGAR: MECHANISING THE HARVEST

Perhaps the best example of this technical view as it affected the design of Cuban planning is the programme for harvesting 10 million tons of sugar. When this goal was conceived in 1964, its achievement was viewed as depending on the mechanisation of the sugar harvest. Mechanisation was seen as possible if enough new equipment was provided, and consequently large investments were directed toward this end.

Yet, by 1970, very little progress had been made towards a mechanised harvesting of the crop. In the 1970 harvest, less than 2 per cent of the cane was cut by mechanised means. (It should be noted, however, that nearly 90 per cent of the harvested cane was being mechanically loaded for transport in the 1970 harvest.) In the early 1970s, significant advances would be achieved in the mechanisation of the harvest; but the failure to accomplish the task by the 1970 harvest cannot be dismissed, and it provides a focal point for interpreting certain difficulties of the period.

To begin with, the failure to mechanise meant that a much greater mobilisation of labour was required for the harvest than had been originally anticipated. Consequently the harvest placed a severe strain on the organisational capacity of the nation, and this strain had its impact throughout the economy, but especially in the sugar mills.

Moreover, there is the matter of explaining why mechanisation was not accomplished when the leaders of the government thought it could be accomplished. Their error most likely lay in an insufficient emphasis on social factors—as opposed to technical factors—in both their formulation and implementation of the plan. Mechanisation is not only a matter of machines, but also requires the establishment of sufficient organisational capacity for the effective development and utilisation of mechanical processes. Technological change is fundamentally a matter of how *labour* is utilised. Yet the Cuban plan placed no direct emphasis on transforming the organisation of labour so that modernisation could be accomplished. By failing to recognise the need for focusing on labour organisation in their analyses of constraints on development, the Cubans overestimated what could be accomplished. By failing to focus their efforts on transforming labour organisation, they did not accomplish as much as they could have.

SUGAR: THE STRATEGY OF UNBALANCED DEVELOPMENT

A recognition of the organisational limits on development would have led to a rather different balance in the sectoral emphasis of Cuba's planning programme. The adoption of an extremely unbalanced development strategy seems particularly inappropriate when organisational capacity is an active constraint on development.

As we noted in Chapter 18, the experience and skills which constitute organisational capacity are not readily transferable from one activity to another. Dock workers or office personnel, for example, can be taken to the cane fields, but they have no familiarity with the work organisation, let alone the technical skills, involved in the cane harvest. The administrative officials in the Ministry of Sugar have no experience in directing and coordinating a massive influx of workers to the mills. Transport workers and administrators are not knowledgeable concerning the special tasks of a mass harvest mobilisation. And the existing corps of skilled mechanics and maintenance workers cannot handle a huge and sudden increase in the use of machinery. People can learn to handle these various tasks. But learning takes time. The amount of labour available in a particular sector can be rapidly increased. But increasing the organisational capacity in a particular activity is a slower process.

Difficulties which developed in the sugar mills reflect the problems of unbalanced expansion most clearly. There was no lack of workers in the mills, with 127,000 people working in the sugar industry in 1970 as compared to 92,000 in 1958. And, according to Castro's analysis of the situation, there was no shortfall in the actual amount of equipment installed in the mills. The problem lay in effectively using that new capacity. He states for example: 'We saw that the mills with large installations of new capacity were holding things up, because they reduced the grinding rate, and because they were going to lengthen the harvest and affect the yield.' Also: 'While we had 20 mills in Oriente with new machinery and all 20 of them were giving us headaches, other mills in which no expansion work had been done, did not receive all the attention or all of the maintenance required.' Castro sums up his analysis as follows:

Three factors have made their influence felt in the low yield: number one, the new equipment; number two, maintenance, which was not up to par in many mills; and number three—and to tell the truth, it's an open question whether this is really factor number three or the principal factor—inefficient management of the mills.
. . . our ignorance of the problem of the sugar industry kept us from realizing as soon as was necessary . . . the different types of problems of a subjective nature, of skilled workers and other problems, so as to take necessary measures in time.

It is reasonable to conclude that the industrial segment of sugar production could not absorb the investment and labour power which was devoted to it in the big push for 10 million tons. The complementary input of organisational capacity was insufficient. Had investment and labour been distributed in a more balanced manner, little, if any, production would have been lost in sugar, while gains elsewhere might have been substantial.

The seriousness of this imbalance error was all the greater because so little attention was given to cost considerations in investment programmes once the overall design of the strategy was established. Estimates made during the process of expansion in the 1960s indicated that expansion from the existing capacity of about 7 million tons of sugar to a capacity of 8.5 million tons would require some 300 million pesos of investment—half in the industrial sector and half in agriculture. To expand to a 10 million ton capacity would require another 700 million pesos. While these figures reveal rapidly diminishing returns in sugar, the actual situation was far worse since the 10 million tons was, in fact, not obtained. Organisational constraints meant that investments were even less effective than anticipated.

OTHER PROBLEMS OF SUBSTANCE AND IMPLEMENTATION

In large part, the problems of the Cuban economy of the 1960s appear in terms of these substantive deficiencies of the plan's design—an overemphasis on technical consideration and a failure to recognise the limits to unbalanced growth. There are other substantive deficiencies in a plan calling for Cuba's continued subjugation to the uncertainty of weather, dependency on a narrow export base, difficulties with labour supply, and an implicit limit on programmes for transforming the nature of labour organisation. However, these problems accompany success as well as failure, and it accordingly seems more appropriate to discuss them in the context of evaluating Cuba's development in the 1970s (see below, Chapter 28).

In addition to plan substance, the form of plan implementation, especially in its overcentralisation, had serious shortcomings. The central planning authorities articulated plans for the agricultural sector that were often so detached from the possible as to become inoperative. Annual plans for particular areas sometimes had to be revised two or three times in the course of a year. And in some cases, the plan was simply inoperative, and local units operated on their own, independent of any overall plan.

OVERCENTRALISATION: PROBLEMS IN PRIVATE AGRICULTURE

One manifestation of overcentralisation seems to have been an insufficient emphasis on secondary crops, particularly those crops in which the small private peasants played an important role. (It should be noted, however, that official statistics—as pointed out in Chapter 8— make it difficult to judge production levels since they include only that share of private production purchased by state agencies.)

Table 19.1 includes data for the 1962–70 period on the collection of four major categories of secondary crops—grains, tubers, vegetables, and fruits. In each case, the end of the period shows a marked deterioration of the total collected. Moreover, the decline in collections

TABLE 19.1 Collection of selected categories of agricultural commodities, 1962–70 (000s tons)

	1962	1963	1964	1965	1966	1967	1968	1969	1970
Grains									
total	340.2	319.7	174.6	82.3	96.6	117.1	111.5	189.3	299.4
private	140.6	116.5	52.2	39.0	32.6	31.4	20.0	16.2	11.0
Tubers									
total	345.2	429.7	440.6	402.2	545.9	393.5	410.5	326.2	196.7
private	249.8	288.5	261.0	225.5	252.8	171.8	160.3	130.8	75.3
Vegetables									
total			195.0	220.4	230.9	282.7	216.7	126.7	136.2
private			142.4	161.2	162.4	188.4	138.7	82.1	62.7
Fruits									
total		365.6	291.7	325.4	321.3	318.1	385.0	297.4	289.7
private		268.9	184.0	224.9	217.7	213.1	240.1	171.0	125.7

SOURCE
Cuba (1970c) pp. 70–8.

from the private sector is far more pronounced. There is no way to determine to what extent the decline shown for the private sector represents an actual production decline, and to what extent it represents a delcine in the share of private production collected by the state. In either case, however, the declining role of the private sector in supply is significant, especially because after the second agrarian reform in 196? the private sector's share of agricultural land did not decline significantly in these years.

It would be difficult to explain the decline in deliveries from the private sector on the basis of either the labour shortage or a shortage of modern agricultural imputs. The small size of most farms made the general labour shortage of limited significance for the private sector. The limited reliance of the private sector on modern inputs at the beginning of the period and their rising supply during the period rules out an explanation along those lines.

It is only possible to conclude that the private sector was not being offered sufficient payments for its products. The central authorities did not develop a pricing system that could elicit the supply of these secondary crops. In addition, a money-pricing system alone could not have dealt with the problem; with rationing and the non-market allocation of various goods, money prices had a limited relation to the real value of payment received by private producers.

The direct supply to the public of commodities produced by private farmers was sharply restricted in 1968 when small private retail operations—including 3700 street vendors—were eliminated. The rationale for this move, taken in the context of 'The Revolutionary Offensive', was to prevent profiteering at a time when a major emphasis was being placed on the development of moral incentives. Yet no sufficient mechanism was introduced to replace the private retailers, and the problem of supplying consumer goods was seriously aggravated. This action, aside from the question of its political justification, provides a further example of the alienation of the planners from local activity, and undoubtedly contributed to the disruption of agriculture. While the government was attempting to follow a policy of encouraging the role of small farmers, it was taking actions that indirectly undermined that policy.

As the problems of production became severe in the late 1960s and as it became apparent that they were associated with considerable disorganisation, the initial response of the government was to further entrench itself in a highly centralised form of control. The military, for example, began to take on significant responsibilities in the 10 million

ons campaign. In the 1970 sugar harvest 100,000 soldiers participated
.nd many others worked in cultivation and construction. The army also
an the machinery sector of the public enterprises, and military officers were
placed in administrative positions on many state farms. The entire sugar
aarvest in 1968, 1969, and 1970 was carried out as a national campaign,
vith the highest government officials directing the effort. (Certain
bservers, particularly Rene Dumont and K. S. Karol, have interpreted
he military's role in this period as indicating a general militarisation
—seen as the opposite of democratisation—of Cuban life. Without
lenying either the importance of the military in the harvest campaigns,
r the problems that reflect it, I would argue that to jump from there to a
picture of a militarised Cuban society is a gross error. Support for my
position will be apparent from the discussion in Chapters 24 and 25.)

20 Labour Motivation and Organisation

Running the sugar harvests of the late 1960s as national campaigns was in part a response to the continuing deficits in the plan. But the Cuban leaders also saw the campaign atmosphere as being a positive component in the process of creating moral incentives. By treating the economic struggle as comparable to a military struggle, the leadership hoped to create the kind of national élan, solidarity, and effort that usually is associated only with wartime.

Indeed, the economic struggle was not only likened to a war effort; it was also described as part of a continuing struggle to establish the revolution in the face of the imperialist threat. The threat was, of course, a real one, and it, along with the social accomplishments of the revolution and the early economic successes, had contributed to widespread enthusiasm. This revolutionary enthusiasm had been a powerful force in building support for the special programmes, such as the literacy campaign, and in leading many Cubans to give their all for the development of the country with little regard for personal gain.

But in the late 1960s, it became apparent that enthusiasm was not a substitute for discipline. Cuban's system of moral incentives, however supported by political exhortation and a campaign atmosphere, was showing serious weaknesses. These weaknesses appeared throughout the economy, but attention here will be focused on the agricultural sector.

One manifestation of the failure of the incentive structure to sufficiently motivate Cuban workers was the general disorganisation noted above. When tractors lay idle, undelivered or unrepaired, no individual or specific group paid a price. When transportation services were inadequate, the costs were not felt by those responsible. The only incentive to solve these problems was a commitment to the society at large, a political or moral sense of obligation. Yet when organisational structures are weak, when experience is lacking, the task is all the greater and the commitment must be more powerful. Apparently, the commit-

nent was insufficient to overcome the disorganisation in the circum-
tances of the late 1960s.

The commitment or motivation difficulties were not the only con-
equence of a deficient incentive system. An effective incentive system
provides direction to workers as well as motivation. It tells people not
only how hard to work, but also what to work on. This point will be
developed further below and more fully elaborated in Chapter 25.

THE RISE OF ABSENTEEISM

A major manifestation of the insufficiency of Cuba's incentive structure
was the rise in absenteeism in the period. For example, in the May–June
period of 1969, absentee rates reported for the permanent farm
labourers in Camaguey Province did not fall below 35 per cent. And at
the height of the 1970 *zafra*, the rate of absenteeism—justified and
unjustified—was found to be almost 29 per cent. (One analyst,
Archibald Ritter, commenting on these data, states that the high rate of
absenteeism among farm labourers is 'surprising, in that the agricultural
proletariat has been the group to gain most from the changes wrought
by the revolution'. What Ritter fails to note, however, is that by gaining
most, farm labourers were also the group that had their traditional
incentives most thoroughly undermined. Ritter's 'surprise' implies that
absenteeism can be equated with political dissatisfaction. I would
instead take this example to imply that political support for the
revolution is, by itself, an insufficient base for motivation.)

It is necessary to emphasise that the absenteeism problem was by no
means confined to agriculture, but was an economy-wide phenomenon.
Studies of the construction industry, for example, found a 17 per cent
absentee rate in 1969, and studies conducted during 1968 and 1969 in
more than 200 state enterprises showed that up to 40 per cent of the work
time was being lost in some sectors, with absenteeism as the principal
source of the problem. By late 1970, absenteeism was recognised as a
most serious economic difficulty. (Archibald Ritter quotes Castro as
stating on 2 September 1970 that: 'Absenteeism is the thing we must
tackle with everything we've got right now.' Carmelo Mesa-Lago notes
that in August 1970 absenteeism reached 20 per cent of the labour force.
This statistic, however, raises a problem about all of the absenteeism
data, namely, what is a high rate of absenteeism? In the month of
August, following the 1970 *zafra*, 20 per cent does not seem a shockingly
high absentee rate. In pre-revolutionary days, unemployment rates for

August often ran close to 20 per cent of the labour force. It would be useful to have more basis for comparison in evaluating these data.)

MOTIVATION'S CONNECTION TO ORGANISATION

The matter of motivation should not be separated from the problem of organisation. To begin with, as pointed out above, in the context of economic disorganisation, moral or political commitment must be all the more powerful since the tasks become more difficult. But, in a more positive sense, it is organisation of one sort or another that is the key to any system of incentives.

In a capitalist society, pre-revolutionary Cuba for example, the market simultaneously provides the basis for organisation and motivation. If an alternative system of incentives was to be developed in Cuba, it would require some institutional structure to substitute for the organisational–incentive function of the market. The Cuban leaders were not ignorant of this problem: in 1969, a Cuban Communist Party Commission on Revolutionary Orientation explained the absenteeism problem by noting that socialism in Cuba had not yet developed methods of its own to replace the market system of checks and incentives that was previously the motivating force behind production.

Economic planning *per se* does not constitute a solution to the problem of organisation. Indeed, for economic planning to be effective, it is necessary to have accomplished a solution to the organisation problem. A plan can be articulated by a central authority, but without effective mechanisms to coordinate the operations of various enterprises, and without a system for organising work, motivating workers and directing their activity, a plan remains little more than an expression of official aspirations.

Moreover, new organisation itself cannot be viewed in a mechanistic manner—for example, as a new structure of responsibility and new lines of communication. A new system for organising work requires extensive political education and the alteration of social consciousness. New organisation is not new formal structures; it is a new, time-consuming process of socialisation.

THE ROLES OF MORALE AND EQUALITY

Once problems of disorganisation and absenteeism begin to develop, as they did in Cuba during the late 1960s, they take on a self-exacerbating quality. This is especially true in a system which relies on individuals' commitment to their work as the basis for motivation. When workers recognise that their labour is ineffective because of disorganisation—spare parts are unavailable, inputs do not arrive on schedule, finished goods await transportation—their commitment is undermined. Consequently further problems of disorganisation developed. Also, when some workers are less motivated and either stay away from work or do not exert themselves, yet those workers share in the fruits of collective labour, the morale of the entire work force is undermined. And with low morale, there is less commitment and consequently less work accomplished.

The matter of morale is fundamental to any system of motivation relying on workers' commitment to their task. If workers do not feel good about their tasks, they can hardly remain committed to them. For this reason, it is widely recognised that equality is not only a consequence of organising a work system without personal incentive, but in addition, it is a foundation for the effective functioning of such a system. If workers see that their efforts are leading to the enrichment of an élite, they cannot be motivated by the belief that their work is aiding society in general. The existence of inequality would destroy morale and hence destroy incentive.

Given the relative equality of income in Cuba (see Chapter 12) one might expect the incentive system to have had greater success in the late 1960s. However, the concept of equality, in so far as it affects peoples' attitudes towards society and towards their work, is broader than what is measured by income distribution. The concept usually includes a sense of fairness as well. For example, a person works all day and receives the same rewards as a person who loafs; that is not equal. Their money incomes are equal, but the situations are unequal. The loafer is the recipient of a special privilege. Such a situation may undermine morale as thoroughly as a situation in which an élite obtains high incomes and special privileges. And, just as élite need not be particularly large for its existence to have a profound impact on social attitudes, neither must the number of loafers be large to have a deleterious effect upon the social commitment of others.

As with the problem of deficiencies in the functioning of economic planning, one of the responses of the Cuban government to difficulties of the incentive programme was to further entrench itself in centralised forms of control. The direct role of the military and the reliance on campaign rhetoric were increased as part of the attempt to make moral incentives more effective. Regulations were established to curb 'loafing' and more thoroughly regulate the movement of the labour force.

But there was, prior to 1970, no modification of the Cuban line on incentives—no programme, for example, to buttress the moral in centives with any re-emphasis of the role of traditional incentives. Nor was any major effort, other than the use of military forms, directed toward the development of organisational structures that might sub stitute for the traditional coordinating and incentive roles of the market

21 Political Foundations of Economic Problems in the 1960s

The failure of the Cuban government to move more positively in the 1960s towards reorganising economic structures reflected political weaknesses. The construction of economic structures to replace the market might have been accomplished by the development of more active participation of the Cuban people in political affairs. Yet in the 1960s forms of mass political participation were being weakened rather than strengthened.

ALTERNATIVE SYSTEMS OF ORGANISATION

The process of the socialisation of work activity, as it has taken place in capitalist societies, has been an essentially top-down process, in which the market serves as the instrument of coercion and direction of workers' activity. The elimination of the market *per se* or the restriction of its role does not necessarily alter the position of workers in this process. Within the context of economic planning, a top-down system of socialisation can still operate. Indeed, in the Soviet Union and much of Eastern Europe, such has been the case. However, when planning is carried out in a top-down manner, when workers are not active participants in decision-making processes, their activity is either directed by wage differentials—a limited labour market—or by coercion, or by both.

To employ a top-down system of organisation would seem to be incompatible with maintaining relative equality (except perhaps for a case in which substantial coercion is involved). In the absence of either significant wage differentials or strong political identification with, and commitment to, the general welfare, workers would have nothing to motivate their activity. Yet such identification and commitment would

149

be difficult, if not impossible, to maintain if workers themselves were not thoroughly involved in decision-making processes. Thus the option of maintaining equality while using a top-down system of decision-making and direction would not appear to be viable. Yet in the 1960s equality with top-down decision-making seems to have been the Cuban option and consequently it should not be particularly surprising that production difficulties were severe.

In other words, regardless of whether economic activity is basically organised through markets or by planning, there would seem to be two mechanisms for organising and directing work activity: inequality and some form of labour market or equality and mass participation in social decisions. (These alternatives need not necessarily be seen as mutually exclusive. Any system in which one alternative was dominant would be likely to include elements of the other. This would be especially true in any transitional society.) The former mechanism is the traditional one, and requires no explanation here. The latter, however, requires further attention.

The socialisation of economic activity, as has been noted earlier, is a process during which certain behavioural traits and sets of social relations are established whereby people coordinate their economic activity in a productive manner. Mass participation provides one avenue for the development of the human traits that can accomplish this task. Through participation, people develop experience in exercising responsibility. In working within groups, and in coordinating the activity among groups, people learn ways to be self-reliant, to identify problems, and to see the relation between their own actions and the solution (or exacerbation) of problems. In addition, when individuals at the local level participate regularly in the decision-making processes, the programmes they choose are not likely to conflict with either local conditions and needs or their own interests. Finally, there is strong evidence that the greater a person's participation in a decision-making process, the more committed she or he will be to carrying out the results of the decisions.

CUBAN WORKERS AND THEIR POLITICAL–ECONOMIC ROLES

The Cuban working class was, by no means, totally lacking such decision-making experience. Prior to 1959, Cuba had a relatively highly developed working-class movement. Trade unions were widely organised, and working-class activity had played an important role in Cuban politics at various times. However, agricultural labourers were less thoroughly involved in this activity. Also, Cuban workers generally did not participate in economic decision-making. Their economic activity was controlled in the usual top-down manner.

Furthermore, during the 1950s the political activity of the working class was severely restricted. Of particular importance, the Cuban working class did not play the leading role in the struggle for power. Thus the revolution itself did not provide Cuban workers with significant further development of their self-organisation, nor did it place them in a dominant position in social affairs. The Cuban working class benefited from the revolution, and it supported the revolution, but it did not make it. (See Chapter 4 for more on those points regarding the pre-1959 period.)

After 1959, Cuban workers became active participants as implementers of the programmes of the revolution. But the role of the working class in the initiation of activity, in decision-making processes and in taking responsibilities for social affairs was limited. Thus the development of working-class self-organisation was limited.

The entire land-reform process and the creation of state farms is an illustration of these limitations (see Chapters 6 and 7). Rural labourers did not take the initiative in the expropriation of estates. They had no basis to establish their own operation of the new farms, either as cooperatives or as worker-managed state farms. And they accepted the process by which INRA ran the new enterprises from above. It was not a process by which the central authorities took control from the workers; the workers never established control.

There were some programmes of the revolution that began to build foundations for mass participation. The literacy campaign (see Chapter 11) involved thousands of working people in an experience which built their capacity for self-organisation. To be sure, the literacy campaign was conceived and directed by central authority, but in its operation people at all levels had to make decisions and take on responsibilities.

Various other programmes of the revolution had a similar impact. The special youth brigades, involved in agricultural production, and the Committees for the Defence of the Revolution, which organised a variety of neighbourhood activities, are further examples. Also, several aspects of the growing educational system were structured to promote participation (see Chapter 23 below). But these activities were limited in size, and they were not characteristic of the every-day activity of Cuban workers. Furthermore, the experience in organisational activity developed in these programmes was often drawn off into higher-level institutions. When, for example, the literacy campaign revealed particu larly effective organisers, they would be given new assignments in the government. They would not provide the leadership for the self-activity and organisation of the Cuban working class.

None of this is to say that Cuban workers took no part in decision-making processes. Even when matters were formally controlled from above—as with INRA and the state farms—workers often took an active role in determining what happened. The revolution had created a sense of power among Cuban workers. The official ideology of the revolution encouraged workers' activity. And the reduction in material and social inequality provided a basis for workers' power. Nonetheless, the formal mechanisms, the organisational structures for the positive exercise of this power, were limited.

Perhaps of most significance, Cuban labour unions during the 1960s increasingly became instruments of the state rather than organisations of the workers, and, even as such instruments of the state, they played an ever-decreasing role in the organisation of production. Officially, the function of the trade unions in the 1960s included the roles of taking part in the development of production plans and the development of political consciousness among the workers. These activities, however, tended to be subordinated to the unions' other functions of encouraging greater work effort and maintaining discipline. While in the early 1960s, the labour unions played a role in handling workers' grievances, this function was transferred to separate labour councils in 1965. In general, in the late 1960s the unions became less and less important. Moreover, even at the local level, union officials were being appointed from above. Hence, the union played little role in developing those social traits which lead to an effective socialisation of the work process in a non-traditional manner.

THE IDENTITY BETWEEN POLITICAL AND ECONOMIC PROBLEMS

The lack of organisational activity developing the decision-making role of the Cuban masses can be seen as inhibiting the development of the incentive system as well as limiting the effective socialisation of work activity. The early accomplishments of the Cuban revolution, the implementation of reforms and the general redistribution of income, created wide political support for the government and the programmes it put forward. This political support provided a basis for the functioning of moral incentives. But, regardless of political support, people's motivation in any activity seems to be strongest when they have been involved in the decisions surrounding the activity and are responsible for its success or failure.

In capitalist society, the wage, an external incentive, substitutes for the motivation that might be provided by participation. But in Cuba, with limited wage differentials and limited participation, motivation was severely weakened in spite of worker support for the government. And as workers began to recognise the ineffectiveness of productive effort as a consequence of the general disorganisation, it is small wonder that the motivation problem became so serious.

The example cited on p. 145 above, of the high absentee rate among agricultural labourers, underscores the insufficiency of political support as a basis for moral incentives. There is no question regarding the support by this group for the government; perhaps more than any other group, they were the beneficiaries of the revolution's programmes. But in being the most complete beneficiaries, they were also the group that had the old basis of their work effort most thoroughly undermined. The fear of insecurity and deprivation was no longer a motivating force, but no other forms had been created to lead them towards more effective socialisation of their activity. They were the objects of the revolution but they were not the initiators of action.

Thus the economic problems and the political problems of the Cuban revolution were basically the same. The leadership was becoming separated from the masses of the people. In spite of explicit campaigns to the contrary, bureaucracy was becoming a serious problem and threatened to become an institutionalised form of operation. If the Cuban revolution were to maintain its commitments to equality, and to overcome the production difficulties of the late 1960s, changes would have to take place in the way in which power was being exercised.

In the early 1970s, several important changes in political and economic organisation were to take place. They would be accompanied by a major expansion of the Cuban economy. Though the expansion had roots beyond the organisational changes, this combination of political and economic events would significantly alter the nature of development in Cuba.

Part Six

Progress and Redirection of Cuban Socialism in the 1970s

22 Progress and New Policies in the 1970s

The failure to harvest 10 million tons of sugar in 1970 and the numerous economic maladies of the late 1960s led to a general re-evaluation of development strategy. The situation was similar to that of the early 1960s when, out of the production crisis of 1962–4, the agriculture-based strategy had been formed. As in the earlier period, economic crisis forced a re-examination of sectoral priorities, the role of incentives, and the structure of planning.

However, as is often the case, before new structures and strategies could be formed and have effect, the situation began to change. As has been noted above, although the 10 million ton goal was not attained in 1970, the large harvest which was brought in led a major spurt in the economy—see Table 22.1 but note that data for years after 1975 are

TABLE 22.1 Annual growth rates, 1969–75

	Gross social product*	Gross material product	Agri-culture	Industry	Construc-tion	Transpor-tation*
1969	−1.3	−1.7	−3.8	1.5	−14.8	−1.0
1970	15.5	21.4	18.9	25.9	−2.6	30.4
1971	7.3	4.2	−8.4	4.4	31.5	0.5
1972	16.2	9.7	5.3	6.7	40.1	3.7
1973	14.4	12.5	4.3	11.9	27.8	2.2
1974	10.3	8.3	4.0	8.2	14.3	2.8
1975†	9.0‡	8.1	4.0	8.0	15.0	12.0

NOTES
* Sectors not included in GMP are in current prices.
† Based on rates for first half of the year.
‡ Does not include commerce.

SOURCE
Table A.2.1.

157

incomplete. (It is clear that growth did slow substantially after 1975, but expansion did continue—see Chapters 26 and 27 below.)

The industrial sector as a whole grew by 25.9 per cent between 1969 and 1970. The sugar industry, to be sure, jumped more rapidly—by 35 per cent. But between these two years the sugar industry's share in the value of industrial output rose only from 16.4 to 17.5 per cent. Other industries were also showing strongly.

In agriculture, sugar's role was more central. In 1970, sugar accounted for 48 per cent of the value of production in agriculture. The previous year, sugar had accounted for only 41.4 per cent. And during the 1965–9 period, sugar's contribution to the value of agricultural output had on average amounted to only 35.8 per cent. Still, some other parts of agriculture did not do badly between 1969 and 1970. Livestock, for example, recovered somewhat from its earlier decline.

It seems clear that something was happening to the Cuban economy in 1970, which went beyond the direct effects of the large sugar harvest. Growth did subside somewhat in 1971—largely as result of the decline in sugar production—but expansion was re-established and maintained up to at least 1975—see Table 22.1. A major rebalancing of the Cuban economy as beginning, and the dimensions of this process will be examined in Chapter 26.

FOUNDATIONS FOR GROWTH IN THE 1970s

The foundations for the expansion of the 1970s lay in the period of stagnation, and, it will be argued, the new policies adopted in the early 1970s solidified that foundation and created conditions for continuing growth.

The most obvious foundation for growth established in the 1960s was the huge expansion of the nation's capital stock. The high rate of investment in plant and equipment, probably increased capital stock by 50–75 per cent during the 1960s. In using the new capital, the progress may have been slow but the Cubans began to overcome their errors of the 1960s. For example, the drive to mechanise the sugar harvest had had almost no pay-off by 1970; but by 1975, slightly more than 25 per cent of the harvest was mechanised.

Furthermore, however slowly and however much it had lacked explicit attention, the basis for a more effective organisation of the work process was developing in the 1960s. The expansion of the education system was most important in this regard. Primary schools were graduating four times more students in 1970 than at the time of the revolution. While quantitative progress at the higher levels was less marked, the educational level of the work force as a whole was being significantly altered. Also, various special programmes and the labour mobilisations—the short-run production ineffectiveness in some cases notwithstanding—had served as training grounds for the Cuban work force. In Chapter 23 we shall examine the educational system and the special programmes and discuss their relation to the organisation problem.

THE DUAL POLICY SHIFT OF THE EARLY 1970s

But perhaps the developments of greatest significance relating to the changes of the 1970s have been the reshaping of the political process and the restructuring of planning and incentives. These two matters will be taken up in detail in Chapters 24 and 25, respectively. Here, however, it will be useful to introduce these two extremely important and in-terrelated developments and to comment on the reasons for these particular redirections of the Cuban economy.

In the realm of politics, two processes were initiated which created mechanisms for a widening of participation in decision-making. First, the various mass organisations—the unions, the small farmers (ANAP), the neighbourhood organisations (the CDRs), the women's federation (the FMC), the student organisations—were re-emphasized. Various steps were taken to give more responsibility and, hence, more authority to these organisations in a wide range of economic, social and political affairs. Second, a move was begun to establish a comprehensive, formal electoral system in Cuba. From a narrowly economic point of view, the importance of these political processes was that, as we have argued above, political participation is an essential element in the effective functioning of a system based on general equality and associated limitations on personnel, material incentives.

In the realm of planning and incentive structures, the Cuban government simultaneously moved toward a decentralisation and a greater use of personal, material incentives as a basis for economic organisation. In and of themselves, these economic policies would seem to constitute a basic redirection of Cuban socialism. Seen in com-bination with the political changes that were taking place, however, they take on a rather different meaning. Also, economic reality had changed rather substantially since the beginning of the 1960s, when the earlier policies were formed; more emphasis on material incentives and decentralisation took on a very different meaning in the context of the 1970s than they would have a decade earlier.

The arguments behind these assertions should become clear in later chapters. Here it is necessary only to re-emphasise the dual nature of the policy shift that took place in the early 1970s. If the political changes are seen in isolation, they may seem purely formalistic or, perhaps, idealistic. If the economic policy is examined alone, it would imply a rejection of a large part of what had previously constituted the Cuban approach to socialism.

BASIS OF THE POLICY SHIFT

Before examining the various developments of the 1970s more thoroughly, one further point requires attention. We will argue through the course of the following chapters that what had happened in the 1970s amounts to movement toward working-class strength and authority in Cuba. Why? Why was the political direction of the 1960s, which was towards a weakening of the working class and a growth of bureaucratic control, changed? It would seem that an answer lies along the following lines:

First of all, while the movement was toward bureaucratic control in Cuba during the 1960s, bureaucracy had by no means become firmly established. Changing directions did not mean throwing out (or throwing over) an entrenched strata. The development of bureaucracy had been limited on two sides. From below, while the working class had not established its own institutions of authority in the 1960s, neither was it thoroughly excluded from power. Its active and positive participation, however limited in terms of decision-making, was essential to the functioning of the Cuban system. Also, the ideology of the Cuban revolution remained a powerful force encouraging working-class activity. And the equality—of status as well as income—reduced the gap between an incipient bureaucratic strata and the Cuban masses. From above, the highest leaders of the Cuban revolution were relatively independent of the bureaucracy. The political authority of the leadership—especially Fidel Castro—had remained above and outside the bureaucracy. In the long run such independence of leadership is not viable, and in the short or the long run it can have negative aspects (vis-à-vis participation). But it can also serve as a check on the institutionalisation of bureaucratic control.

The nature of the Cuban leadership has, in itself, also been an important factor in determining the redirection of policy. Whatever their other characteristics, the Cuban leaders have consistently placed a very high priority on equality. They pursued policies which drastically altered income distribution in Cuba. Consequently, regardless of the good will (or otherwise) of the Cuban leaders in the 1970s, they were thoroughly entrenched in a system based on equality. To take actions which threatened equality—which threatened the reforms that had been implemented—would have been likely to arouse considerable resentment and disillusionment among the Cuban people. Thus the necessity of a continuing commitment to equality was a fact of politics in Cuba.

And the commitment to equality, combined with the need to achieve economic growth, provides a key in the explanation of the changes of the 1970s, as, indeed, that same commitment was a central factor shaping the policies of the 1960s. In the 1960s, growth with equality had led to moral incentives and centralisation of planning (see Chapter 14). An essential missing ingredient in the earlier policy had been participation, and the problems of the 1960s forced this issue to the surface. Had there been no move toward more widespread participation, growth would have been inhibited or the commitment to equality would have had to have been abandoned.

The conditions of the early 1970s, however, facilitated the move toward participation. The political foundations of the Cuban revolution were well secured by this point. Both external and internal threats had been thoroughly overcome. Whatever problems might be generated for the leadership by the political changes, they would not pose serious threats to the stability of the system. Also, the Cuban people had had ten years of common political experience which prepared them for the reshaping of political institutions. A new political culture had been created in the processes of the reforms, the building of the education system, the special programmes, and the general process of revolutionary change. The creation of a new political culture assured a unity and stability that otherwise would have been lacking in the political process. Finally, the economic growth of the early 1970s itself facilitated the political reforms in that it both strengthened the government and created the need for new administrative forms—forms that would be part of the political structure.

These various factors—the basic weakness of a bureaucratic group, the nature of the Cuban leadership, the entrenchment of equality, the evolution of political and economic life—all contribute to an explanation of why changes in the direction of greater working-class power were possible in Cuba at the beginning of the 1970s. We are not able to judge, however, how the actual process of redirection took place. Most importantly, there is no evidence as to the degree to which positive actions of the working class itself played a role in the change. The negative actions of the working class—the absenteeism of the 1960s, for example—had forced the issue. But, at least from outside Cuba, it appears that the positive initiation of the changes came from the leaders of the Cuban revolution. Any complete explanation of the change would require more information on these matters.

23 The Development and Extension of Organisation: Education and Special Programmes

The economic changes of the 1970s resulted in part from the accumulated experience attained in programmes which had been pursued since the triumph of the revolution. But it had taken time for that accumulated experience to reach sufficient proportions to have an impact on the way the economy operated. In particular, the growth of the educational system and the continual importance placed on special programmes can be seen as contributing to the organisational development of Cuban workers. (The organisational impacts of formal education and special programmes were probably inhibited in the 1960s because of the particular economic and political context of those years. The political and planning reforms of the 1970s—see below Chapters 24 and 25—probably allowed education and special programmes to have their full impact on participation and organisation in the 1970s.)

The roles of education and special programmes bring out how, in the Cuban context, political development and organisational development are two combined aspects of the overall process of social transformation. In focusing its attention on education and special production mobilisations and social campaigns, the Cuban government emphasised a political goal: its desire to advance a socialist ideology among the populace. In serving this political end, these programmes have also been creating a labour force with experience in group interaction, shared responsibilities, and discipline. (Practical motivating factors were also involved: in the case of education, the need to expand technical skills; in the case of the special programmes, the need to accomplish certain otherwise unattainable tasks. Furthermore, the expansion of education was motivated by the Cuban revolutionaries' belief that education was a human right, aside from its role as a mechanism for social transformation.)

EDUCATION AND SOCIALISATION

The process of formal education—almost regardless of content and form, but more on that shortly—trains people in such seemingly prosaic behaviour patterns as coming on time, following directions, accepting authority, working in coordination with others and striving toward established incentives. These sorts of behaviour traits, and the social relations which their collective operation constitutes, are very close to being those which make up the socialisation of the work process. They need to be learned or acquired in one way or another, if labour is to function most productively. Formal education is neither the only way these traits can be developed, nor is it even an essential mechanism, but it serves the function.

While simply involving people in the group process of education is central to organisational development, content and form are by no means irrelevant. The content and form of education play a role in determining the particular nature of the organisational skills which emerge. For example, if group activity is to be effective, people must learn to accept authority. But the origins of that authority and its justification can be different in different social systems. Aside from ethical judgements about the proper origins of authority, it should be recognised that an educational system will not be economically effective if, through its content and form, it teaches different attitudes about authority from those which operate in the work place. If students are taught in school that authority should derive from an outside power over which they have no control, they will be ill prepared for a work environment in which they are expected to play an active role in decision processes. Similarly the incentive structure of the school system, if it is to prepare production workers, must parallel the incentive structure of the work place.

In Cuba, the form and content of the educational system are still evolving. But there have been major efforts—the work-study programme and schools in the countryside which will be discussed below—to develop a type of curriculum and a form of education which prepare students for participation in the reality of Cuba's egalitarian society. In so far as these efforts are successful, the educational system is all the more effective in expanding the country's organisational capacity.

THE EXPANSION OF EDUCATION

The emphasis which the government placed on education from 1959 onwards resulted in some impressive quantitative achievements. During the 1960s these achievements included the following:

—enrolment in primary schools (grades 1–6) grew from 717,000 in 1958–9 to 1,558,000 in 1969–70; in secondary schools, from 88,000 to 256,000.

—adult education, almost non-existent at the time of the revolution, included 356,000 persons in 1969–70; it had peaked at 848,000 in 1964–5 but declined in importance as the regular system expanded and was especially low in 1969–70 because of the great effort in the sugar harvest.

—throughout the latter half of the 1960s total enrolment in the educational system averaged 2,166,000, more than 25 per cent of the entire population and more than the number of workers in the labour force.

Special efforts were made to reduce the rural–urban differential in Cuban education. While urban primary-school enrolment increased from 501,000 in 1958–9 to 926,000 in 1969–70, rural primary education rose more than twice as rapidly from 217,000 to 632,000. Rural areas have received special attention in adult-education programmes, with the result that, by 1967, 236,000 adults in rural areas were enrolled in the worker–peasant education programme, making up more than half the total. Also, the government developed a scholarship programme (providing room and board) primarily for children from the countryside to attend boarding schools in the cities or at rural educational complexes. By 1970, this programme included 277,500 pupils.

The Cuban education system did have deficiencies. Teachers were under-trained and over-worked, drop-out rates were high and educational techniques were often backward and slow to be changed. Yet, especially from the point of view of the schools' role in establishing new social relations and behaviour patterns, simply the fact that so many people did pass through the system is of great importance. Aside from whatever intellectual skills they developed and whatever new ideological outlook they adopted, students learned through experience to take part in the organisational process of education. (Of course, the Cuban educational system has also served some very tangible functions. As intended, it has been producing large numbers of technically skilled people who can play important roles in the modernisation of the economy. For example, the faculties of agriculture in Cuba's universities graduated 29 persons in 1959–60 (veterinarians and agronomists); but in 1969–70 the figure has risen to 392. And the graduates of the faculties of technology rose from 88 in 1959–60 to 825 in 1969–70. These people were the human counterparts of the new machinery and equipment in which Cuba had invested. They embodied not only technical skills but also years of experience which prepared them for playing roles in the effective organisation of the economy.)

Education, however, takes a long time to have its economic impact. In the period immediately following the revolution the expansion of primary-school enrolment came first, followed by an expansion of secondary-school enrolment. Enrolment in higher education actually declined substantially in 1959–60 and 1963–4 (from 24.8 thousand to 15.1 thousand). But then as the students who had earlier accounted for the expansion in lower-level enrolments entered colleges, the system expanded rapidly (to 29.6 thousand in 1969–70). It takes many years to produce an educated worker and many more to produce an educated work force. And it was only in the early 1970s that the huge expansion of education was having a substantial impact on the nature of the labour force.

NEW EDUCATIONAL PROGRAMMES IN THE 1970s

During the early 1970s, the educational system had become a regular part of the lives of Cubans. With the educational system well established, the most rapid growth of enrolment between 1969–70 and 1973–4, was in the upper levels: higher education expanded by 64 per cent and secondary by 50 per cent, as compared to a 22 per cent expansion of primary enrolment. One government report summarised the situation as follows: 'Approximately one inhabitant in every three was involved in a study program in the academic year 1973–4, either within the regular education system or in one of the technical training courses run by one of the State institutions and agencies. In the same year the level of school enrollment was 99.5 per cent of children between six and 12 years old, and 71.7 per cent of young people between the ages of 13 and 16 years.' The continued expansion of the educational system has been associated with the introduction of new programmes integrating academic and production activity and placing special emphasis on agricultural work. At the secondary-school level there was a major development of schools in the countryside (*escualas en el campo*). At the university level, half-time production work was made a regular part of matriculation. These programmes deserve emphasis here because they advanced the role of education as a mechanism in preparing people for effective participation in production. They also illustrate the close connection between organisational and political development.

In the late 1960s secondary-school students had been included in the major labour mobilisations for the sugar harvest (and other work in agriculture) through the schools to the countryside programme. In this programme, students would go to the countryside to work for 45-day periods. At the First National Congress on Education and Culture in 1971, however, the schools *to* the countryside programme was criticised because problems had developed with the coordination of academic work, with production being ineffective because of its temporary nature, and with production interrupting classroom progress. Consequently the Congress proposed that secondary boarding schools be built *in* the countryside so that students could integrate their studies and productive labour on a continuing and regular basis. (The schools *to* the countryside programme was viewed as providing the experimental foundation for the schools *in* the countryside programme.)

During the 1971–5 period, over 300 such boarding schools were constructed, each having a capacity of roughly 500 students. The development of the schools in the countryside programme, which involves each student working for three hours a day in the schools' fields, was motivated by several factors. Greatest stress has been placed on the importance of involving students in manual labour so that, while acquiring intellectual skills, they will not acquire an élitist self-concept. The dignity of physical labour, and especially agricultural labour, was seen as a major component in creating an egalitarian ideology; and combining work with study was seen as a way to reduce the cost of education, and thus allow its nation-wide development.

From the point of view of advancing the socialisation of the work process, the schools in the countryside also seem especially effective. The student is trained not only in the classroom but also in the work process itself, so that the values of academic and practical education are combined in behavioural as well as intellectual development.

In the universities, a parallel programme of integrating work and study has beem developed whereby each student spends 20 hours a week at productive labour. The purposes and functions of the university work-study programme are the same as those of the schools in the countryside programme. It need only be added that at the university level a student's productive labour is often tied to his or her academic pursuits. A chemical engineering student might work in the laboratory of a sugar mill, and an economics student might work in the mill's accounting office. Consequently, upon completion of an academic programme, a student has also achieved some learning by doing. Of course, there is nothing unique to Cuba in such an approach to education, but what is unusual in Cuba is developing such a programme as a nation-wide practice and stressing its role in developing egalitarian attitudes.

These new programmes in the Cuban educational system simply highlight the general role of education in the Cuban economy and the ways in which education is playing a greater role in the transformation of the work process. The entire process was begun at the outset of the revolutionary period, but in the 1970s the weaknesses in the process (drop-out problems, for example) have been reduced, while the pay-offs are beginning to come as those trained in the new system become economically active, and the new programmes are increasing the system's effectiveness.

THE CONTINUING ROLE OF SPECIAL PROGRAMMES

Similarly, Cuba's special programmes have been a factor effecting a transformation of the work process. In Chapter 11, the literacy campaign—the prime example of a special programme—was given considerable attention. Its social roles of developing new cadre, new organisational practices and new attitudes towards social problems were emphasised. Various other special programmes served similar functions in the 1960s—the youth brigades working in agriculture, for example. (However, the most extensive special programme of the 1960s, the labour mobilisation for the sugar harvest, was reduced in its social effectiveness because of the economic problems of that period. New cadre or positive new attitudes, for example, do not emerge as well from failures as from successes.) One of the major justifications of the special programmes was their role in the general policy of applying and building moral or collective incentives. And in the 1970s, in spite of the decline in emphasis on moral incentives (see Chapter 25 below), the special programmes have not been abandoned.

The role of the 'micro brigades' in the 1970s provides a good illustration of the way special programmes have continued to effect the work process through the development and extension of organisation. Elsewhere, I have described the micro brigades by focusing on one of their major projects:

On the coast about eight miles east of Havana is a small town called Alamar. It is the site of a large construction project where over 2000 people are erecting hundreds of small apartment houses and the schools, stores and other service buildings that go with them.

The new city at Alamar is being built by 'micro brigades'. A micro brigade is a group of 30 to 50 workers from a particular work centre or closely related group of work centres. The formation of a brigade follows a process of discussion in the work centre (factory or office, for example) regarding who can and should be assigned to the brigade, how the rest of the centre will make up the work of those who enter the brigade, and what the priorities of the brigade should be. Finally, the brigade is selected from volunteers and begins work on construction—sometimes at large sites like Alamar, but also on smaller projects.

From each micro brigade working at Alamar, 8 or 10 persons are assigned to the social tasks of the project—school buildings, the furniture factory, the cement-block factory. The remaining 25 or so brigade members work together on a particular building. Upon completion, the apartments in that building are allocated—primarily on the basis of need and work record—to people from the work centre where the brigade originated.

When I visited Alamar in October 1972 I was told that people there work hard and long hours. The way workers discuss their project, it sounded like a bunch of people at an old-fashioned roof raising. One day shortly before my visit, I was told, a certain micro brigade had reached the point where all that was left to complete its building was the painting. That night, along with several additional volunteers from their work centre, the micro brigaders painted and in the morning the job was done.

Micro brigade workers do not receive any over-time pay for the long hours they put in. They get the same salaries they were getting in their work centres prior to joining the brigade. The only 'bonus' they obtain is an earlier move-in date for their fellow workers, and, of course, in many cases for themselves.

In the period 1971–5 construction micro brigades built about 21,400 housing units. At the beginning of 1976, 1127 brigades were active and had a target of completing 27,000 units in a 12-month period. Towards the end of 1975, Castro summed up the work at Alamar as follows:

> . . . this community is the result of one of the most notable efforts made by the revolution in the past few years.
>
> . . . this method of construction is being put into effect in 26 places in Havana, but this is the principle zone of construction. A total of 100 micro brigades are working here. They have built 167 apartment buildings—a total of 4600 apartments—and are working on more than 100 more. They have also built six elementary semi-boarding schools; six children's day care centers, and are now building more of them; three shopping centers; a furniture factory; a garment factory; a movie theater; an amphitheater; and a poly-clinic for the medical care of 30,000 persons. The number of residents already comes up to more than 20,000.
>
> As you can see, this concept of urbanization implies the solution to all of the communities' social problems . . . [It will be noted that, implicit in Castro's data, is a larger number of people working on the Alamar project—somewhere between 3000 and 4000 persons—than indicated in my own statement quoted above—A.M.]

The micro brigades have been part of a general expansion of housing construction that has been undertaken in the 1970s, including the construction of new towns in the rural areas. It may be recalled (see Chapter 7, page 48) that one of the justifications for maintaining the large estates as unified production enterprises was that it would allow concentrating the rural population in towns where services could be provided. Even though the costliness of construction inhibited such development in the 1960s, between 1959 and 1971 some 246 communities were constructed in rural zones on which 132 had more than 40 housing units. Since 1970 the programme has been stepped up and involves the construction of communities integrated with local agricultural-production plans (e.g., a new dairy complex, a new citrus-fruit project) under the direction of the Community Development Group of the Agency for Development of Social and Agricultural Construction. Between 1971 and 1975, 50 new communities including 6027 family units were built and some 70 more communities were being built or were in the planning stage at the end of 1975. According to a description in the Cuban press, the programme provides that:

Community housing will be built in relation to a well-defined agricultural development plan. The rural community will have all necessary social installations and will constitute a self-ruled administrative and political unit, closely linked to its adjoining development plan. The plan's work force will be drawn from the inhabitants of the new town who will also help out in the construction of housing and other social buildings.

The role of the micro brigades during the early 1970s is a useful antidote to misinterpretations of the changes in Cuba's approach to incentives (again, see Chapter 25). The reliance on the micro-brigade approach for a major social task and the importance attached to the brigades, indicates a continuing reliance on non-traditional forms of incentives in Cuba.

MICRO BRIGADES AND DEVELOPING ORGANISATION

Also, the micro brigades illustrate the close connection between altering incentives and developing organisation. For the micro brigades have been a major exercise in new forms of socialising the work process. Workers have been brought together in a situation where they must develop new leaders, make decisions about the hours and methods of their work, and bear direct responsibility for their actions. The continued reliance on this form of labour involves a continual training of workers in decision-making processes.

Moreover, the micro-brigade programme forced workers in the regular work place from which the brigade members were drawn to focus their attention on organisational problems. According to one account in the Cuban press:

While some workers were engaged in construction, all forces had to be utilized back in the work center to increase the productivity of the collective. At the beginning, workers made up the deficit with voluntary over-time. Gradually they started to work with greater efficiency and better methods of organization until they were able to do all the work of the commrades who were in the mini brigades during regular work hours.

This showed that in most cases it was possible to make more efficient use of the labor force, thus lowering the cost of production, and at the same time, improving work organization and increasing productivity. This is shown by the fact that more than 28,000 workers have shifted from production and service to construction without unfavorable repercussions in the quantity and quality of goods and services available to the people.

Thus, the micro brigades and the other special programmes create a pressure that can further the process of transforming the organisation of work.

One further aspect of work reorganisation exhibited in the micro brigades has been the integration of women into types of labour traditionally considered men's preserve. By approaching the work process in a new way, the micro brigades have created the opportunity for old ideas about work to be set aside. Regarding a construction project in Sancti Spiritus, for example, another Cuban press article reports as follows:

> An intensive political campaign is being carried out in the region with the aim of incorporating women into such jobs as interior finishing, painting, and the handling of heavy and other equipment. A total of 445 women are doing construction work, mainly in [building] the primary education teacher training school, the pedagogical school in Cabaiguan, the Zaza Hotel, and the junior high school in Las Pozas. While working, all of them acquire training and skills in construction work.

The point here is not simply the progress in the position of women. Equally important, such progress is but one example of manner in which the micro brigades programme has been affecting work organisation in Cuba. It is an indication of the general advance in the socialisation process being achieved through special programmes.

24 Reorganising the Political Process

In Chapter 17, it was argued that the nature of the political process is closely related to the socialisation of the work process. And further, the weakness of the organised role of the working class in social decision-making was a basic factor accounting for the organisational weakness, and hence the economic weakness, of the Cuban economy in the late 1960s. Of course, the Cuban working class was not totally denied a role in decision-making processes, but its role was very limited and deteriorating. Consequently it is of special significance that the roles of the mass organisations in Cuba have been re-emphasized in the 1970s and new political forms have been developed which involve the Cuban working class in decision-making.

RE-EMPHASIS OF THE MASS ORGANISATIONS

Cuba's mass organisations include the neighbourhood club—such as Committees for the Defence of the Revolution (CDRs), the labour unions which include workers on state farms, the Association of Small Farmers (ANAP), the Womens' Federation (FMC), and the various student organisations. All of these played an important role in implementing the programmes of the revolution. But during the 1970s there has been a re-emphasis on the mass organisations, a widening of their activities, and an increase in their decision-making role. (The concept of a 'mass' organisation in Cuba means an organisation with open membership. It is to be distinguished from the concept of a select organisation—the Communist Party of Cuba. To enter the Communist Party a person must be selected by the other members of his or her work place—or in some cases, the other members of a mass organisation—and approved by the Party.)

In the 1960s the central function of the mass organisations was that of mobilising the masses. ANAP's function, for example, was to encourage small farmers to associate themselves with the plan and meet production goals. Labour unions had the primary task of getting people to work harder and more efficiently. But in spite of their importance, the role of the mass organisations was to carry out policy, not to formulate it.

The re-emphasis of the mass organisations has meant most importantly that they have begun to have a decision-making role. Specifically, for example, a new practice has been developed of circulating draft laws for discussion and amendment among the local units of the relevant mass organisation. These draft laws include items ranging from specifics of new regulations on maternity leave (discussed in trade unions) to a whole gamut of civil regulations (discussed in the block clubs).

Labour unions are taking a more active role in plants, offices and farms. Local union officials are being elected rather than appointed from above, as had been the case in the past. These changes have not given the trade unions new areas of authority. They continue to concentrate on solving problems in the work place and on mobilising the workers for greater productivity—for example, by handling the political offensive against absenteeism. Still, it seems likely that with the increased activity comes increased authority, and authority that is enhanced by the re-establishment of local elections. The fact that local elections are contested—as they in fact are—does not in itself assure the primacy of workers' interests in the activities of their officials. However, the general nature of the Cuban political process (which will be discussed shortly) seems to give those elections some significance. (Since much of this discussion of union elections is based on information provided in an essay by Carmelo Mesa-Lago, it should be noted that Mesa-Lago himself is sceptical of the extent to which the changes in the labour unions will lead to any effective political participation on their part.)

The trade unions have been the first of the mass organisations in this new period to hold a nation-wide conference. The trade union congress which took place in autumn of 1973, undertook the formulation of policy on such fundamental issues as incentives and wage structure. Moreover, the congress was preceded by extensive discussions at the local and regional levels. There were, to be sure, limits on the extent of this discussion. Carmelo Mesa-Lago has pointed out that the context for the discussion preceding the congress was determined by the issue of nine theses by the central authorities of the labour unions. Furthermore, he offers the following statement by a leader of the labour unions as an indication of the limits of the pre-congress debate.

During the discussion [of the theses] every worker who wanted to criticise the administration about concrete aspects of its work was given a chance to do so. . . . No political, moral or any other pressures were applied to him. . . . The criticism voiced in the assemblies [however] cannot be viewed as the expression of any anti-administration trend, because, if such were to develop, the CTC would be the first to oppose it. . . . [The kind of criticism expressed was] in line with the role which the trade union movement can and should play. [The speaker quoted is Lázaro Peña. CTC stands for the Confederation of Cuban Workers. The brackets in the quote are Mesa-Lago's—A.M.]

Nonetheless, in spite of such limitations this involvement of Cuban workers in decision-making was a major change from the situation of the 1960s.

The extension of decision-making procedures to include the masses has been accompanied by an increase in the responsibilities of the mass organisations. The increased activity of the labour unions has already been noted, but it is in the CDRs—the neighbourhood clubs—that the increase in local authority seems most apparent. Today the CDRs—the most all-inclusive of Cuba's mass organisations, including upwards of 70 per cent of all Cubans over 14 years old (the eligible age)—take the responsibility for innumerable local tasks: from organising the in-oculation campaigns to keeping the streets clean and in repair; from organising night guard duty to recycling bottles and newspapers; from organising neighbourhood political discussion groups to making sure women have had recent pap smears.

The significance of the increased role of the CDRs—and for the other mass organisations—is that it is combined with their increased role in decision-making. The two developments are mutually dependent or at least mutually reinforcing. The increased decision-making power at the local level means that people identify more thoroughly with the programmes for which they are responsible. And the wider the realm of local responsibility the more it becomes necessary—almost automatic—to include local units in decision-making.

In the case of the small farmers, it does not appear that ANAP's role altered significantly in the early 1970s. However, in the light of the government's goal of eventually eliminating private farming, it is noteworthy that ANAP retained its functions and its membership. Though the land held by the small farmers declined (from 37 per cent of cultivable area in 1963 to 30 per cent in 1975) there were still 232,000

ANAP members (162,000 farm owners, the rest being family members). The organisation is still heavily relied on to encourage production and procurement and to carry out political education among its members. For these purposes, the membership is grouped into 6162 primary units. Thus, even though there has been a shift in the 1970s toward a greater use of prices as a mechanism for coordinating activity (see below, Chapter 25), there continues to be a heavy reliance on the organisation of the small farmers.

In all branches of society, the reliance on organisation has been a central theme of Cuban development in the 1970s. And this reliance on organisation—whether in neighbourhood affairs, in worker's involvement in production, or in coordinating small farmers with the plan—can be expected to further the general process of socialising work activity. In addition, the various mass organisations are now operating within an overall context of direct political involvement by the masses.

CREATING PODER POPULAR

The creation of a new system of political organisation—known as 'Poder Popular' (Peoples' Power)—has been an event of considerable importance. On one level, it would appear that Poder Popular is simply the introduction in Cuba of a form of electoral politics similar in structure to electoral systems in several other countries. Local assemblies are popularly elected; they elect district assemblies; and so on up to a national assembly. However, even if there were nothing unusual in the Cuban electoral system, its introduction after many years without mechanisms of popular participation would indicate a significant shift in Cuban politics. Poder Popular, at the very least, constitutes an institutionalisation or regularisation of political organisation in Cuba and this by itself would enhance the overall organisational capacity of the population in economic affairs as well. But there are factors which distinguish Cuba's new political system and make it have more effect upon the country's organisational problems. (These factors also make Poder Popular a more effective instrument of democracy, but that is not my primary concern here. However, I should note that were Poder Popular a sham in terms of democracy, its effect in expanding organisation would be greatly limited. If people did not feel the political system was working, they would become alienated from it, participation would wane, and it would not play a role of training people in organisational practice.)

First, the process of political institutionalisation of the revolution was :plicitly seen as a factor in strengthening the recovery of the economy. he leadership was aware of the connection between the economic roblems of the 1960s and the separation of the masses from political Tairs. In analysing the problems of the 1960s, Castro noted on 23 ugust 1970 that:

> The formulas of revolutionary process can never be administrative formulas. . . . Sending a man down from the top to solve a problem involving 15,000 or 20,000 people is not the same thing as the problems of those 15,000 or 20,000 people—problems having to do with their community—being solved by virtue of the decisions of the people, of the community, who are close to the source of those problems. . . . We must do away with all administrative methods and use mass methods everywhere.

'hus Poder Popular, as well as the re-emphasis of the mass organi- ations, was explicitly seen as having an economic function as well as a olitical one.

Second, in the operation of Poder Popular, politics has been defined ᴐ include economic affairs. The local assemblies of Poder Popular have uthority over local enterprises—for example, local retail outlets, onsumer services, facteries (perhaps a bakery) producing for local onsumption. District assemblies have authority over district enter- ⸱rises, and so on up to the National Assembly which, as the highest ᴇgislative authority, exercises control over national economic matters. Γhis means that the realm of decision-making in the Cuban political ⸱rocess is much wider than in many nations, and, as compared with ⸱olitical processes in capitalist nations, is not constrained by the ndependent activity of economic units. Consequently the role of ⸱olitical participation in developing economically useful organisational .bilities is all the greater. (It should be noted that the role of Poder ʾopular is not confined to economics and the traditional realm of ⸱olitics, but, according to Raul Castro, speaking in 1974 about the ᴵevelopment of the system in Matanzas Province, the Poder Popular ʾepresentatives 'are going to direct and orient the administration of ᴇconomic activities, culture, recreation, and the general services of the nunicipalities, the regions and the province'.)

Third, the operation of Poder Popular is integrated with the activities ᴐf the mass organisations. Consequently political participation for the ᴐrdinary citizen is not confined to taking part in periodic elections of representatives. In addition, on a continuing basis, each citizen involved through the mass organisations in implementing programme of Poder Popular, in passing information, advice and criticism on t representatives, and in political discussion of the entire operation. Thu Poder Popular and the mass organisations should be seen as com plementary components of the system involving the Cuban people i political affairs and involving them in organisational tasks.

Poder Popular, and Cuban politics generally, are not immune fron criticism as vehicles or democracy. The rights of opposition are seriousl limited in Cuba. The Cuban Communist Party dominates politic; affairs, and there is no pretence that the electoral system allows leewa for altering that basic fact of Cuban life. Cubans justify their one-part system in a traditional manner: they cite the continued threat of counter revolutionary actions backed by the U.S.; they argue that a need exist for decisive and uninhibited leadership in carrying out their struggl against underdevelopment; and they point to the meaninglessness c formal opposition in the capitalist nations.

My purpose here is neither to elaborate those justifications nor repea the now-familiar critiques of such a system. I do however, wish to mak two points, one of fact and the other of interpretation. First, to ente Cuba's Communist Party, a person must be elected by the othe members of his or her workplace (or in some cases, mass organization as well as accepted by the Party itself. In a context where the workers role in decision making is expanding, it would seem reasonable t< assume that such elections are not simply rubber-stamp procedures What I have been told about assemblies where such elections take plac tends to support that assumption. Second, regardless of forma authority, elections to the Party and so forth, the hegemony of the Communist Party remains a mechanism or a procedure. If workers are deprived of power by the nature of the organization of the economy, the Party will exacerbate that condition. If, however, the economy i organized along lines that tend to enhance workers' power, the Party might well serve the purpose it claims for itself—the purpose of leading the masses and of administering power on their behalf. For example, i workers have power in production, they are less likely to be cynical in politics; accordingly elections to the Party can take on a real meaning. I can be argued (as I have done elsewhere) that certain factors in the organization of the economy do favor the continued development o democratic relations in Cuba. For example, the pervasiveness o equality and of an ideology stressing the transformation of socia relations would seem to be important factors.

Here, however, an overall appraisal of the effectiveness of Cuban democracy generally and Poder Popular particularly as models for democracy is not the central issue. Indeed, a thorough appraisal of Poder Popular might be premature; the system was developed experimentally in Matanzas Province in 1974 and only extended to the entire nation in 1976. It is clear, however, that the new electoral system, combined with the development of mass organisation, involves a significant extension for mass participation in social decisions. As such it is creating a new context for the organisation and development of the Cuban economy, and for the restructuring of planning and incentives.

25 Restructuring Labour Motivation and Planning

During the 1960s, the Cuban economy suffered from over-centralisation of planning and an ineffective system of incentives. These problems did not arise, however, simply from erroneous decisions about economic structure. As pointed out in Chapter 14, the Cubans were pushed along the route of centralisation and moral incentives by the circumstances and contradictions operating in the early 1960s. The process of destroying old structures and instituting social reforms created labour shortages and general economic disruption. Only by abandoning the socialist goals of the revolution could these problems have been eliminated by a reintroduction of market relations and traditional incentive structures. And in the absence of a functioning market, there appeared to be little alternative to centralisation, since at that time the political structures did not provide a viable basis for an alternative approach. Moreover, with the general disruption of the revolutionary process, centralisation probably provided the only avenue of control open to the government; other routes might have led to greater instability.

Nonetheless, there were errors made in structuring planning and incentives during the 1960s. While the decisions to centralise and to develop moral incentives may have been dictated by circumstances, greater attention might have been given to altering the circumstances and thereby widening the options. The expansion of education—dictated by other factors as well—was the main programme that would widen the options. But political structures of mass participation were neglected. In addition, while centralisation and limitations on material incentives were in large part imposed by existing circumstances, they were treated as unmitigated virtues. Accordingly the centralisation was extreme and little attention was given to constructing a system of material incentives to buttress the moral incentives. (It is useful to compare the attitude of the Cubans in the mid-1960s with that of certain individuals in the Soviet Union during the period of War Communism.

There were some economists who viewed the War Communism period as a short-cut to communism. They made a virtue out of the necessities of rationing and the elimination of money in that period. It seems—though perhaps on a lesser scale—the Cubans repeated this sort of error in the 1960s.)

In the general re-evaluation of policy at the beginning of the 1970s, these past weaknesses seem to have been recognised. Also, some of the circumstances affecting the earlier decisions had altered. Consequently, in the 1970s, there have been major changes in the incentive system and the structure of planning.

THE RETREAT ON LABOUR INCENTIVES

Since 1970 more and more stress has been given to the use of traditional material incentives. The ideological justification for this switch in policy has been provided by the principle, well established in Marxist theory, that in the transition to socialism the economy should operate on the basis of: 'From each according to ability, to each according to work.' The position was clearly and thoroughly articulated at the national congress of the Cuban labour unions in late 1973, where a series of resolutions was adopted calling for linking pay more closely to work and for reducing the free distribution of certain goods and services. The new position on incentives, however, was not a total alteration of the basic strategy of development in Cuba; it would more accurately be interpreted as a tactical retreat or a rationalising of the strategy.

The wage–price structure of pre-1959 Cuba, affected as it was by monopoly and political factors, had not been a particularly useful basis for an economically rational allocation system. Moreover, the dramatic alteration of income distribution and fundamental economic structures made the pre-1959 wage–price system have little connection to economic rationality in the 1960s. During the 1960s little attention had been given to structuring wages to reflect productivity or to structuring prices to reflect scarcity. Furthermore, the extreme scarcities of the 1960s and the non-market distribution of goods that was extended to maintain equality (see Chapter 12, pp. 89–91) made wages and prices have even less connection to economic rationality.

Thus one of the tasks that was central to the 'retreat' of the 1970s was attempting to connect wages more closely to productivity and prices more closely to scarcity. It seems that this has not meant any marked increase in inequality of money wages. Instead, adjustments have been made within the framework of the existing wage spread to 'norm' wages, or tie them more directly to output. (However, there is no data available to support – or contradict – this statement. I have based this conclusion on inference from a variety of statements by Cuban leaders and on informal interviews.)

In part, such adjustments took place automatically in the early 1970s. To some extent, money-wage differences in the 1960s had been tied to productivity differences, but the scarcity of consumer goods and non-market distribution meant that money-wage differences were not equal to real-income differences. In the 1970s, the expansion of the economy has increased the availability of consumer goods, so the money-wage differences have come to be differences in real income. The greater output of the Cuban economy can thus be viewed as providing the material basis for the new structure of incentives without the creation of serious poverty. More goods means that the lower limit on incomes can be maintained and that greater productivity can be materially rewarded.

The shift away from non-market distribution has had important limits. Free health care and education, for example, have been maintained. Employment and old-age security are still guaranteed. Housing is kept free or cheap and is rationed. And many food items are still rationed. Also, central components of the moral–incentive system have been maintained. The special programmes—as discussed above—continue to play an important role; volunteer labour is still encouraged on the basis of political motivation; and, in work places and schools, a stress is placed on collective action, political commitment, and hard work for the general welfare.

The task is now seen as one of *developing* a new incentive structure rather than imposing it by fiat. As Castro stated in his speech to the late 1973 labour-union congress: 'We must use material incentives intelligently and combine them with moral incentives, but we must not be deluded into thinking we are going to motivate the man of today, the socialist man, only through material incentives because material incentives no longer have the validity they have under capitalism, in which everything—even death—requires money.'

NEW PLANNING STRUCTURES

The changes in the structure of planning which have accompanied the incentive changes also involve a retreat from the 1960s and have been

ade possible by changes in material circumstances. The new approach
b planning involves a considerable decentralisation. The foundation of
otivation and coordination in the decentralised system is to be a
ombination of material incentives and mass participation.

A central purpose of the decentralisation has been to increase local
ccountability in order to raise productivity. By introducing more
orough receipt-and-payment relations at all levels, errors and in-
fficiencies will be more readily identified. Under the old system, in
hich local production units were grouped together into sector-wide
nterprises (see Chapter 14, p. 107), local receipt-and-payment relations
ere neglected. In addition, with achievements more clearly measured,
ewards can be tied to those achievements. A system of limited bonuses
as been introduced in which a share of a unit's profits remains in the
ands of the collective of workers, to be used for solving the social
roblems of that collective and rewarding the most outstanding
orkers.

Using profits as an indicator of success means that a more important
ole has been given to prices in coordinating activity. Prices, however,
re not to be determined in the market. Prices are the instruments of
ontrol used by the central planners. Thus they can be used to influence
ocal decisions in line with the overall social goals of planning. Allowing
rices to be determined on the market would, instead, mean that (given
upply conditions) local decisions were determined in accord with
eoples' demands—that is, their wants as made effective through their
ontrol over income. In Cuba the planning process is dominant and is
lesigned to make price represent a political choice process rather than
n economic, or market, choice process. In a major article in the Cuban
ournal *Economía y Desarollo*, two Cuban economists, Armando López
Coll and Armando Santiago, initiate their discussion of Cuban planning
with the statement:

> The economic system of Cuban society has, as one of its most im-
> portant characteristics, that the development of the relations of pro-
> duction is realized in a conscious manner; in accord with the workers'
> interests, economic processes and the reproduction of the economic
> system are jointly directed, for which [reason] profit and the market
> are no longer guiding elements. The foregoing implies that the
> movement of the economic proportions is regulated through the
> appropriate institutions and mechanisms . . . . The instrument that
> regulates the proportions in the Cuban economy is the plan.

Prices and local decisions based on prices are not the basis fo
investment decisions in the Cuban planning system. Aside from limi
ted expansion or modernisation programmes initiated at the loca
level, investment decisions are determined by central-planning pro
cesses.

By using plan-determined prices as guides and profits (computed wit
those prices) as indicators of success, it is possible to induce actions i
line with the plan goals. The system of the 1960s, organised on the basi
of centrally determined quantitive targets, was insufficient to induc
efficiency. The centre could not provide sufficient targets to assure cos
minimisation in each unit, and the unit had no incentive to minimise cos
on its own. Even where political consciousness was high, efforts t
increase efficiency could not be effectively directed; the local unit did no
know what to conserve. The planning changes of the 1970s are designe
to eliminate the waste inherent in that old system.

BUILDING ON MATERIAL CHANGES

The planning change stems in part from a recognition of past errors—
what Castro has termed 'idealistic mistakes' based on 'utopian attitudes
and 'a contempt for the experience of others'. And by correcting thos
errors the changes are likely to expand the basis for economic growth
However, the planning changes are also the consequences of materia
changes, including those connected with growth itself.

First, the expansion of the education system is again important. A
more and more people equipped with the organisational experience o
education enter the labour force, the workers and managers at the loca
levels are more able to handle the tasks of operating their units and
integrating them with the general economy. In addition, there are more
accountants and economists who can operate the formal aspects of a
decentralised system.

It is often argued that a decentralised system requires less, not more,
administratively skilled operatives than a centralised system. Such an
argument may be correct when coordination is accomplished via the
market and the driving force in the system is uninhibited self-interest.
But in a system like Cuba's decentralisation is a mechanism for
planning, and local operatives must be capable of coordinating their
activities within a planning system. And neither the market nor
personal-gain incentives are allowed to operate in an unmitigated
manner.

Furthermore, education has not only equipped new operatives in a technical sense, it has also begun to prepare them for their tasks ideologically as well. One potential danger of a decentralised system, relying significantly on highly trained personnel, is that a new, bureaucratic strata of experts may emerge. In the 1960s, had a more decentralised system been employed, this danger might have been especially serious. (This argument is related to Guevara's points noted in Chapter 14 above.) In the 1970s, however, partly as a result of the educational system and partly of the general political maturity of the revolution, the danger is reduced and decentralisation becomes a more attractive option. Still, the potential development of a new élite is a danger which should not be dismissed lightly. The main guard against this danger becoming an active problem is the sort of political development that has, in fact, been taking place. This point will be elaborated shortly.

A second material development contributing to the planning changes is that, in spite of the problems of the late 1960s, a certain amount of stability had been attained by the beginning of the 1970s. The dislocation of international trade, for example, was no longer such a severe problem. Consequently decentralisation and evaluation of the production units on the basis of their profits no longer ran up against problems created by instability (supply uncertainty, for example).

A third important factor is that the unemployment problem has been overcome. In the early period, it seemed important to encourage units to expand employment, and measuring success via profits with wages tied to productivity would have pushed things in the opposite direction. Also, decentralisation in the conditions of instability might have led production units to follow conservative employment practices. Through the 1960s, and especially in the 1970s, it has become apparent that labour is wasted and in short supply. The planning change is designed to correct this problem.

Finally, the political developments of the 1970s have radically altered the context, and therefore the implications, of the entire planning process. Had decentralisation been introduced in the absence of well-organised workers' (and other mass) organisations, it could have led in the direction of increasing managerial authority within the enterprise, encouraging worker alienation, and worsening inequality. In the centralised system of the 1960s, the central authority pre-empted the development of local-based administrative authority. This was precisely the intent of the Cuban leaders—especially Guevara—when they opted for the system of the 1960s.

Now, however, the increased role of the Cuban masses in all types of decision-making means that a decentralised system may be an effective mechanism for developing socialist social relations, as well as raising production. The problem of emerging élites is, of course, an ever-present one is the process of transition to socialism. But the problem is neither created nor solved via planning structures. Ultimately its resolution depends on the effectiveness of the peoples' control over political affairs. (As stated in Chapter 14, this is the central point, I believe, that comes out of the well-known debate between Paul Sweezy and Charles Bettelheim. In his synopsis of the new Cuban system, Castro has stated: 'But, under socialism, no system can be a substitute for politics, ideology, and the peoples' consciousness, because the factors that determine efficiency in a capitalist economy are different, and can never operate under socialism, so that the political aspect, the ideological aspect, and the moral aspect continue to be the crucial factors.')

26 Rebalancing the Cuban Economy

The restructuring of planning in Cuba and the political changes on which it is based apply to the operations of all sectors of the economy: agriculture as well as non-agriculture. State farms are treated in the same manner as industrial production units, and the new forms of operation should have similar impacts on all such units. The private operators in agriculture are, of course, separate entities. But they, too, as will be discussed below, are being affected by the planning changes.

It is not only the form of planning, however, that has changed in the 1970s. The content of Cuban planning has been significantly adjusted so that the roles of sugar and of agriculture generally are no longer so heavily emphasised. Industry is being moved into a position of higher priority, though not in such a manner as to create a new imbalance in that direction. Furthermore, the 'big push' approach to growth appears to have been abandoned. Investment rates have been substantially reduced and, in spite of the rapid growth of the early 1970s, target growth rates for the 1976–80 period are not high.

THE PATTERN OF EXPANSION IN THE EARLY 1970s

Even with the policy changes and growth of the early 1970s, some difficulties remain. During the 1971–5 period, sugar production averaged 5.6 million tons, and thus showed no departure from the industry's long-run stagnation. A favourable harvest in 1977 and a very large 1978 harvest have raised the average for the 1970s to 5.9 million tons. But, while these two harvests offer a basis for optimism, they hardly establish a clear upward trend (see Table 26.1 and Chart 26.1). Although weather has been relatively unfavourable in the 1970s, it would appear that problems of effective organisations persist.

On the other hand, significant progress has been made in raising productivity in both the cane fields and the sugar mills. As noted above,

TABLE 26.1 Sugar output, 1949–78 (million tons)

1949	5.1	1964	4.5
1950	5.4	1965	6.2
1951	5.8	1966	4.5
1952	7.3	1967	6.2
1953	5.2	1968	5.2
1954	5.0	1969	4.5
1955	4.6	1970	8.5
1956	4.8	1971	5.9
1957	5.7	1972	4.3
1958	5.9	1973	5.3
1959	6.0	1974	5.9
1960	5.9	1975	6.4*
1961	6.9	1976	5.7*
1962	4.9	1977	6.3*
1963	3.9	1978	7.3

NOTE
* These data are not from official Cuban sources and their validity is questionable.

SOURCE
1949–50, Table 1.1; 1951–73, Cuba (1973) p. 124; 1974, Cuba (1975) p. 54; 1975–76 Economic Intelligence Unit (1977) p. 9; 1977, estimated on the basis of information in Fidel Castro's 24 December 1977 speech as printed in *Granma Weekly Review* of 1 January 1978 and in Economic Intelligence Unit (1978), p. 9; 1978, *Granma Weekly Review*, 2 July 1978.

more than 25 per cent of the harvest was mechanised by 1975, and 39 per cent of the harvest was mechanised by 1978. Also, preparation of the land for sowing is totally mechanised as is cane lifting and loading. Consequently, since 1970 there has been a sizable reduction in the labour force. During the 1975 harvest, there were only 180,000 cane cutters, or roughly half the number involved in the pre-revolutionary harvests; and in 1978 there were only 161,000. In the industrial phase of sugar production, total employment dropped from 120,000 in 1970 to 89,000 in 1975. There have also been increases in the use of herbicides and pesticides, an expansion of total land cultivated and land under irrigation, and an increasing use of high-yield varieties. Still, there is no strong and continuing growth of sugar output.

Elsewhere in agriculture, the picture has been more favourable. Non-cane agriculture (excluding livestock) expanded at a rate of 8.4 per cent per year between 1970 and 1974, thus surpassing output in all previous years. The livestock sector expanded at an average rate of only 2.3 per cent per year during the early 1970s, and had not (in 1974) yet re-attained its previous peak. For the entire agricultural sector, 1971 saw a

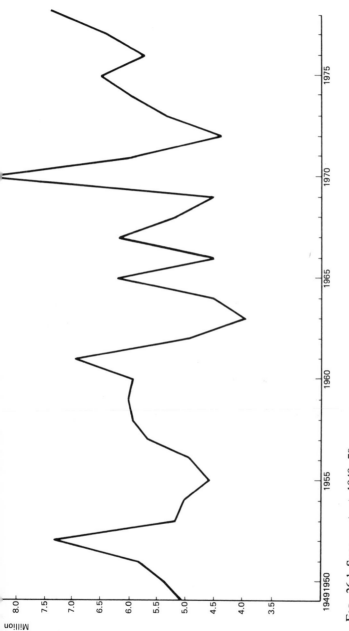

FIG. 26.1 Sugar output, 1949–78

SOURCE
Table 6.2.

8.4 per cent output decline, resulting primarily from the large drop in sugar production, but from 1971 to 1975, overall agricultural output steadily expanded at between 4.0 and 5.3 per cent per year. In spite of these positive aspects of the agricultural situation, however, the output data do not indicate by the mid-1970s any decisive break from the pre-1959 agricultural stagnation. The continuing weakness of agriculture, in the face of extensive modernisation, raises a number of questions which will be discussed shortly.

The big difference in the Cuban economy during the early 1970s, as compared to earlier years, was that expansion of the rest of the economy appears to have become firmly established independently of agriculture. The industrial sector expanded at close to 8 per cent per year between 1970 and 1975; and this followed a 28 per cent increase in output from the poor showing of 1968 to 1970. Construction, however, was the leading sector, tripling between 1970 and early 1975, though this followed a 25 per cent decline between 1967 and 1970.

The differential growth rates of the agricultural and non-agricultural sectors significantly altered the economy's structure. In the period 1962–9, agriculture accounted for between 20.8 per cent and 22.5 per cent of Gross Material Product; there was only a very slight downward trend in agriculture's share of GMP. After 1969, however, the decline in agriculture's share of output was large and steady. By early 1975 agriculture accounted for only 14.8 per cent of GMP. The same shift is apparent if agriculture is taken as a share of Gross Social Product. The shift is shown in Table 26.2.

The changing structure of the Cuban economy reflects a shift in planning priorities. The shift in the balance between agriculture and non-agriculture sectors was greater than intended, however, because of the relatively poor performance of agriculture. Nonetheless, it is clear that decisions were made after 1970 to shift the emphasis in development strategy from sugar particularly and agriculture generally towards the other sectors of the economy.

The rapid expansion of construction, for example, was induced by decisions to attack the housing shortage, to expand educational facilities (e.g., the schools in the countryside), and to extend infrastructure development. The growth of industry was the result of a general diversification and expansion programme. The most notable change was the rapid growth of the metallurgy and machinery industry, which accounted for 9.7 per cent of industrial output in 1974 as compared to 5.6 per cent in 1970 and 4.4 per cent in the early 1960s. Chemicals and construction materials were also rapidly growing sectors, the former

TABLE 26.2 Agriculture's share in total output, 1962–75

	Agriculture as % of GMP	Agriculture as % of GSP
1962	22.1	14.7
1963	21.7	14.2
1964	21.7	14.0
1965	22.5	14.9
1966	22.0	14.3
1967	20.8	13.9
1968	21.4	13.9
1969	21.0	13.5
1970	20.6	13.9
1971	18.1	11.9
1972	17.3	10.8
1973	16.1	9.8
1974	15.4	9.3
1975	14.7	8.8

SOURCE
Table A.2.1

accounting for a larger share of industrial output (11.6 per cent) in 1974 than sugar (11.5 per cent). The growth of the service sector reflects decisions to increase consumption.

The rise in consumption was associated with a decline of the rate of investment. In 1970, when the effort was made to harvest the 10 million tons, investment was cut back sharply from the high levels of the preceding years, and it amounted to only 11.8 per cent of GMP. In 1974, the investment rate was up to 21.1 per cent but was still below the staggering levels of the late 1960s.

CONTINUING PROBLEMS IN SUGAR

Difficulties of sugar production that have continued through the 1970s are a serious weakness in the Cuban economy. In spite of notable progress with mechanisation and the exceptional 1978 harvest, the problems of the 1960s continue to exist. From one perspective, these problems can be seen as resulting from a continuing labour shortage. The rapid expansion of other sectors in the 1970s has drawn labour out of agriculture and into new activities. The role of mass mobilisations in the attempt to solve the labour-shortage problem has been drastically reduced since 1970. There were 60,000 fewer volunteers involved in the 1971 harvest than in the 1970 harvest, still 35,000 less in 1972, and still 25,000 less in 1973. Also, as noted above, the programme of sending students to the countryside to work for extended periods was cut back in the early 1970s. Apparently, these mobilisations were viewed as an ineffective solution to the labour shortage in sugar; the experience of the late 1960s could hardly be interpreted otherwise.

From another perspective, the sugar problem can be seen as the result of insufficient technical progress, or insufficient progress in transforming the organisation of work. A number of attempts have been made to speed up the mechanisation process in cane cutting and to find other methods for raising productivity. Several different types of harvesters were tried in the late 1960s and early 1970s before significant progress was attained. The roughness of the terrain and maintenance problems were continual difficulties.

By 1973, a harvester-combine satisfactory for Cuban conditions had been designed by Soviet and Cuban engineers based on their earlier experiences. The machine, the KTP–1, was to be manufactured in Cuba beginning in 1976. However, the anticipated annual production rate is 600 units, and may be far less; several times that number, in working order, are needed to harvest the entire crop. Moreover, the existence of machines will not eliminate the administrative and break-down problems that plagued the use of tractors in the late 1960s.

There has also been some experimentation with the Australian method of cane harvesting, which involves burning the fields prior to cutting. This eliminates the tasks of cleaning and stacking the cane, and it reduces the cane's weight. While the Australian method seemed to yield significant positive results—saving upwards of 60 per cent of manpower where it was used—it precipitated new sorts of difficulties: the terrain had to be prepared, a special variety of cane had to be used, more frequent and more precise planting was required, and special fertiliser was needed; the burning of cane had to be carefully planned and carried out; cutting, loading, and transport had to be reorganised; and finally, burned cane loses its sugar content more rapidly than regularly cut cane and hence must be transported to the mills more quickly.

It is not clear to what extent the Australian system has been developed in Cuba. But the process is mentioned in neither Castro's report to the 1st Congress of the Cuban Communist Party nor in the comprehensive economic report issued on the 25th anniversary of the National Bank of Cuba. In any case, the Australian method has clearly not provided a general solution to the productivity problem in the cane fields.

The problems associated with the Australian method are particularly interesting, because, in one way or another, they are fundamentally problems of organisation. They illustrate the way in which technological change is basically a matter of using labour in new ways, of reorganising the work process. Indeed, both the inadequacies of the Australian method and the delays in mechanisation underscore the continuing importance of organisational difficulties in sugar production. And this, in turn, suggests a point that will be discussed further below, namely, that organisational progress appears to be most difficult in those branches of the economy which have long histories as significant sectors. Cuban agriculture in general has its problems. But it is cane production (and cattle raising) that seems most dominated by backwardness and hence most difficult to modernise. (By contrast, rice production in Cuba has been developed as a new activity since the revolution. It is relatively detached from traditional Cuban agriculture. While the new rice cultivation has had problems, mechanisation has been complete.)

Backwardness is also entrenched in the sugar industry. Its capital stock is old, although extensive modernisation was carried out in the 1960s. Except for four new mills which began operation in the 1978 harvest, Cuba is still working with mills the newest of which was built in 1927. And along with the old structures and equipment are old, backward forms of organisation that are not easily renovated.

One problem exists in simply keeping the old mills going. In 1969 there were 152 mills operating in Cuba, as compared to 161 at the time of the revolution. (The decline in number may have been as much the result of consolidation to achieve economies of scale, as of deterioration.) After the 1970 harvest, four more mills were out of operation, and frequent break-downs took place in 1971. During the 1972 harvest the number of mills operating varied between 136 and 144.

Other difficulties are indicated by the low recovery rates, i.e., the sugar obtained as a percentage of the weight of the cane. Between 1951 and 1958 the recovery rate averaged 12.85 per cent and was never below 12.56 per cent. Between 1959 and 1963, the rate went from 12.57, to 12.51, to 12.66, to 13.31 (higher than any year in the 1950s), to 12.36. Until 1969 the rate hovered just above 12 per cent, but then the following rates were realised (more recent data are not available):

1969	11.02 %
1970	10.71 %
1971	11.49 %
1972	9.93 %
1973	11.07 %

While the higher final production of sugar during the subsequent years indicates the likelihood of some improvement in the recovery rate, the weight of these data is impressive. They reflect a failure to organise the activities effectively in the mills, in the fields, and in transporting cane from fields to mills. It would appear that the old methods of work organisation had been broken down, but new organisation, a new socialisation of the work process, had not been thoroughly established. (It should be noted, however, that weather has also been a factor in the low recovery rates of the early 1970s.)

THE LIVESTOCK SECTOR

The livestock sector grew, but only slowly, during the early 1970s. And its problems again illustrate the persistence of organisational difficulties in agriculture. (The livestock sector was also hurt by CIA-sponsored sabotage in the early 1970s – see p.34.) Since the early 1960s, a major effort has been under way to improve the genetic composition of Cuban cattle. Yet by the mid-1970s there had been no appreciable success in increasing the size of the nation's herds or raising output of beef. Between 1967 and 1970, the herds were reduced from 7 to 5 million head. According to Carmelo Mesa-Lago: 'Various technical reports published in 1969–71 by British genetic advisors of the Cuban government suggest a bad performance in this sector due to failures in the breeding and artificial insemination programs, poor quality of fodder, cattle illness and drought.' During the early 1970s a restrictive-slaughter policy was followed in an effort to increase the herds; but the short-run impact was a 16 per cent decline in beef production between 1970 and 1974. (Experience elsewhere suggests that to initiate the expansion of cattle herds by genetic improvement is likely to yield poor results. Existing herds are probably adapted to the existing environment, and the success of introducing new genes will depend on improving that environment. Although Cuba has made efforts along these lines, events suggest that efforts were overbalanced in favour of genetic improvement as opposed to improving the environment on cattle ranches, e.g., through disease control, feed supply, etc.)

By contrast, other branches of livestock production did not do badly during the 1970s. Poultry production rose by 28 per cent between 1970 and 1974, and thus accounted for a greater value of output than did beef production. Egg production, which had already done well in the 1960s, rose by 20 per cent in this period. Pork production, in spite of the sabotage noted above, increased by almost 50 per cent (but the value of ork production is still only 20 per cent of either poultry or beef production). And, even while beef production has done badly, milk production has risen by 16 per cent. (Available data, unfortunately, do not allow us to answer some of the more interesting questions about these changes: What is the extent of public-sector and private-sector responsibility in these various branches of livestock? And to what extent has the expansion of output—especially in poultry and egg production—depended on imported feeds? Without a firm answer to this latter question—an answer indicating the existence of domestic sources of feed—the conclusion of 'success' is tenuous.)

A major factor that distinguishes beef production from the other branches of the livestock sector is that beef production was well established prior to the revolution; and moreover beef production was carried on in a complex relationship among small, medium and large-scale producers, each handling different aspects of the process. The other branches of livestock production have all been developed in large part since 1959. This again suggests that new forms of organisation can be most readily established where they do not have to compete with established patterns, old forms, of organisation. The expansion of the poultry sector provides particularly striking positive support for this hypothesis. Successful poultry production requires relatively modern techniques of organisation. Yet here is an area where Cuba has had considerable success, having begun to develop poultry and egg production anew after the revolution (though as noted above, data limitations make any appraisal tenuous).

PRIVATE AGRICULTURE IN THE 1970s

The private operators in agriculture do not appear to have done badly since 1970. Table 26.3 reports data on collection of various categories of crops in which the private sector plays a significant role. (The table overlaps with and may be compared to Table 19.1.) Two conclusions can be drawn from these data. First, the general fall of the 1960s in the collection of these food crops has been reversed in the 1970s. Second, the notable decline in the role of the private sector, which took place in the 1960s, has halted.

Data on tobacco and coffee production reveal similar positive developments in the 1970s. Both tobacco and coffee production rose about 35 per cent between 1970 and 1974. (Though 1970 was not a particularly good year for either.) Data on the private – state breakdown for these two crops are not available. In the case of tobacco,

TABLE 26.3 Collection of selected categories of agricultural commodities, 1969–74 (000s tons)

	1969	1970	1971	1972	1973	1974
Grains						
total	189.3	299.3	297.2	251.0	244.0	347.7
private	16.2(9%)	11.0(4%)	15.1(5%)	19.2(8%)	13.7(6%)	n.a.
Tubors						
total	326.2	196.8	239.3	383.5	397.5	289.5
private	130.8(40%)	75.3(38%)	82.6(35%)	168.1(44%)	181.9(46%)	n.a.
Vegetables						
total	126.7	136.2	172.2	150.0	239.8	265.9
private	82.1(65%)	62.7(46%)	74.0(43%)	63.3(42%)	123.6(52%)	n.a.
Fruits						
total	297.4	289.6	296.9	372.4	434.0	463.4
private	171.0(57%)	125.7(43%)	130.1(44%)	161.7(43%)	207.9(48%)	n.a.

SOURCE
1969–73. *Anuario Estadistico de Cuba. 1973* pp. 91–3. For 1974, crop values in constant prices are reported in Cuba (1975) p. 40. The per cent increases were used to obtain these 1974 volume figures. These 1974 data may not be consistant with the figures for other years.

however, it is known that production continues to be primarily (85 per cent) in the private sector.

It is possible only to speculate on the reasons for the better performance during the 1970s in secondary crop production generally and in the private sector particularly. Several factors seem to be involved. To begin with, these crops (with the important exception of rice) are in general cultivated in relatively small units and require intensive cultivation. Such processes are not effectively directed by central authorities out of touch with local conditions. The general trend toward decentralisation in Cuban planning may thus have been particularly important for these secondary crops.

In particular, there has been a move towards the development of a variety of types of locally organised development plans, involving both state and private producers. These plans serve, on the one hand, as a mechanism of decentralisation; on the other hand, within the local context, they appear to tie the private producers more closely to the state. Thus the production practices of the private sector can be improved and the state can more readily gain control of the output.

The control attained through the local plans is part of a general effort by the government to limit sales outside the state procurement system. Such sales were apparently an issue of controversy at the 1971 congress of ANAP, but the policy of moving toward their reduction seems to have been firmly established. More important than a policy line, however, is that the increased availability of consumer goods has provided an inducement to the peasant to trade within the official network. Regardless of any formal adjustment in procurement prices the situation has been automatically adjusted in the same way that wage differentials have been automatically adjusted (see above, Chapter 25).

In addition, by the early 1970s the stability of private agriculture and the sincerity of the government's pledge not to eliminate the small farmers had been well established. Since 1963 the attrition of the private sector had been gradual. At the close of 1963, after the second agrarian reform, the private sector held 37 per cent of the cultivated land. While later data are not clearly consistent with either this base figure or with one another, they seem to indicate the following shares of cultivated land in the private sector:

1963	37%
1966	35%
1971	32%
1975	30%

The decline of the private sector has resulted from the death o
retirement of owners and government purchases of some farms (in orde
to integrate them in larger units, e.g., for rice cultivation). (However, it i
not clear that the decline in share of cultivated area is the same as
decline in the absolute position of the private sector, since total lan
under cultivation has increased. But no total break-downs exist. Dat
on the total number of private farms is even more difficult to interpre
The total number of private farms just prior to the second agraria
reform was 164,000; some of these must have been eliminated in th
reform. José Acosta reports that in 1967 there were 218,000 persons i
ANAP, and 16,000 unassociated peasants. He later reports 203,00
peasants in 1971, but is unclear whether this refers to all peasants or onl
those in ANAP. Acosta also says nothing to distinguish farm owner
from other ANAP members—that is, family members. Castro in hi
speech to the 1st Party Congress, reported 232,000 ANAP members i
1975, of which 162,000 were farm owners and the rest were members o
families. On the basis of all this the whole situation remains somewha
unclear.)

While the government maintains the position that private cultivatio
will eventually be eliminated, there would appear to be little pressure i
that direction on the private farmers. Indeed, Castro has stated that the
government simply does not have the organizational capacity to take
over the private sector, and that the private sector's role will be
indispensable for some time to come.

These various factors explaining the favourable developments with
secondary crops carry relatively positive implications for the future. It
seems that at least in this part of agriculture a stable and organised
foundation for continuing growth may have been established. Likewise,
in the traditionally secondary branches of livestock, the prospects are
positive. The situations with sugar and beef are not so auspicious.
Nonetheless, if major policy changes of the 1970s continue to have the
positive impact they seem to have had to date, even the stagnation in
sugar and beef production may be overcome. (Aside from the question of
production in general, it would be useful to determine the extent to
which Cuba has been moving towards self-sufficiency in the production
of food. Available data, however, do not allow a thorough appraisal.
The emphasis on eggs and milk production and the output successes
achieved in these areas are positive, albeit very limited, indication.
Likewise, the high priority given to rice cultivation is important because
rice is such an important part of the Cuban diet. Nonetheless, through
the early 1970s, it appears that Cuba was still importing as much rice as

t was producing; but with the investments that have been made in rrigation facilities and the development of large-scale rice farming, this picture might be expected to improve shortly. Also, the improvement in he production of secondary crops noted above and the seemingly mproved integration of peasants in production programmes would seem to augur well for improvement of the domestically produced food supply.)

27 Directions of Development in the Late 1970s

The 1st Congress of the Communist Party of Cuba in December 1975 provided the occasion for a political celebration of the economic success attained in the preceding years. It also provided an opportunity to consolidate—or at least clearly articulate—the policy changes of the early 1970s and set the directions for Cuban development in the subsequent period.

With regard to policies on economic, political and social organisation—policies which, as we have argued in preceding chapters, provided much of the foundation for growth in the early 1970s—the congress did not mark any significant changes. Indeed, one of the primary functions of the congress seems to have been the institutionalisation of the new approach to planning and incentives, the new forms of political participation, and the continuing reliance on social programmes.

Nonetheless, some important adjustments in Cuban development strategy did emerge from the congress, and they would have an impact on the economic plan for the late 1970s. To begin with, in his speech to the congress, Fidel Castro announced that in the subsequent years the tempo of economic expansion would be substantially reduced. From the 10 per cent per year rate of expansion in the first half of the decade, the plan would call for a reduction to a 6 per cent growth rate in the 1976–80 period. Furthermore, a switch in emphasis from agriculture to industry, long anticipated, would guide Cuban strategy in the late 1970s; industrial development would now have first priority. (With regard to all aggregate growth rates in Cuba, the following comments by Castro, made when he announced the 6 per cent target, deserve special note:

'It should also be taken into account that, according to socialist methodology, only material production is considered in the growth percentages. Services, like education and public health, are not included in the gross social product, as is the practice in the capitalist countries. Otherwise, our growth estimates up to now and in the coming five-year period would be much higher, for the abundant resources and the material and human investment that the Revolution has made into these activities are well known.')

Because of the lack of sufficient data, it is not possible to appraise in any thorough manner the economic course of the Cuban revolution since 1975. We do know that global social product increased 4 per cent in 1976 and 3.8 per cent in 1977. The forcast growth rate for 1978 was 7.4 per cent, and with the very large sugar harvest this rate may have been attained. Beyond these very aggregate sorts of data, however, it is necessary to speculate, and a more meaningful examination of this period will have to be postponed to a future date.

TOWARDS AN INDUSTRIAL EMPHASIS

In establishing a target growth rate of 6 per cent per year for the Cuban economy in the 1976–80 period, the Cuban authorities revealed some qualitative as well as quantitative changes in their approach to economic development. They appear to have overcome the crude over-optimism of earlier years and to have accepted the economic limits imposed by local conditions. In addition, the decision to reduce target growth rates was connected to the decision to give industry the leading role in Cuban development. Because industrialisation would require substantial foreign exchange, a lower overall growth rate was probably dictated by expected export earnings and limits on foreign loans. In his report to the Party Congress, Castro introduced the new role for industry in the following terms:

'In the coming five-year period, the industrialization process in the country is to be significantly accelerated. During the first years of the Revolution, there was no other alternative but to concentrate on agricultural production. At this stage, the closest attention is to be given to agriculture, but the main emphasis is to be on industrialization. Contracts have already been signed for most of the factories to be set up in this period, and the rest are being negotiated [i.e., with foreign concerns and governments—A.M.]. This industrialization program falls short of solving many of our difficulties, but it will mean an important advance.'

(The issue of foreign loans raises a number of questions concerning Cuba's relationship with the Soviet Union and the significance of that relationship for both Cuba's development policy and broader political matters. I will offer some comments on these questions in the following chapter.)

The particulars of the Cuban industrialisation programme call for an expansion closely tied to agriculture. To begin with, the industrialisation programme relies on a continuing important role for sugar. 'Consolidation and modernisation of the sugar industry' is a central component in foreign-exchange planning. Emphasis on food processing and on textile goods industries are also part of the industrialisation programme; these industries are intended to perform both consumption and export roles. And the linkages of industry to agriculture in the provision of agricultural inputs have an important place in the programme.

The industrialisation programme for the late 1970s rejects the 'big push' approach to development. An emphasis is given to the production of consumption goods and there is a minimal role for investment goods industries. Aside from those activities tied directly to agriculture, the only roles for heavy industry in the principal tasks are the expansion of nickel plants (in connection with export promotion) and the continued development of industries related to construction.

In maintaining the approach of developing industry in connection with agriculture, the plan for the 1976–80 period is in line with the long-range programme established in the early 1960s. Moreover, that long-range plan anticipated a switch towards an industrial emphasis by the end of the 1970s. The long-range plan, however, anticipated switch as following from the successful attainment of goals in the agricultural sector. Most important, the long-range plan called for sugar output running at or close to 10 million tons per year in the 1970s and an additional export base developing in other branches of agriculture. These accomplishments were supposed to provide the foreign-exchange base for industrial expansion.

The emerging industrial emphasis in Cuba is a response not to the strength of agricultural growth, but to its weakness. While the severe agricultural problems of the 1960s have been overcome, progress has been uneven (see Chapter 26). And it appears likely that in the late 1970s the agricultural situation is one of continuing unevenness, though the plan and information so far available do hold out some reasons for positive expectations.

CONTINUING IMPORTANCE AND PROBLEMS OF SUGAR

The central importance of agriculture, especially sugar, to the Cuban economy is nowhere more clear than in the data on export earnings. Table 27.1 shows trade data for the 1970–5 period, with exports broken down by type of commodity until 1974. During the years 1970–3, exports of sugar and its derivatives accounted for roughly 75 per cent of each year's foreign-exchange earnings. This was basically the same as in the pre-revolutionary period. In 1974, the rise of world sugar prices lifted Cuba's total export earnings by over 90 per cent in one year, and sugar made up 86 per cent of the 1974 total. For the first time in over a decade, Cuba ran a foreign-trade surplus, but only by increasing its reliance on sugar.

TABLE 27.1 Cuba's trade balance, imports and exports, 1970–5, and percentage break-down of exports by type of product, 1970–4

	1970	1971	1972	1973	1974	1975
In millions of pesos:						
Trade balance	−261.5	−526.3	−418.9	−314.0	3.7	−138.4
Imports	1311.0	1387.5	1189.8	1467.0	2225.9	3071.7
Exports	1049.5	861.2	770.9	1153.0	2222.2	2933.3
As a percentage of exports:*						
Sugar and its derivatives	76.9	76.4	74.1	75.4	86.5	n.a.
Minerals and concentrates	16.7	15.8	14.9	13.9	6.4	n.a.
Tobacco and its products	3.2	3.7	4.7	4.5	2.7	n.a.
Fish products	1.8	2.5	3.4	3.0	2.3	n.a.
Other	1.4	1.6	2.8	3.2	2.2	n.a.

* Total will not always be 100.0 due to rounding.

SOURCE
For 1970–4, *Economiá y Desarrollo* (1976a); for 1975, *Economiá y Desarrollo* (1976b).

Cuba's export earnings continued to grow rapidly in 1975, rising by 32 per cent over the 1974 level. (Imports grew by 38 per cent, however, and the trade surplus was transformed back to a deficit.) Although a breakdown of export earnings by type of products is not available for 1975, it may be safely assumed that sugar's role remained fairly stable.

With a continuing weakness of world sugar prices since 1975, the country's export earnings have undoubtedly suffered. Not having established an alternative source of earnings, Cuba remains as dependent as ever on sugar. (We are forced to speculate here, however, because trade data for the post-1975 period are not yet available. Cuba, of course, sells much of its sugar outside of the world market in contract agreements with the Soviet Union and other nations. Still, the prices in those contracts are adjusted up and down to some degree as world market prices change. Also, Cuba does sell a substantial share of its sugar on the world market.)

Yet in at least one respect, the relation between sugar and the rest of the economy is changing in the 1970s. Mechanisation of the sugar harvest continues to progress. As reported above, by 1978 39 per cent of the sugar cane was mechanically harvested. The current plan anticipates that 60 per cent of the harvest will be mechanised by 1980, and this target, while optimistic, is not totally out of line with the progress made through 1978. In large part, meeting the target will depend upon the successful production of the KTP-1 combine and its operation in the fields (see Chapter 26, p. 192, above).

Mechanisation of the sugar harvest, it should be emphasised, will greatly alter the implication of sugar's important role in the Cuban economy. Because of the seasonal nature of the demand for labour in sugar cultivation, its large role means that in the absence of mechanisation the labour force of the entire country must be structured to meet the needs of sugar. Such was the case before 1959, when the labour needs of the sugar sector meant severe unemployment for large segments of the population much of the year and when the up and down of the sugar cycle created an up and down of the whole economy. Mechanisation, however, is now beginning to break this link, and the social structure of the nation need not be subordinated to sugar. For this reason the continuing major role of sugar in the Cuban economy does not have the same negative implication as in the pre-revolutionary era, though, as will be pointed out in the subsequent chapter, there do remain some important difficulties associated with sugar's continuing centrality.

In addition to the advances in mechanising the sugar harvest, there appears to be continuing progress with regard to irrigation, the introduction of new cane varieties, the uses of chemicals (fertilisers, pesticides, herbicides), efficiency in the use of fuel for processing, and overcoming transport problems.

The failure to attain a sustained expansion of output, in spite of these positive developments, may be attributed in part to poor weather in the early 1970s; average rainfall for the 1971–5 period was 13 per cent below the 1966–70 average. The weather issue should not be forgotten; its significance will receive comment in the following chapter. Nevertheless as we have suggested in the previous chapter, labour shortages and organisational factors are probably of major importance. And these continuing problems indicate some shortcomings of Cuban planning. Inconsistent goals seem to have been established. On the one hand, Cuban authorities are pushing an industrialisation programme (including the rapid expansion of construction), providing opportunities which draw labour out of the agricultural sector. On the other hand, they plan to finance industrialisation with agricultural exports (sugar) which can only be produced by maintaining the agricultural labour force, or at least allowing it to decline only at a slower rate. This apparent inconsistency could have its roots in a variety of relationships. The problem may simply indicate that, for the time being, industrialisation goals have been set too high. Also, it may reveal more particular imbalances, such as an overemphasis on construction activity (a relatively labour-intensive process) or poor setting of relative wage rates in different sectors of the economy.

In the plan for the 1976–80 period there is some recognition of the need to establish a consistency between agricultural and industrial expansion. For example, in the plan, heavy emphasis is placed on raising productivity in agriculture so that labour can be released for industrialisation. And, most important, keeping the overall growth-rate target as low as 6 per cent should provide some relief on the labour-supply front.

Whatever problems persist, there is no evidence that the problems of the 1970s are either nearly as severe or as much characterised by general economic disorganisation as were the difficulties of the 1960s. The steady—albeit slower than hoped for—progress with cane-cutting mechanisation is evidence of considerable success in overcoming the worst symptoms of disorganisation. Likewise, the industrial expansion of the early 1970s and general economic success of those years should have greatly changed the context in which economic shortfalls have their impact. Once begun, the process of improving the organisation of production gives itself a certain momentum, just as the lack of progress had a self-perpetuating character in the 1960s.

This generally positive appraisal not withstanding, it is still questionable whether or not the plan goal of 8 to 8.7 million tons of sugar in 1980 will be attained. It is likely that the severe output fluctuations that resulted from general disorganisation may be eliminated; and with the progress in mechanisation, productivity in cane production will continue to rise. But a substantial share of the productivity increase is likely as in earlier years, to result in releasing labour rather than in raising output. Such speculations (to say nothing of the world-market situation) lead toward the conclusion—which we will discuss more thoroughly in the next chapter—that a continuing heavy reliance on sugar is a poor base for Cuban industrial expansion.

ECONOMIC EXPANSION AND THE POSITION OF THE PEASANTRY

Elsewhere in agriculture (with the exception of cattle) the experience of the 1970s seems to have been more favourable. The information which is available—covering the years up to the end of 1975—was discussed in the preceding chapter. In spite of the fact that 1975 itself was not a year of rapid expansion for the traditionally secondary agricultural activities there are reasons to expect the generally successful experience of the early 1970s to continue into the latter half of the decade.

The factors which we offered to explain the success in the 1970–5 period (see Chapter 26, especially pp. 195–9) seem to have been firmly established. The decentralisation of planning allows local conditions to play their necessary role in crop management and planning. The more effective integration of the peasantry with local plans facilitates the modernisation of their practices as well as a more thorough control over their product by the government. The greater use of prices in planning (part of the process of decentralisation) provides a greater incentive both in the private and public sectors. And the rising availability of non-agricultural consumer goods—a part of the sharp increase in national output—has meant that the agricultural sector is able to obtain real remuneration for raising the supply of its products. All of these processes are illustrated in the accelerated development of local rural communities tied in with the formation of agricultural mini-plans (see Chapter 23, p. 170).

In the *Theses and Resolutions Concerning the Agrarian Question and the Relations with the Peasantry* which came out of the Party Congress the general lines which had been followed up to 1975 were affirmed, clarified, and put forth as the continuing policies of the revolution. Of course, the theses and resolutions are statements of policy and may well differ from actual events since 1975. Nonetheless, as a first guide to events, it is worth noting several points which are emphasised in the official document. These may be paraphrased as follows:

1 With regard to the peasants' role in the economy, there are two 'roads' which can be followed towards 'superior forms of production': one is the road of integration of the peasants with the plan; the other is the development of peasant cooperatives. Both roads are viewed as legitimate routes, and the answer to the question of which to follow should be determined by an examination of concrete conditions in each zone of the country. Factors to be considered in the choice include: the importance of large-scale investments; the proximity of peasant holdings to state lands; the need for intensive cultivations versus the need for large-scale operation; and the particular political conditions in the region.

2 While there are two legitimate roads to follow, the goal of both is the eventual incorporation of the lands of the peasantry in the state system. Incorporation is the 'superior form of production' because it represents ownership by all the people, because it allows the advance of productivity, and because it facilitates raising the conditions of rural life.

3 Movement toward the 'superior forms of production' should be a gradual and voluntary process. Incorporation will allow the backwardness of small-peasant cultivation to be overcome in the long run. But until new forms of production and organization are consolidated, the small operations must be relied upon. Moreover, violating the principle of voluntary change would undermine the political foundation of the revolution. (Voluntary change, of course, includes change induced by such mechanisms as the availability of better housing and social services in the state sector and by a credit system favouring the move toward incorporation.) It is the role of ANAP to continually encourage the move toward incorporation and to create the political and organisational base for its accomplishment.

4 As long as the private peasantry exists, it will be encouraged to play a positive role in production, and, in particular, the state will supply it with productive inputs. Although the peasant farm is primarily dependent on family labour and, to an extent, on mutual aid, the state sector will assure a sufficient supply of labour during periods of peak activity; use of labour in the private sector will thus be accomplished without the reintroduction of a private wage-labour system. In addition, the state will supply the peasantry with modern inputs (e.g., fertiliser) and will assure the availability of credit and

reasonable procurement prices. The private peasantry is thus to operate within the system—indeed, within a planning framework—rather than in an alien and possibly antagonistic relation to it.

5 'The worker–peasant alliance is not a temporary pact, a tactic, but is the strategic and lasting union between these two classes, the final objective of which, as affirmed by Fidel, is "to advance the revolutionary process until all, absolutely, belong to a society without classes, a society of workers with equal rights."'

The positive general policy toward the small peasants which is embodied in these points has been followed, in one form or another, since 1959. Unlike other important aspects of Cuban economic, political and social policy, the policies on relations with the peasantry have been remarkably stable. This stability, no doubt, is one reason for their apparent success. It is also a reason why, in so far as the small farmers are responsible for secondary activities in agriculture, the favourable production record of the early 1970s is likely to continue in the late 1970s.

If such success does continue, however, it may contain certain political contradictions. In the late 1960s, Leo Huberman and Paul Sweezy called attention to the political danger implicit in the Cuban revolution's heavy reliance on production by the private farmers (see Chapter 12, pp. 88–9). Huberman and Sweezy argued that some peasants were becoming relatively wealthy and constituted a potential political threat to the revolution—not necessarily through direct action, but through having the economic power to force the adoption of a particular set of policies. In the absence of any general economic success in that period, the enrichment of a segment of the peasantry was surely a very limited phenomenon. And there is not evidence that serious political conflict evolved (though there does appear to have been relatively heated exchange over matters of policy at the 1971 ANAP conference).

The production success of the early 1970s may have altered the situation somewhat. Associated with that success, a relatively large number of small farmers has undoubtedly obtained substantial material returns (though the term 'enriching themselves' may be an exaggeration). It is by no means unreasonable to assume that such a group would resist policies which would eliminate the foundations of their personal success. There is still no evidence of serious conflict along these lines, but the whole issue is one that cannot be ignored, and there is some indication that during 1977 the government increased its efforts to bring small farmers into a closer relation with the system. The extent to which this intensification was in response to any active or passive resistance remains open to speculation.

A PERIOD OF RELATIVE STABILITY

It is still too early to form any definitive judgements concerning the path of the Cuban economy in the late 1970s or about the success of new policies, e.g., the industrialisation policy. It is relatively clear, nonetheless, that economically the Cuban revolution had entered a period of relative stability. Since the beginning of the decade, there have been no sharp changes in the political, economic and social policies which—as we have argued—form the foundation of economic progress and policy.

Moreover, the shift in the sectoral emphasis which has taken place has not had the character of earlier policy shifts. The extreme emphasis on sugar and the consequent imbalance of the economy seems to be a policy approach of another era. The current emphasis on industry does not involve any abandonment of agriculture. Current policy seems to be best described by the world 'balance', both in the technical and philosophic sense of the term.

This is not to say that significant changes and serious contradictions are all things of the past in Cuba. Both the internal development of the economy and international events (political and economic) will create pressures and bring about alterations of Cuban society. Yet it seems a certain period has passed in Cuba. It is probably true that in any revolutionary process there is a time when the laws of motion of the old society have been destroyed and new modes of operation and organisation have not been firmly established; and during that time the explicit decisions of revolutionary actors are particularly important and changes in policy and direction are especially sharp. It seems likely that, as the Cuban revolution ends its second decade in power, this time is past. And it is consequently a particularly opportune moment to draw out some of the lessons of the Cuban experience.

Part Seven

Lessons of Agriculture and Development in Cuba

Lessons of Agriculture
and Development
in Cuba

'Cuba is above all an agricultural state. Its population is largely rural. The city depends on these rural areas . . . The greatness and prosperity of our country depends on a healthy and vigorous rural population that loves the land and knows how to cultivate it.'

'With the exception of a few food, lumber and textile industries, Cuba continues to be a producer of raw materials. We export sugar to import candy, we export hides to import shoes, we export iron to import plows. Everybody agrees that the need to industrialize the country is urgent.'

In these words from his famous 1953 speech 'History Will Above Me', Fidel Castro expressed a part of his indictment of the capitalist system which dominated Cuba at that time. Capitalism, he maintained, kept the rural areas impoverished and prevented industrialisation; only a revolution could change all that.

These same words, however, expressed a contradiction which would continue to confront Cuban economic development long after the political triumph of the Cuban revolution. Cuban development requires both a vigorous agriculture and industrialisation. Ultimately agriculture and industry are complementary, mutually dependent activities. But they are also—and especially in the period of initiating a new development strategy— competing activities, standing in contradiction with one another. Each requires the organisational attention, labour supply and other resources which are in such short supply.

But the contradiction is one which transcends technical problems of resource allocation. It is as much a social and political problem as an economic problem. It is the conflict between town and country as well as the conflict between industry and agriculture.

Almost all of the central issues of Cuban development which have arisen since 1959 are closely tied to this contradiction. For example, the early conflict between the industrial–urban and agricultural–rural priorities of the revolution appeared in terms of an emerging labour shortage in the early 1960s; and this labour shortage was the prime factor behind the sharp debate over incentives. The entire development strategy of the 1960s—the 10 million tons and the big push—was an effort to overcome the agriculture–industry conflict and transform it into a relation of complementarity. And the 'organisation problem'— which has received so much attention in earlier chapters and which was embodied in all the social, political and economic programmes of the revolution—has been defined in large part by the rural and under developed situation of much of the Cuban proletariat.

In the 1970s, the centrality of this contradiction between town and country lives on in the effort to find a satisfactory balance between agriculture and industry in Cuba's national plan. The 1976–80 Cuban plan calls for a lower growth rate in order (among other things) to ease the conflict between the two main sectors of the economy. The plan also embodies an effort to give first priority to industry without abandoning agriculture. Indeed, those industrial branches given greatest emphasis are, with few exceptions, ones closely tied to agriculture.

The continuing evolution of the rural–urban relationship provides a useful—if not essential—back-drop against which to review some of the lessons which can be derived from Cuba's experience with socialist development. To do so in this chapter I am going to discuss first the weaknesses of Cuban agriculture as a leading sector. This brings me to some remarks concerning Cuba's international economic, and political relations. Finally, I shall re-examine some of the important socio political issues involved in Cuban development.

The issues discussed here are by no means unique to Cuba. In each nation where socialist forces have attempted to guide economic development, the agriculture–industry relationship with its complex overtones of class relationships has been at the heart of political and social problems. As Paul Sweezy has noted in a discussion of Soviet history:

> . . . at the heart of the great debates and decisions in the USSR in the 1920s were issues which . . . were immediate and crucial: How could the USSR feed its cities, provide itself with the needed agricultural raw materials, and acquire foreign exchange, with which to buy vital imports? And these are questions which faced China in the 1950s.

Cuba in the 1960s [and 1970s—A.M.], and Vietnam today. They are likely to face practically all countries which in the future embark on a socialist course.

In the USSR these questions were answered with collectivisation and a 'huge-push' industrialisation programme. The contradiction between town and country was resolved by an almost total subordination of the latter. The process appears to have been an important factor contributing to extreme centralisation of political authority, bureaucratisation, and lack of mass participation in the USSR. Moreover, this resolution of the rural–urban contradiction seems to have eliminated whatever worker–peasant alliance had once existed. As we have suggested in earlier chapters, these events are most usefully understood as consequences of the particular nature of Soviet (Russian) history and of the Soviet revolution; the separateness of rural and urban socio-economic organisation was exacerbated by the revolutionary process.

In China, where the revolutionary process contributed to overcoming that society's rural–urban separation, the town–country contradiction has evolved in a rather different manner. The creation of a socialist agriculture was much less abrupt and disruptive than in the Soviet Union. And the Chinese government has continuously maintained a political base in both rural and urban areas. The Chinese have described their policy as one in which agriculture is the foundation and industry is the key, a policy of 'walking on two legs'. Still, the rural–urban contradiction has continued to play a role at the centre of Chinese development strategy, and continues to create tensions in the formulation of all major policies. (For example, wage and incentive policy is greatly affected by continuing inequality between city and country. Also, the emphasis placed on young people moving to the Chinese countryside is a reflection of problems arising from differential development of rural and urban areas. In the social realm, disputes over the questions of who should have access to higher education also reflect the town–country division, as well as other contradictions.)

In Cuba, the problems emanating from this contradiction also play a continuing role. In the political realm, the Cubans appear to have been fairly successful, with the government maintaining a strong base in both rural (public and private) and urban sectors. The relatively integrated nature of pre-1959 urban and rural economic activity in Cuba facilitated a political integration as well. In the realm of production, however, Cuba's success in resolving the agriculture–industry contradiction has been limited. Among the lessons which may be drawn from the Cuban difficulties are those concerning the weakness of agriculture as a leading sector.

THE WEAKNESS OF AGRICULTURE AS A LEADING SECTOR

To begin with, let us review the facts. On the one hand, Cuba has devoted tremendous resources to the development of its agriculture since 1959. Huge investments have been made in water control and mechanisation; there has been a great increase in the use of modern inputs. The social reorganisation of agriculture has been a linch-pin of change. And major labour mobilisations have been aimed at achieving agricultural output goals. Through the 1960s, agriculture, especially sugar, was at the centre of Cuban development strategy; it was viewed as both the foundation and the key to economic growth. In the 1970s, while formally replaced in the first priority position by industry, agriculture retains a leading role in the Cuban strategy.

On the other hand, agricultural production has not done well in Cuba. Total agricultural output in the 1960s was basically stagnant; per capita agricultural production at the end of the decade was substantially below its level of the 1950s. During the 1970s, there has been considerable improvement; agricultural production in 1975 stood 60 to 70 per cent higher than in the mid-1960s, and growth has been fairly steady. Still, per capita agricultural output in the middle of the 1970s was little (perhaps 5 to 10 per cent) higher than in the 1950s. No clear upward trend in sugar output has been established, and cattle production (Cuban agriculture's traditionally number 2 branch) has also done poorly.

The record with social change in the countryside has been far better. Rural illiteracy has been reduced to near zero, and the formal educational system is thoroughly incorporating the rural population. Health services have been dramatically improved, and some headway has been made with housing. Perhaps of greatest importance, Cuba's agricultural population is becoming involved in the political life of the nation. Yet, whatever foundation these social and political developments provide for future economic growth, their agricultural production pay-off has so far been limited.

Traditional Issues: Weather and Prices

Official Cuban government statements point to poor weather as an important contributing factor in the less than desired performance of agriculture (especially sugar) during the early 1970s. Also, in at least one important government document, it is noted that 'if' the international price of sugar had been a bit higher, the Cuban economy would have been considerably stronger.

These points, however, do little to justify a policy of dependence on agriculture—quite the contrary. Indeed, the oldest argument against an agricultural orientation for Cuba (and for many other poor nations) is that such a strategy makes the welfare of the country depend on the vicissitudes of the weather and of international commodity prices. These problems are all the greater when one crop plays a central role, as has been the case with sugar in Cuba. Any development strategy which relies on 'good luck' is hardly satisfactory. But for a small nation like Cuba, dependence on favourable weather and international prices is reliance on luck.

The weather problem can be partially overcome by the extension of irrigation and water-storage systems. Cuba has certainly moved in this direction. Between 1958 and 1975 irrigated land was increased from 160,000 to 508,000 hectares, and water-storage capacity was increased from 39 million to 4400 million cubic metres. Such steps can reduce, even if they cannot eliminate, susceptibility to weather conditions.

Also, the long-term sales agreements with the Soviet Union (and some other nations) have partially insulated the Cuban economy from international market fluctuations. The international price of sugar dropped from its 8.34 cents (US) per pound of 1963 to a low average of 1.81 cents in 1966; and it did not attain an annual average of above 4 cents per pound until 1971. However, from 1963 on, the Cubans sold sugar to the Soviets at the constant price of 6.11 cents per pound (though the price was paid in roubles, not hard currency). Over 40 per cent of the Cuban sugar crop went to the Soviet Union at some points in the 1960s. In the 1970s, as the international price rose, the Cuban–Soviet price was adjusted upward. The price data are shown in Table 28.1.

Water-control programmes and long-term trade agreements do not, however, solve the problems associated with Cuba's heavy reliance on sugar (and agriculture generally). Weather had continued to play a significant role in the 1970s, in spite of the investments in dams and irrigation. And the drop in the world sugar price from its 27 cents per pound average in 1974 has had a detrimental impact on Cuba. Moreover, in so far as Cuba has been able to protect itself from the extreme effects of sugar-price fluctuations, it has built a heavy reliance on the Soviet Union. Some of the implications of this reliance will be discussed shortly.

TABLE 28.1 World market sugar prices and prices of Cuban sugar sales to the USSR, 1961–74 (in US cents per pound f.o.b.)

	World market price	Cuba to USSR price
1961	2.75	4.09
1962	2.83	4.09
1963	8.34	6.11
1964	5.77	6.11
1965	2.08	6.11
1966	1.81	6.11
1967	1.92	6.11
1968	1.90	6.11
1969	3.20	6.11
1970	3.68	6.11
1971	4.50	6.11
1972	7.27	6.11*
1973	9.51	12.02
1974	26.69	19.64

* Does not take into account the devaluation of the dollar in 1972; i.e., the rouble per pound price was not changed when the devaluation took place.

NOTE
Although Soviet purchases of Cuban sugar are reported in US cents per pound, payment is in Soviet roubles instead of hard currency.

SOURCE
Cuba (1975) pp. 31–2.

Labour Issues: Supply and Transformation

In any case, even with good luck, good water programmes, good prices and good relations with the Soviet Union, Cuba would still have weaknesses in its agricultural sector. During the entire period since 1959, labour supply has been a nagging problem in the rural areas. Also, the tasks of more effectively organising the work process and raising productivity are hindered by an agricultural emphasis.

The agricultural-labour shortage in Cuba may have been in part created by policy errors or poor planning. For example, as pointed out in the preceding chapter, the Cuban plan for 1976–80 seems to embody a set of conflicting goals for agriculture and industry which may be aggravating the agricultural-labour shortage. There are, however, more fundamental factors which contribute to the labour-supply problem.

The equalisation of income in Cuba brought about by the revolution's major reforms has undoubtedly undermined the effectiveness of tradi-

:ional material incentives in Cuba. For agricultural wage labourers and small private farmers, their very survival was continually at issue prior to 1959. These poorest segments of the Cuban population were thus forced to perform the most onerous tasks. Yet in the 1960s, the real income of these groups rose dramatically, perhaps by as much as 100 per cent, while income of the society as a whole remained roughly constant (see Chapter 12). In such circumstances, there would be every reason to expect the development of an agricultural-labor shortage. (I would like to emphasise that these observations do not imply that growth and income equalisation are necessarily in conflict with one another. It is true that within the context of a traditional incentive structure equalisation may undermine growth. But equalisation may also have some positive effects on growth even within traditional structures. And, of course, incentive structures can be changed. This issue will be discussed below shortly.)

The problem can be—and to some extent has been—off-set by the development of an alternative incentive system. Yet, at the very best, the development of new forms of labour motivation takes time. Most important, the formation of a new incentive structure is closely linked to the organisation problem that has been so heavily stressed in this essay. A thorough and effective socialist incentive structure in Cuba would depend upon the operation of socialist modes of work organisation— that is, modes of work organisation in which workers themselves play a central role in controlling the production process. There is evidence that the Cuban working class is beginning to play such a role in the 1970s, and forms of organisation are emerging which can facilitate the functioning of new incentive structures.

These changes, however successful, will be slow to have their impact on worker motivation. And, in addition, there are many reasons to believe that the entire process of transforming labour organisation and work processes will be most difficult and slowest within the agricultural sector. The relative isolation of rural life and agricultural work, both traditionally and in the current era, inhibit the development of new organisational forms and of an ideology which could facilitate the transformation of work. Moreover, such factors as lower rates of participation in education and lower female labour force participation rates in the countryside exacerbate the difficulties. Traditional attitudes and practices remain powerful forces in rural Cuba.

Although certain types of agricultural production may be extremely important quantitatively, it is hardly reasonable to expect agriculture to play a leading role in transforming the social foundations of economic activity in Cuba. In so far as new organisational forms can be created, the conditions of urban life and industrial activity are more likely to provide a fertile field for progress. It is in these conditions that the Cuban working class is most thoroughly developed and separated from traditionalism, and, thus, under these conditions it is most readily involved in political and work-place organisation. If the Cuban working class is going to lead in the process of economic development (and what other meaning can socialist development have?), it seems to follow that those activities in which it is strongest and most advanced must become the leading sectors.

Changes which have taken place in the Cuban economy and in Cuban planning during the 1970s are, more or less, in line with these general conclusions about the weakness of relying upon an agricultural emphasis for the country's development strategy. By designating industry as first priority, the Cuban government has given it a qualitatively central role—the lead role—even while agriculture remains quantitatively very important. In addition, the advance of agriculture is being thoroughly tied to industrial advances. In Cuba, the idea of agricultural progress has meant modernisation—mechanisation, ferti- liser, etc. In the 1970s, reality is beginning to approach this idea; industry is becoming the key to agricultural progress.

But, of course, to say that agriculture's role should be diminished is only the most general sort of guideline. A policy of ignoring sugar production or attempting an overly rapid diversification (as in the early 1960s) would be as harmful as an extreme over-balance in favour of agriculture (as in the late 1960s). The fact that the Cuban authorities have in the past jumped from one extreme to another on the question of sectoral balance underscores the fundamental nature of the agriculture– industry contradiction in socialist development (rather than any special short-comings of the authorities themselves). And there is no reason to suppose that a resolution of the contradiction and a correct sectoral balance have been permanently achieved.

The sorts of difficulties the Cubans have encountered would be likely to exist in one form or another for any poor, agricultural nation simultaneously attempting to achieve a socialist social transformation and economic growth. The Cuban experience appears to provide some evidence for the conclusion that in such countries agriculture is unlikely to be an effective leading sector. At the same time, in countries in which a large segment (if not the majority) of the population is rural and agriculture is the base for industry (via raw-material inputs and foreign- exchange earnings), agricultural expansion and rural social transfornation must be important parts of the development process. The problem continually revolves around striking some sort of sectoral balance, which is to say that it revolves around attempting to resolve the contradiction between town and country in a non-antagonistic manner.

THE IMPORTANCE OF EXTERNAL ASSISTANCE

In the Cubans' attempt to reduce the antagonism between town and country, the availability of considerable foreign assistance has played a major role. Most obviously, the availability of foreign funds has made it possible to achieve high rates of investment without placing severe pressure on some segment of the population (the peasantry, for example). Also, the availability of foreign funds has made it unnecessary to wait for the progress of domestic industry in order to begin the process of agricultural modernisation.

The actual extent of foreign assistance is difficult to measure for any country, because it often comes in terms of tied aid and soft loans. The precise value of the former is never clear, and any appraisal of the latter would require some judgement (usually arbitrary) regarding the availability of other sources of credit. In the Cuban case, these difficulties are compounded because many details of economic relations with the Soviet Union are not public information. Thus, for example, it is difficult to determine the meaning of any particular price of sugar which the Cubans receive from the Soviets, since the Soviets pay in roubles and the prices which the Cubans pay for Soviet goods are not available.

Nonetheless, while precision is not possible, the general situation is clear. Cuba has received a very large amount of foreign assistance. One crude measure of this assistance is the size of the foreign-trade deficit. During the ten years 1962 up to the end of 1971, the Cuban trade deficit averaged 33 per cent of the value of imports. In absolute terms, the deficit averaged 346 million pesos per year. In 1972, the deficit remained large, and, then, as the sugar crop improved somewhat and the price of sugar jumped up, the deficit dropped to 21 per cent of imports in 1973, was transformed to a small surplus in 1974, and was only 5 per cent of imports in 1975. With the exception of these last few years, Cuba's trade gap has been large compared to the trade gaps of other aid-receiving nations.

But Cuba's experience, measured in terms of the percentage of imports financed with foreign funds, is by no means unique. Cuba's 1962–71 decade, when the trade deficit averaged 33 per cent of imports, can be compared with the same figure in, for example: Mexico, during the 1966–75 decade, 37 per cent; Pakistan, during the 1960–9 decade, 41 per cent; and India, during the 1959–68 decade, 39 per cent. And of course there are such countries as Israel, the Republic of Korea, and the former Republic of Vietnam. But these cases are all extreme as is the Cuban case. Especially when computed on a per capita basis, the amount of foreign funds received by Cuba during the 1960s was exceptionally high by international standards.

Information on the sources of Cuba's foreign credit is not available, but it is a safe assumption that the Soviet Union is responsible for the lion's share. In addition to its role in providing credit (and other aid), the Soviet Union is also Cuba's largest trading partner by far. In the 1970–4 period, for example, on average 47 per cent of Cuba's trade was with the USSR.

Any judgements of Cuba's achievements since 1959 must be viewed in the context of these large quantities of external assistance and trade ties to the USSR. This is not to say that Cuba's successes can be dismissed as but the products of the Soviet connection. Assistance *per se* does not assure development as there are ample cases to illustrate. Moreover, it could be argued that the Soviet assistance has but offset the costs of the economic actions taken against Cuba by the US government (to say nothing of the military actions). But whatever successes Cuba has achieved, attaining a firm economic independence has not been among them.

It is only possible to speculate here about the political and economic questions that are raised by this close tie to the Soviet Union. To what extent has Cuban economic and social policy been influenced by the Soviet Union? And to what extent has Cuban foreign policy been shaped by Soviet interests? It would be naive to suppose that the economic relationship with the USSR has not affected Cuban policy. As Fidel Castro himself has stated: ' . . . historical experience, even our own experience, shows that once economic bonds are established between two countries, any responsible government, any government truly concerned for its people, does take into consideration those interests and those bonds, and in one way or another they do exercise a certain influence in the governments' attitudes.'

Yet there is no way to determine clearly the extent to which Soviet influence has led to Cuban policies being different from what they would have been in the absence of that influence.

In this essay, however, I believe there is ample evidence to explain the evolution of Cuba's major internal policies without reference to Soviet influence (aside from the obvious fact that Soviet aid and trade created certain possibilities that otherwise would not have existed). The strategy of the 1960s, with its heavy emphasis on sugar and high investment rates may have been encouraged by Soviet advisers, but there is reason to believe the Cubans would have chosen such a path in any case. Likewise, the re-emphasis of personal, material incentives would seem in line with the type of policy the Soviets would have urged on Cuba; yet, as I have argued, Cuba's experiences on their own are probably sufficient to explain the policy shifts of the early 1970s. In addition, although the forms of incentives and planning adopted in the 1970s bear substantial similarity to a 'Soviet model', the combination of those institutions with the political and social developments of the period gives Cuban policy its own special qualities.

It is my judgement that Cuba's foreign policy has been more seriously affected by Soviet influence. In some cases, of course, Cuba's own interests coincide with those of the Soviet Union. In Latin America, as the armed struggles for power by revolutionary movements came to naught in the late 1960s, Cuba's own interests dictated a move toward a more 'united front'-type policy. Also, Cuba's involvement with the liberation struggles in Angola and other former Portuguese colonies has well-established roots in the independent formation of Cuban foreign policy. Still, there are matters on which it is difficult to explain the Cuban position without reference to Soviet interests and influence. Castro's statement of support for the Soviet intervention in Czechoslovakia in 1968, although tempered by criticism of the Soviet Union, is a case in point. And ten years later, Cuba's involvement in Ethiopia would at least raise questions about the independence of its policies.

In the 1970s there appears to be some reduction in the extent of Cuba's economic ties with the USSR. The decline of the trade deficit in the 1973–5 period, though in large part the result of unusually high sugar prices, may indicate a move toward reducing dependence on foreign funds. The lower target growth rate for the late 1970s should also reduce the need for external assistance. And the shift toward an industrial emphasis along with the advances in non-sugar agriculture should contribute to a diversification of Cuba's trading patterns. (Some diversification of trading partners did appear in the early 1970s, but it is not clear whether this resulted simply from the unusual sugar prices or from lasting changes.) Finally, if significant change takes place in the political relations between Cuba and the US, the economic options for the former could be greatly expanded.

Whether one's judgement of particular matters of Cuban policy and of the possibilities for future change, Cuba's lack of economic independence can hardly be seen as a positive aspect of its development strategy. Soviet economic assistance has been very valuable to Cuba, and Soviet military protection has probably been necessary for the survival of the revolution. But the Soviet relation surely has its costs. And those costs provide one more argument for moving away from the heavy reliance on sugar exports (and thus on Soviet trade) and on high rates of investment (and thus on Soviet aid).

EQUALITY IN CUBAN DEVELOPMENT

Although the Cuban relationship with the Soviet Union is a particularly close one, Cuba is far from being a small-scale model of the Soviet system of economic organisation. Its path of development and the course of its policies have had their own distinct characteristics.

Among these characteristics, the movement toward economic and social equality stands out not only as an achievement of the Cuban revolution, but also as a mechanism affecting other aspects of the country's development. Over and over again, in examining events and policies in Cuba, we have been drawn back to the overriding importance of the equalising impact of the early reforms. In the final section of this essay, there are two broad issues relating to equality in Cuba that should be drawn together. First, social and economic equalisation in Cuba has arisen in large part out of the particular treatment of the country's rural—agrarian problems. It has consequently created an important part of the foundation for a successful resolution of the rural–urban contradiction in Cuba. Second, relative equality has been a major factor allowing progress toward solving the organisation problem. Therefore, far from conflicting with growth, equality in Cuba appears to be contributing to economic expansion.

At the time of its political triumph, the Cuban revolution could be viewed as an agrarian, rural movement. Active support had existed in the urban areas and among almost all classes; but the military struggles had been in the countryside, and the revolutionary leaders had looked to poor peasants and rural workers as their primary base of support. As the revolution began to take shape in 1959 and the early 1960s, its rural orientation continued in ascendency in spite of the government's formal commitment to industrialisation as the key to development.

The agrarian reform beginning in 1959 was the most important early event giving definition to the social character of the revolution. Also, the employment policies and the social programmes of the revolution—the teracy campaign of 1961 and the general extension of health and ducation—had their greatest impact in the rural areas. Taken together, hese various programmes led to an immense redistribution of real ncome.

In order to appreciate the impact of redistribution, we need to view it ot only as a redistribution from the rich to the poor. It was also a edistribution from the urban areas to the rural areas. Undoubtedly the ural rich also lost and the urban poor gained, but the overriding lirection of redistribution was from the city to the country (especially vhen we take account of the role of social service). Thus, from the outset f the revolution, it was established that the rural population would not e excluded. (Of course, many of those who were among the urban rich wed their wealth to rural origins—the owners of sugar estates, for xample.)

One of the primary elements of the general contradiction between own and country, as it has operated historically in Cuba and elsewhere, as been the exclusion of the rural population from the benefits of conomic development. The city and industry traditionally grow by the xtraction of surplus from agriculture and its transfer out of the rural reas. And in many cases this process is a prime factor effecting rural nderdevelopment and poverty. There are strong tendencies in econ- mic growth—whether guided by capitalist or socialist forces—for this rocess to continue, for industry to develop at the expense of the rural opulation, for the gap between town and country to widen. The esulting imbalance can manifest itself in social and political instability s well as in the economic weakness of an important sector, and the mbalance can thoroughly disrupt economic growth.

By the early redistribution from town to country, the Cuban revolution pre-empted tendencies toward such an exacerbation of the rural–urban contradiction. Had industrialisation instead of redistri- bution received highest priority in 1959, the Cuban revolution might have been led to extract surplus from the rural areas in order to finance development. But the early programmes which were in fact pursued gave the rural population a stake in the revolution and secured the revolution's political foundations in the countryside.

These steps, of course, did not eliminate the conflict between town and country in Cuba. But the revolution's early programmes did a lot to overcome the traditional impoverishment of the Cuban countryside, and thereby they established the possibility of resolving the con- tradiction by creating a complementary—a balance—between agricul- ture and industry.

In class terms, the improvement in the conditions of rural life helped in building a worker–peasant alliance. Similarly, the stress on equality in Cuba created a material basis for unity within the Cuban working class. And working-class unity is essential for attaining a socialist solution to the organisation problem.

A socialist solution to the organisation problem, as we have stated earlier, requires that the working class take control over production and over political life. In so far as objective divisions exist within the working class, this task will be hindered. In particular, large income differences and associated social-status differences between various groups within the working class—skill groups, occupational groups, regional groups—would most effectively subvert unified action. Groups in the most privileged positions would tend to seek ways to preserve their own status. And individual members of the working class would tend to become concerned with their own advancement rather than with the interests of the class as a whole. In such circumstances a socialist solution to the organisation problem would be highly unlikely if not impossible.

Cuban reality, however, is not characterised by substantial objective differences within the working class (at least when compared with most other nations or with Cuba's own historical experience). Consequently the interests of the class are relatively unified and the likelihood of effective collective activity is increased. And, in so far as that collective activity can achieve a solution to the organisation problem, economic expansion can proceed apace. In addition, the objective unity of the working class and its collective activity interact with political education and the transformation of people's social consciousness. The existence of equality makes people perceive their social position and interests in a new way and increases the likelihood that they will be motivated by more than personal well-being. In these ways, equality, far from being in conflict with economic growth, can be a principal mechanism for its achievement. (The same conclusion may also be reached by focusing on incentives. Indeed, I have argued earlier—in Chapter 20—that inequality would undermine a system of collective or moral incentives because workers would recognise that their efforts were serving an élite rather than the general society, the collective. Conversely, if general equality does exist, workers efforts do serve the collective and they are more likely to give their all; they are then working in a system with which they can identify and feel a part of. However, as I have stressed earlier, effective incentives depend upon an effective organisational structure; thus, I have chosen to focus on the organisational issues above. It would e possible to infer from my argument that within the context of a capitalist system of organisation and incentives, inequality is the key to growth. All I wish to say, however, is what I have said: within a socialist framework equality can contribute to growth through its positive impact on the ability of the working class to effectively organise social, political and economic activity. Within a capitalist framework, the relationship between equality and growth is complex. It is easy to conceive of ways in which inequality can hinder as well as facilitate the functioning of such a system. All that is well beyond the scope of my argument here; I raise the matter simply to avoid unwarranted—often pernicious—inferences.)

A review of Cuban experience discussed in earlier chapters seems to give some credibility to this line of argument; it also gives an indication of the limits of the argument. During the early 1970s, the Cuban economy experienced relatively rapid economic growth. And this growth took place following a massive redistribution of income. Also, the growth took place in a period during which the effective organisation of the working class was in ascendency.

But economic growth did not follow directly upon the massive income redistribution. The 1960s were a period of disorganisation and stagnation (though a great deal of investment was accomplished which would eventually become productive). Also, in the 1970s, when growth did take place, it was associated with a more effective structuring of traditional incentives; in so far as inequality continued to exist, it was tied more directly to worker productivity.

These various points indicate the complexity of the relationship between equality and growth in a society undergoing a major social transition. Certain conclusions seem clear: rapid growth certainly can take place after a massive redistribution of income; but equalisation will not automatically yield growth. Furthermore, these events do suggest that equality may bring growth only when it has had the time to affect working-class organisation. But, also, they suggest that extreme equalisation can have detrimental effects on work incentives, except when the inequalities which remain are tied to productivity.

Cuba's experiences will not put an end to disputes about the relation between equality and economic growth. But these experiences do begin to provide useful lessons about the central role of equality in socialist development. I have focused here on the relation of equality to the rural—urban contradiction and to the formation of working-class organisation. And there are surely other ways in which equality intertwines with the major issues in Cuban development.

For, as I have stated, equality stands out not only as an achievement of the Cuban revolution, but also as a mechanism affecting other aspects of the country's development. The agrarian reform and the literacy campaign, programmes of equalisation, are examples of major achievements of the revolution. They are also major elements in the country's history, affecting current and future policy and progress. The history of imperialism and underdevelopment still weigh heavily on Cuba. But Cuban agriculture, and Cuban development generally, will more and more be shaped by experiences such as the agrarian reform and the literacy campaign, by the history of the socialist era.

Appendix 1 Quantifying the Redistribution of Income, 1958–62: a Crude Estimate

The overall picture of income redistribution in Cuba is difficult to quantify in the absence of any comprehensive data. Still, a very crude quantitative estimate of the overall change of income distribution can be made.

To begin with, a crude approximation of the pre-1959 income distribution in Cuba can be obtained by using the average of distribution data for a few other Latin America nations: Mexico 1950, 1957, 1963; Argentina 1953, 1959, 1961; and Puerto Rico 1953, 1963. The resulting hypothetical distribution of income by quintiles of families is shown in column A of Table A.1.1. The associated hypothetical Gini ratio is 0.47. (The Gini ratio is a standard of measure of income

TABLE A.1.1 Crude estimation of the change in the distribution of income, 1958–62: family income in quintiles

Percentiles of family recipients	(A) Hypothetical 1958 distribution	(B) 1962 Case 1	(C) 1962 Case 2	(D) USA 1974
0–20	5.7	11.4	9.5	5.4
21–40	8.9	14.6	12.2	12.0
41–60	12.5	16.1	13.5	17.6
61–80	18.3	18.3	18.3	24.1
81–100	54.6	39.6	46.5	41.0
Gini ratio	0.47	0.27	0.35	0.36

SOURCES
(A) has been obtained by calculating the average for Mexico (1950, 1957, 1963), Argentina (1953, 1959, 1961) and Puerto Rico (1953, 1963) from data presented by Weisskoff (1971) p. 312.
(D) is obtained from Ackerman and Zimbalist (1978) p. 298.
(B), (C) and Gini ratios for all except (A) have been calculated as explained in the text.

229

inequality. If share of total income received by each share of the
population is graphed, a picture like the following would be obtained:

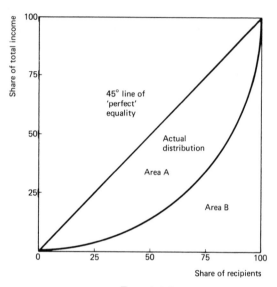

Fig. A.1.1

In this example, the graph indicates roughly that the lowest 25 per cent
of recipients receive 5 per cent of total income, that the lowest 50 per cent
receive 15 per cent, that the lowest 75 per cent receive 35 per cent. The
greater the inequality, the further the Line L will be from the 45° line.
The Gini ratio is defined as the ratio of Area A to the total area under the
45° line (A + B). Thus the Gini ratio can theoretically vary from O,
complete equality, to 1, where one recipient receives all income. In fact,
actual Gini ratios for almost all nations lie between 0.30 and 0.60.)

It is then possible to use some of the particular facts presented above
to move from the quintile distribution of column A to estimates of the
1962 quintile distribution.

Case 1 (column B) is a rather extreme estimate. It incorporates the
following assumptions: that the income of families in the lowest quintile
doubled between 1958 and 1962, based on the quoted statement by
Amaro and Mesa-Lago regarding agricultural labourers; that 15 per
cent of national income was redistributed from the top quintile to the
bottom three quintiles, based on one of Pazos's statements; that the
share of income going to the next to highest quintile did not change; and

that the ratio of the differences between (a) the shares of the second and third quintiles and (b) the shares of the third and fourth quintiles did not change. (The calculations are simplified by the fact that 1962 national income was roughly the same as that of 1958.)

Case 2 (column C) is a more conservative estimate, which begins by using the statement of Pazos and Seers to yield a rise in the income of the bottom three quintiles by 30 per cent. Again, it is assumed that all of this increase comes from the highest quintile, and the share going to the second highest quintile does not change. Also, it has been assumed that the relative positions of the bottom three quintiles is the same as in Case 1. (Case 2 would not be greatly altered had the income of the lowest groups been raised by 25 instead of 30 per cent.)

In column D, US data for 1974 have been shown to provide an additional point of comparison. Also, Gini ratios have been calculated for each quintile distribution. (The Gini ratios have not been calculated directly from the quintile distribution. Instead, they have been adjusted to approximate the Gini ratios which would be obtained were they calculated from (roughly) continuous, rather than interval, data.)

These estimates—and it must be re-emphasised that they are very crude estimates—indicate that the Cuban Gini ratio dropped by at least 25 per cent, and perhaps by as much as 43 per cent, during the first few years of the revolution. This change is in line with the conclusions expressed in the last paragraph of Chapter 12. Of course, the data in Table A.1.1 are simply an extrapolation of the various particular points presented in the chapter. They only serve the function of allowing a crude aggregate quantification of the situation.

Appendix 2　Cuban Global Social Product and Gross Material Product by Sector, 1962–75

Table A.2.1 presents data on Cuban global social product and gross material product by sector for 1962–75. These data have been collected from several official Cuban government publications, and there are some problems of completeness and consistency. Explanatory notes in those publications are rather limited, and it has been necessary to proceed on the basis of reasonable assumptions in order to fill in gaps and make the data as consistent as possible. Before listing the steps which were taken in preparing the table, it will be useful to quote the following from the economic report issued on the 25th anniversary of the National Bank of Cuba (i.e., Cuba (1975) p. 23, one of the sources of these data):

> By 'global social product' is meant the value of all goods and productive services generated in the country in the course of a year. It is equal to the sum of the value of gross production of all productive sectors.

> The global social product is determined in Cuba according to the 'system of material production' accepted by the Statistical Office of the United Nations. See *Studies in Methods*, Series F, No. 17, 1971. This indicator does not include the value of services such as financial, housing, personal and professional, public health, education, public administration, defense and other similar ones, which are classified as consumption in Cuban methodology. The global social product is expressed in the table [and in Table A.2.1] in 'current prices' because in the Transportation and Trade sectors gross production has been calculated using the prices and tariffs of the current year. In all other sectors constant 1965 prices are used.

On the other hand, the concept of total [gross] material production of the country is obtained by deducting from the global social product shown in the table the value of the activities of the Transportation, Communications and Trade sectors.

In Table A.2.1, I have reported both the global social product and gross material product figures because, while the former is a more complete aggregate, only the latter is available in constant prices.

The following steps were taken to construct Table A.2.1:

1 Global social product data by sectors were obtained from the following sources: (a) for 1962–5, Cuba (1970c) pp. 30–2; (b) for 1966–9, Cuba (1972b) pp. 30–2; (c) for 1970–2, Cuba (1973) p. 35; (d) for 1973–4, Cuba (1975) p. 23; (e) for 1975, *Economia y Desarrollo* (1976b).

2 In these sources, agriculture was defined to include forestry and fishing, but in Table A.2.1 these branches have been reported as a separate sector.

3 In the period 1962–9, the original data included a category 'agricultural services' (*servicios agropecuarios*) within the agricultural sector. However, after 1969, no such separate category is reported. It appears that after 1969, this category was merged within the commerce sector. Accordingly, in the table agricultural services has been merged with the commerce sector for the 1962–9 period as well.

4 For 1974 the components of the agriculture sector were obtained by applying the 1970–4 growth rates reported in Cuba (1975) p. 40 to the 1970 components.

5 Data for 1975 are reported in *Economia y Desarrollo* (1976b) for all sectors except commerce. The commerce figure was estimated by assuming the ratio of commerce to the total was the same as in 1974. Thus, it was possible to obtain the estimate of gross social product.

6 *Economia y Desarrollo* (1976b) also reports both a 7.3 per cent and a 5.3 per cent 1974–5 growth rate for livestock. One must be a misprint. On the basis of more detailed data provided for physical output of various sub-branches, it would appear that 7.3 per cent is the misprint, and 5.3 per cent has been taken as the correct figure.

7 Also, for 1975, growth rates are given for total agriculture and for all its components except 'other agriculture.' Therefore 'other agriculture' was computed as a residual.

TABLE A.2.1 Cuban global social product and gross material product by sector, 1962–75 (millions of pesos)

	1962	1963	1964	1965	1966	1967	1968
Global social product	6082.1	6013.2	6454.9	6770.9	6709.3	7211.6	7330.9
Gross material product	4038.3	3929.1	4167.8	4474.8	4369.3	4832.8	4746.4
Agriculture	891.9	856.0	906.7	1012.9	960.0	1004.1	1018.0
Sugar cane	267.0	235.1	265.5	367.1	268.6	352.9	394.2
Livestock	309.4	325.1	362.7	387.5	393.9	360.6	314.5
Other agriculture	315.5	295.4	278.5	258.3	297.5	290.6	309.3
Forestry and fishing	30.3	24.1	25.9	27.1	33.3	46.1	72.7
Industry	2746.2	2700.7	2813.5	2913.0	2858.5	3185.1	3129.9
Construction	369.9	348.3	421.7	521.8	517.5	597.5	525.8
Transportation	289.9	297.7	339.5	348.1	372.5	384.5	610.9
Communications	45.2	48.2	48.8	51.5	55.7	56.6	60.3
Commerce	1708.7	1738.2	1898.8	1896.5	1911.8	1937.7	1913.3

	1969	1970	1971	1972	1973	1974	1975 estimate
Global social product	7236.1	8356.0	8966.5	10417.9	11921.8	13149.0	14745.4
Gross material product	4667.8	5666.2	5903.4	6477.6	7286.5	7893.1	8807.2
Agricultural	979.1	1164.6	1066.5	1122.7	1171.3	1217.9	1292.8
Sugar cane	406.3	559.2	471.0	457.5	n.a.	479.6	512.7
Livestock	298.2	345.0	327.8	362.9	n.a.	378.3	398.3
Other agriculture	274.6	260.4	267.7	302.3	n.a.	360.0	381.8
Forestry and fishing	62.7	65.0	86.1	92.9	100.2	106.4	99.0
Industry	3178.0	4000.3	4177.0	4458.3	4988.3	5395.6	6010.7
Construction	448.0	436.3	573.8	803.7	1026.7	1173.2	1404.7
Transportation	604.6	788.5	792.6	822.3	840.4	864.3	1042.3
Communications	60.6	66.9	67.9	71.5	73.4	73.5	78.4
Commerce	1903.1	1834.4	2202.6	3046.5	3721.5	4318.1	4817.5

NOTE
Gross material product and its components are in 1965 prices. Figures for transport and commerce are in current prices. Global social product is reported as the sum of these constant and current price components.

There are no Cuban national accounts for 1959 through 1961. The limited availability of data often leads to using 1962 as a reference-point year. If this is done, it should be kept in mind that 1962 was a rather poor year for the Cuban economy.

Notes

CHAPTER 1

The general data in the opening paragraphs, along with other useful data, are pulled together in Seers (1964). Unemployment figures are thoroughly discussed in Mesa-Lago (1972) and in O'Connor (1970), Appendix B.

For a brief but useful description of the Cuban peasantry and rural scene which develops the points made on page 1 and 2, see Mintz (1964); also see Zeitlin (1970), p. 145. The classical description of these matters is Guerra y Sanchez (1964). But Pollitt (1971), (1972), (1977a) and (1977b) points out data errors that led Guerra y Sanchez and others to overstate the degree of proletarianisation of the Cuban agricultural labourers.

There are many books which establish the points I have noted about the Soviet and Chinese situations. I have found Dobb (1948) particularly useful on developing the concept of dualism in the Russian context, and Deutscher (1967) relates the dual economic structure to Soviet political developments. For the Chinese situation, I have found Moore (1966) useful on economic and social background, while Selden (1971) and Bianco (1971) provide important political analyses.

Data employed in the discussion of agricultural stagnation are either taken from the tables in the text or are from Bianchi (1964), p. 71. O'Connor (1970) provides a general discussion of stagnation in pre-1959 Cuba. In an effort to demonstrate no need for a revolution, some authors argue that the long stagnation was coming to an end in the late 1950s. The most notable among these is the work of the Cuban Economic Research Project (CERP). The CERP data, however, do not support their contentions; see, in particular, CERP (1965), pp. 119–22.

CHAPTER 2

The discussion concerning Cuba's colonial era draws heavily on Le Riverend (1967), Pino-Santos (1964) and Fraginals (1976). Also, an extremely useful source on Cuban history, written with purposes similar to my own, is Blackburn (1963).

The figures on sugar exports in the 1762–1886 period are from Pino-Santos, p. 96; the data on the direction of Cuban exports is from Pino-Santos, p. 95. Pino-Santos provides a useful discussion at that point concerning the growing imbalance in the Cuban economy associated with the rise of sugar.

On the policies of the sugar oligarchy regarding infrastructure, see Fraginals, pp. 70–3.

And the Fraginals quote regarding the absorption of peasants and artisans in the wage-labour force is from p. 19. Regarding the conflict over slavery and the struggle for independence, see Pino-Santos, Chapters 10, 12, 14 and especially 16; also see Le Reverend, Part Four.

On the matter of classes and underdevelopment, Moore (1966) provides a very useful analysis emphasising the different class alliances in capitalist development. An interesting examination of particular political and economic struggles in this context is provided by Ackerman (1974); he also provides a useful comparative analysis of the differences in this regard between the central capitalist powers and underdeveloped countries.

Turning to the era of US dominance, Castro (1976), p. 24 provides data on early US investment in Cuba. His figure for 1923 is slightly less than that reported by the US Department of Commerce—see Jenks (1928), p. 299, footnote 8. Jenks himself reports a total figure of $1 billion for US direct investment in Cuba in 1928. Seers (1964), p. 16, using US Department of Commerce sources, reports a figure of only $919 million for 1929. Variations in accounting procedures and taxation practices mean all of these figures should be taken as crude ones. Here, what is relevant is the general order of magnitude and the rate of growth. Details on the quantity and nature of US investment in Cuba through the first quarter of the twentieth century are provided by Jenks (1928), ch. 15.

Seers (1964), pp. 9–15 provides a discussion of the Reciprocal Trade Agreement, the sugar quota, and related matters. He provides the data on period averages for sugar sales going to the US.

For particulars on the US use of troops in Cuba, see various parts of Jenks (1928) and Nearing and Freeman (1966). For a list of such instances of the use of US armed forces abroad, see the US Congressional Record for 23 June 1969. As to the situation in 1933, and the role of the US at that point, see Aguilar (1972).

The various data on land concentration are taken from Bianchi (1964), pp. 75–8. As to the changes between the time of Bianchi's data and the revolution, at the beginning of 1959, of the 8,522.2 thousand hectares subject to expropriation under the First Agrarian Reform, 73.3 per cent were in 3.6 per cent of the farms. Another 1448 thousand hectares were not subject to the reform. Any reasonable assumptions about the average size of the farms in this latter category support the contention that the degree of concentration had not substantially changed. See Table 6.1, Part B in the text. Regarding Bianchi's figures on the control of land by the sugar companies, he also notes, however, that the total percentage of land controlled directly by all sugar *mills*—not the same as sugar companies— had peaked in 1939 at 27 per cent and had fallen to 21 per cent by 1959.

CHAPTER 3

Data on the low productivity of Cuban sugar estates is taken from Bianchi (1964), p. 91. Likewise, land-utilisation data comes from Bianchi, pp. 83–90. Much of the general argument concerning the nature of large-estate activity is drawn from Bianchi (1964) and Feder (1971). Pearse (1966) also provides a useful discussion, particularly with regard to the tendency of agriculturalists to speculate in urban activity.

Data on the condition of the rural population in Cuba has been obtained from Huberman and Sweezy (1960), ch. 2, Valdés (1972), p. 423, and Cuba (1973), p. 256.

Figures on Cuba's role in world sugar production and supply are obtained from International Bank for Reconstruction and Development (1951), p. 194, and Seers (1964), p. 9. Also, Bianchi's discussion, as cited above, is particularly useful on the pattern of sugar production and market strategy.

Feder (1971), pp. 70–1, provides a more thorough and more general discussion of the large land-owner's economic strategy and of the manner in which it is conditioned by social and political considerations.

Chapter 4

Several sources provide the general material on which this chapter is based: Ruiz (1970), Le Riverend (1967) and (1969), Wolf (1969), Zeitlin (1970), and Guevara (1968).

The quote concerning violence in Cuban political history is from Ruiz (1970), p. 155. On the development of unions and their relation to working-class politics, see Wood (1970), O'Connor (1966), Zeitlin (1970), especially chs 4 and 6, Ruiz (1970) especially ch. 7, and International Bank (1951), ch. 16. Wood, p. 26, argues that the working class was the 'only national class in Cuba'. O'Connor discusses the success of organised labour in obtaining wage gains. The International Bank report, p. 364, points out the inclusion of agricultural sugar workers in the unions.

O'Connor (1966), p. 4, notes the slow organising progress of the unions in the early 1900s and comments as to their educational success. O'Connor and Ruiz in ch. 7 provide useful discussions of the relation of the Communists to organised labour. The International Bank report, ch. 16, also provides useful comments— interesting because of their source as well as their substance. For details of 1933, see Aguilar (1972), in addition to the other sources. The long Ruiz quote concerning 1933 events is from pp. 124–5.

The information on the membership and programme of the Fourth National Labour Congress is from O'Connor (1966), p. 5. Data on Communist Party membership are from Ruiz (1970), p. 128 and p. 132 and O'Connor, p. 7. The quote from the International Bank report is taken from Ruiz, p. 129. On the operation of the unions in the 1950s, see O'Connor and the International Bank (1951), ch. 16.

The Zeitlin quote on the role of rural labourers is from pp. 146–7. The Ruiz summing-up quote is from p. 129.

See Debray (1968) for the views referred to; the Cuban edition of 200,000 is noted in the preface to the English edition. Also, see Guevara (1968) for his views, though they are not put forth in terms of a theory of revolution. The only criticism of Debray's work from the perspective of Cuban revolutionaries seems to be Torres and Aronde (1968), but they explicitly express only their own views (as distinct from those of the Cuban leadership). Wolf (1969) provides a useful sketch of the period of armed struggle. Guevara (1968) also provides useful details; the quote is from p. 197. There does not seem to be an 'official' Cuban history of the events.

CHAPTER 5

Regarding investment and import substitution during the years immediately
preceding the revolution, see O'Connor (1970), p. 16. His points are corroborated by the Cuban Economic Research Project (1964) pp. 621–2.

While 1959–61 saw high levels of sugar production, export earnings from
sugar did not rise along with production because of the low sugar price on the
world market in 1959 and 1961, and because of Cuba's loss of a share in the
higher-priced US market in 1960; see Ritter (1974), p. 114. Ritter states that the
actual value of the sugar crop in these three years was less than that of the smaller
crops of 1957 and 1958; Ritter's source is Economic Commission for Latin
America (1964), p. 275.

Data on the growth of the Cuban economy in the 1959–61 period are taken
from Ritter (1974), pp. 111–16.

Relating to the explanation of the growth in the early period, see Cuba (1972a)
p. 52. O'Connor, p. 269, and Ritter, p. 25, provide data on demand arising from
government spending and private investment.

The figure on the emigration of agronomists is from Gutelman (1967) as
excerpted in Bonachea and Valdes (1972), p. 234. See Guevara (1963), p. 259 on
difficulties resulting from external military pressure. The story of the CIA
sabotage of Cuban pig production in 1971 is reported in *The Boston Globe*, 10
January 1977. For details of the impact of weather in the crisis of the early 1960s,
see Cuba (1972a), p. 181.

CHAPTER 6

The Blas Roca quote is from Roca (1965), p. 4. Roca and Carlos Rafael
Rodriguez—see below—were both important figures in the pre-1959 Cuban
Communist Party (PCC) and have probably been the two most important pre-
1959 PCC figures in the revolutionary period.

The summary of the particular terms of the Reform is based on Acosta (1970),
pp. 95–101 and O'Connor (1970), pp. 91–6. One decisive feature of the law
which did not fall on INRA's shoulders, but was determined by the government
when the law was promulgated, was the method of compensation for
expropriated land. Expropriated land was to be paid for by the government with
20-year bonds paying $4\frac{1}{2}$ per cent interest. The catch came in the method of
determining the land value; the government used the value at which the land had
been recorded for tax purposes—see Acosta (1970), p. 95. All parties recognised
that such recorded values were well below the market values of the lands.

The Rodriguez quote in the footnote is from Rodriguez (1965), p. 64; this
source also provides a useful, brief description and analysis of the land reform.

The dilemma over the speed of instituting the agrarian reform in Cuba is
discussed at various points by Chonchol (1963) and Gutelman (1967). However,
while Chonchol's statement of the problem is similar to that presented here,
Gutelman places less emphasis on the dilemma as such and argues that INRA
moved too rapidly, creating the later serious administrative-coordination
problems.

The discussion of the Soviet and Chinese experiences is based on numerous
sources. See in particular Dobb (1948) and Lewin (1968) on the USSR and

Wheelwright and MacFarlane (1970), Schurmann (1968) and Perkins (1966) on China.

Regarding the details of taking over cattle and sugar lands O'Connor (1970), ch. 5, has been extremely useful. The O'Connor quote is from p. 99 in that chapter. Nove (1969), ch. 7 provides a particularly useful discussion of the livestock slaughter in the USSR. The Rodríguez quote near the end of the chapter is from Rodríguez (1965), pp. 64–5.

CHAPTER 7

Castro's speech of 18 August 1962 is translated and reprinted in Kenner and Petras (1969); the quote is from pp. 36–7. For the quote on the aspirations of Cuban rural workers, see Mintz (1964), p. xxxviii. A similar argument is made by Rodríguez (1965). For criticism, or at least qualification of the Mintz position see Pollitt (1971), (1972), (1977a), and (1977b).

The material on the USSR and China is drawn from sources cited in earlier chapters. The argument vis-à-vis Cuba draws on ch. 4.

See O'Connor (1970), p. 110 for his quote and related argument, which provides much of the foundation for this section.

On the government's commitment to equality, see Castro's speech of 18 August 1962 as cited above. Indeed, there Castro deals with many of these issues.

The subsection on the rapid transformation draws heavily on Bianchi (1964), pp. 105–10. The quote regarding INRA's instructions on how long to continue the practice of appointing managers is from Administracion General de Cooperativas Cañeras, *Cooperativas Cañeras*, 1960, as cited by Bianchi, p. 109; the numbers regarding the different types of cooperatives in 1960 are from p. 106.

The data regarding the 1963 supply and demand for labour is from O'Connor (1970), p. 220. The comparison of 1967 with 1959 is from Mesa-Lago (1972), p. 50. See p. 221 of O'Connor for details of employment growth on state farms. Also, O'Connor's Appendix B and the entirety of Mesa-Lago (1972) give more information and analysis on changes in unemployment. O'Connor, p. 222, is also the source of information on the decline in cane yields and cane cutters' wages. For details of the early expansion and employment, see Seers (1964), p. 51 and Mesa-Lago (1972), p. 48. The long quote on declining labour effectiveness is from Mesa-Lago (1972), pp. 49–50.

CHAPTER 8

For the data in paragraphs two and three of this chapter, see Tables 6.1 and 6.2 and the accompanying notes. O'Connor (1970), p. 119 discusses the failure to bring many peasants' holdings up to the vital minimum. Interestingly, according to O'Connor's data on p. 326, the average of 16 hectares held both for those small farmers producing sugar—slightly less than 45 per cent—and those producing other crops.

The discussion of the development of ANAP is based on O'Connor, pp. 121–7 and Bianchi (1964), pp. 125–8. On the matter of credit, Acosta (1970) was also useful.

The discussion and analysis of the crop data—the distinction between collection and production—is based on the tables and technical notes in Cuba (1973) and similar statistical reports for earlier years. The rise in peasants' own consumption is discussed in Mesa-Lago (1972), p. 49.

CHAPTER 9

The three quotes of Guevara are from Guevara (1964) as reprinted in Bonachea and Valdés (1969), pp. 142, 141–42, and 142 respectively. The role of sugar in Cuba's history is discussed above in chs 1–3.

The diversification policy, its consequences and related events of this period are discussed in Cuba (1970a), pp. 51–7, and in Cuba (1972), pp. 176–88. The particular figure of 200,000 hectares taken out of cane is from Cuba (1970a), p 54; Bianchi (1964), p. 85, reports that in 1958 roughly 1.3 million hectares were under cane.

Data on production in the crisis of 1962–4 are from Ritter (1974), pp. 113 and 202. The events of those years are also discussed with additional data in Cuba (1970a) and Cuba (1972).

CHAPTER 10

The data on nationalisations are from Acosta (1974), p. 79. Detailed accounts of the moves toward the explicit declaration of socialism, of the interaction of political conflict and economic change, are available in numerous sources. My own interpretation is supported by O'Connor (1970), Williams (1962) and Morray (1962). For a very different point of view, see Draper (1962).

The quote from Fidel Castro's 1 May 1961 speech is taken from the English version in Kenner and Petras (1969), pp. 79, 81.

The limits of the First Agrarian Reform, especially with regard to conflict with the larger farmers, are discussed in Rodriguez (1963), Aranda (1968), p. 190, and Acosta (1970), p. 106. Castro's comment on this issue is taken from Aranda, p 191. O'Connor, p. 129, and Acosta, p. 106, discuss the economic non-cooperation of the larger farmers and the problems created by their paying high wages.

CHAPTER 11

In his famous speech of 1953, 'La Historia Me Absolverá', Castro (1960) put forth the idea behind the literacy campaign. Fagen (1969), p. 34 refers to the *Manifesto of the Sierra Maestra*, issued in mid-1957, for a direct statement of the revolutionaries' intent to initiate such a campaign. Statistics in this section are taken from Fagen, pp. 35–50. Also, Fagen's general discussion, ch. 3, has been extremely useful.

Regarding the expansion of the regular education system, data is from United Nations (1959) and Cuba (1968).

The quote for the literacy campaign *Instructor's Manual* is from Fagen, p. 40

Health data is taken from Cuba (1973), pp. 256–7 regarding the number of hospitals, p. 26 regarding infant mortality. On training health personnel and on the health programme's role generally, see Barkin (1972b), who refers to Liebowitz (1969) and Orris (1970), as his sources. It should be noted that while the medical programmes were successful as indicated, malaria reappeared briefly as a serious problem in the early 1970s.

Data on the position of women are obtained from Bengelsdorf and Hageman (1974). Various chapters in Sutherland (1969) are also useful. I am grateful to Dudley Seers for pointing out that in the late 1960s the incentive structure worked against encouraging women to enter the labour force.

Much of the general discussion of this chapter is based on information and impressions gained during my own visits to Cuba in 1960, 1968, 1969, and 1972. In addition to the sources mentioned above, Huberman and Sweezy (1969) provide much useful background discussion and information on the issues covered in this chapter.

Chapter 12

Elsewhere, MacEwan (1975a) and (1975b), I have discussed the relation between equality and power at greater length. Also, Sweezy (1971) suggests the point that equality is a useful indicator of the real distribution of power in a society.

Regarding the pre-1959 distribution of income, Nelson (1950), for example, provides useful information, especially in ch. 8. Pazos (1961), p. 46, in the context of a generally negative assessment of the revolution, lists various negative aspects of the pre-1959 economy. First among these is 'the extreme inequality in the distribution of income to the detriment of the rural areas'.

The Seers statement regarding upper limits on salaries as compared with the minimum wage is from Seers (1964), p. 29. Data on unemployment are taken from Mesa-Lago (1972), whose estimate of the change between the pre- and post-revolutionary periods is a relatively conservative one. Some sources, Huberman and Sweezy (1960) for example, report pre-1959 unemployment rates as high as 25 per cent. Also, data for the post-1959 period is weak, and the 8 per cent unemployment figure for 1963 is probably high. O'Connor (1970), Appendix B, analyses the seasonal employment and unemployment data.

Pazos's estimate on income transfer resulting from the rent reform is from Pazos (1961), p. 48. See Pazos (1962), p. 7 and p. 9, respectively, for the quote and statement regarding the redistribution of 15 per cent of national income. See Seers (1964), pp. 32–3 for the corroborating quote.

See Amaro and Mesa-Lago (1971), p. 361, for their statement. My own report is from MacEwan (1975a). Also see Bonachea and Valdés (1972), pp. 360–5.

Regarding the controversy over the position of the small farmer, see Huberman and Sweezy (1969), p. 118, and surrounding passages; Rodriguez (1965) especially the footnote and material on p. 64; and Amaro and Mesa-Lago (1971), p. 360.

The discussion of non-market distribution is taken largely from MacEwan (1975a). Also, see Barkin (1972) for an extensive discussion of equality in terms of consumption rather than in terms of income. Barkin discusses the health issue at some length; and Bowles (1971) deals with the matters relating to education.

The Castro quote on meals in schools and work places is taken from Kenner and Petras (1969), pp. 267–8.

CHAPTER 13

Edward Boorstein (1968) provides a useful description of the planning process in Cuba through the early 1960s. His personal account provides a useful picture of both the positive and negative aspects of the 'por la libre' attitude.

Much of the general account of the Cuban strategy in the 1960s is based on my own discussions with Cuban economists and government officials during visits to the country in 1968 and 1969. Ritter (1974), Barkin (1972a), Cuba (1969), and Cuba (1970) also provide useful general discussions of the strategy.

The 1964 Guevara quote is from Bonachea and Valdés (1969), pp. 142–3. The Castro quote regarding sugar trade with the USSR is from a speech of 29 May 1970, reprinted in English in Bonachea and Valdés (1972), pp. 263; the discussion in the associated footnote is based on Ritter (1974), p. 212.

The pattern of planned output of sugar from 1965 to 1970 is from a speech by Fidel Castro printed in *Verde Olivo*, 20 June 1965, cited by Auroi (1975), p. 166. The other specific objectives listed for various parts of agriculture are from Ritter (1974), pp. 168–9.

CHAPTER 14

Several central essays in the debate over incentives, planning structure and the related theoretical issues are translated into English and reprinted in Silverman (1971). I have made some comments on this debate and elaborated the discussion of the 'collective' versus 'personal' incentives terminology in MacEwan (1975a).

The quotations from Castro regarding treating 'wealth with more collective political awareness' are from a speech delivered on 26 July 1968, translated and reprinted in Kenner and Petras (1969), pp. 293–4.

Regarding the role of special programmes in affecting political consciousness, see MacEwan (1975a) and (1975b). Also, Fagen (1969), in providing an analysis of the transformation of political culture in Cuba, is, in essence, dealing with the same phenomenon.

The long Guevara quote concerning planning systems is from Guevara (1964), pp. 132–4. For the useful debate on related theoretical issues see Sweezy and Bettelheim (1971).

CHAPTER 15

Most of the data discussed in Chapter 15 are from the tables. The figures on pesticides and herbicides are from Cuba (1970a), (1970b), and Cuba (1972). The data on water storage, irrigation and roads are from Cuba (1972), p. 184, Cuba (1970b), p. 3, Auroi (1975), p. 101, and Castro (1976), p. 72. For more details on the development of scientific agriculture, see Cuba (1972), pp. 186–8.

The Castro quote describing the steps taken in sugar is from Castro (1976). The figures on cane cutters in 1959 and 1967 have been cited above, Chapter 7, p. 10. Data on the 1970 labour mobilisation is from Cuba (1970b), pp. 27–9.

CHAPTER 16

The various output data figure for the late 1960s are taken from the tables or from Cuba (1973). The March 1968 Castro quote is from Kenner and Petras (1969), pp. 248–9. That speech also provides some discussion of private sales; also, see Mesa-Lago (1971), pp. 290–1 on the issue of private sales.

CHAPTER 17

Mesa-Lago (1974) provides an example of the critique which argues the incompatibility of growth and equality. Dumont (1970) and Karol (1970) are examples of writers who emphasise bureaucratic control and the development of a campaign atmosphere in the late 1960s.

The concept of traditionalism and the process of its destruction draws from, among other sources, Polanyi (1957). The most accessible statement of Marx's ideas on the process of capitalist development is the first section of *The Communist Manifesto*. On the issue of socialist revolutions coming in the periphery, Sweezy (1953) provides a useful analysis. Also, see Sweezy (1972) on the relationship between success in the capitalist centre and underdevelopment in the periphery.

Schumpeter's (1961) analysis is a classic statement regarding the role of 'entrepreneurial ability'. Also, see McClelland (1967), W. Moore (1960) and Bendix (1974) provide examples of analysis stressing the need in the development process for workers to fit into a hierarchical mode of production organisation.

The only source I know where the problem of the 'conundrum' for Marxist theory is dealt with in similar terms is Sweezy (1971).

CHAPTER 18

The problem with Soviet combines is reported by Mesa-Lago (1971), p. 305. Castro's 26 July 1970 speech is translated and reprinted in Bonachea and Valdés (1972). See Leontief (1969) for an account of his observations. Numerous examples of investment ineffectiveness outside of agriculture are provided in Castro's 26 July 1970 speech and in various chapters of Ritter (1974) and Mesa-Lago (1971).

CHAPTER 19

Examples of the Cuban's technical view of development are found, for example, in Cuba (1970a) and Cuba (1970b). Also, see Castro (1976) for a discussion of

Cuba's backwardness under imperialism; however, it is in this report that new approaches to development strategy, approaches which depart from the technical view, are most thoroughly articulated.

On the data regarding mechanisation of the sugar harvest, see Auroi (1975) who cites articles from *Bohemia* of 20 November 1970 and 27 July 1973 as his sources. In Cuba (1975) it is reported that only 1 per cent of the crop was harvested mechanically in 1971.

Data on the number of workers in the mills in 1970 and 1958 are from Mesa-Lago (1972), p. 65. And the data on the costs of expanding sugar output are from Gutelman (1967), p. 204.

The Castro quotes regarding problems in the sugar mills are from his speech of 20 May 1970, translated and reprinted in Bonachea and Valdés (1972), pp. 281, 288, 289, 297.

On the general disorganisation resulting from overcentralisation, see Joshua (1968) as cited by Huberman and Sweezy (1969), pp. 176–7.

For details of the 'Revolutionary Offensive' and its impact on retail trade, see Ritter (1974), pp. 236–9. See Perlman (1975) for an analysis of the general importance of street vendors in poor countries.

On the role of the military in the economy see Ritter (1974), pp. 292–3 and Mesa-Lago (1972), p. 64. For the interpretations referred to, see Dumont (1970) and Karol (1970). Some of my own views relating to these issues are contained in MacEwan (1975a) and (1975b).

CHAPTER 20

Ritter (1974), p. 282 provides the May–June, 1969, and the *zafra* peak 1970 absenteeism data. His source is a 20 September 1970 speech by Castro. The data on absenteeism outside agriculture is from Ritter (1974), pp. 282–8 and Mesa-Lago (1972), pp. 61–6.

CHAPTER 21

See Blumberg (1969) and Gintis (1972) for more discussion of the theoretical issues involved in the relation between participation and production. Also, these sources provide discussions of related empirical issues. It should be noted, however, that studies providing evidence on the positive relation between participation and production have been conducted in social contexts rather different from Cuba's.

See Zeitlin (1970) for information on workers' attitudes towards their role in Cuban society. Also, see MacEwan (1975a) and (1975b) for discussion of the relationship between equality and power and ideology and power in Cuba.

Hernandez and Mesa-Lago (1971) provide details on the role of trade unions.

CHAPTER 22

Data on the growth and structure of the economy in the early 1970s are taken

mainly from Table 22.1 and Table A.2.1. However, the shares of output within
the industrial sector are from Cuba (1972b), pp. 31–2 and Cuba (1973), pp. 35–
5. Data on the mechanisation of the sugar harvest are from Cuba (1975), p. 53.

CHAPTER 23

Bowles (1971) and Valdés (1972) provide a good deal of useful information on
the Cuban educational system. Bowles, especially, examines the type of
socialisation issues of interest here. Bowles and Gintis (1976) provide a useful
elaboration of the argument concerning schools' role in the development of
economically important behavioural traits. Their context, however, is the US.
Nonetheless, while the particular context of these traits may vary from one
social system to another, they seem of importance in any system in which output
expansion is a major goal. Gintis (1971), in fact, argues that the main way in
which formal education enhances productivity is through its impact on
behavioural traits rather than cognitive abilities; the context is again the
US.
    Data on the achievements of the 1960s are from Cuba (1970c), pp. 216–17.
Data on the particulars of expansion in rural areas and on rural–urban
comparisons are from Valdés (1972), pp. 430 and 440.
    Various problems of the Cuban educational system in the 1960s are discussed
by Fidel Castro in a 14 April 1972 speech; see *Granma Weekly Review* for that
date. Also, see Bowles (1971) on these issues.
    Data on the expansion of graduates of various types and on the relative
expansion of the different parts of the educational system are from Cuba (1973).
The government report quoted is Cuba (1975), p. 96.
    Regarding schools in the countryside, see the report in *Granma Weekly
Review*, 9 May 1971; Center for Cuban Studies (1975); Castro's speech 'La
Fuerza de la Revolución está en la Unidad', in *Bohemia*, 12 November 1976; and
his speech before the Young Communist League, 14 April 1972, in the *Granma
Weekly Review* of that date.
    The brief description of the work-study programme in the universities is based
on my own interviews in 1972, primarily at the Universidad de la Habana.
    My own description of the micro brigades is from MacEwan (1975a). The
data following that quote and the Castro quote are from an article in the *Granma
Weekly Review* of 21 December 1975, by Orlando Gómez, entitled, 'Plus-work is
the Solution'. The data on new communities' relation to agricultural plans are
from an article in the *Granma Weekly Review* of 1 June 1975, by Marta Jimenez
Almira, entitled, 'Urban Living in the Countryside'. The Cuban press quote on
reorganisation of work in regular work places is from the Orlando Gómez article
cited above. And the quote regarding the changing role of women is from a
Granma Weekly Review article of 29 June 1975, entitled, 'Women's Outstanding
Role in Construction Work'.

CHAPTER 24

Regarding the discussion of draft laws in mass organisations, see, for example,

'Workers to discuss draft laws on maternity', in *Granma Weekly Review*, 27 May 1973.

The discussion of changes in the trade unions is based on Mesa-Lago (1974) pp. 72–89. For his comments on the discussions preceding the trade union congress of 1973 and the quote from Peña, see pp. 81–2.

For details of the activities of the CDRs, see, for example, *Bohemia*, 12 October 1972, and *Granma Weekly Review*, 21 December 1975. The data on ANAP organisation and membership is from Castro (1976), pp. 193–7.

The 23 August 1970 Castro quote is from Bengelsdorf and Locker (1974), p. 8. For a delineation of the realms of authority of different levels of the Poder Popular system, see Cuba (1976c) and *Cuba Review* (1974). See Raul Castro (1974), p. 10, for his article quoted on p. 177.

Regarding the comments on political matters in the final paragraphs of the chapter, I have elaborated these sorts of points in MacEwan (1975a) and (1975b).

CHAPTER 25

In his speech to the closing session of the 1973 trade union congress, Castro provided a thorough discussion of the issues and policy matters, relating to the alteration of the incentive structure; see *Granma Weekly Review*, 25 November 1973. For a useful and succinct statement of the official position on the new forms of planning, see Castro (1976), pp. 132–8. Also, see López, Coll and Santiago (1975); the quote on p. 183 is from the first page of that article.

For Castro's discussion of past errors and his use of such terms as 'idealistic mistakes', see Castro (1976), pp. 123–32. For the debate referred to in the chapter's final paragraph, see Sweezy and Bettelheim (1971). For the Castro quote, see Castro (1976), p. 134.

CHAPTER 26

Data on the sugar-related work force, on mechanisation, on irrigation, on the use of new varieties, and on the use of chemical inputs are from Castro (1976), pp. 75–6 and Cuba (1975), pp. 55–6. See Table A.2.1 for information on the growth of different branches of agriculture. For data on mechanisation and the labour force in the 1978 harvest, see *Granma Weekly Review*, 2 July 1978.

Mesa-Lago (1974), p. 52 reports that on 1 July 1972—following Cuba's worst sugar harvest since 1963—President Dórticos announced that, beginning in 1973, Cuba would no longer attempt to produce large sugar crops, but only the amount of sugar that the country could rationally turn out. See Cuba (1975) and Castro (1976) for more on these decisions. Structure of industry data are from Cuba (1970c).

Investment data for 1970 and 1974 are from Cuba (1975), p. 24. Data on the decline in labour mobilisations are from Mesa-Lago (1974), p. 48.

The discussion of the Australian method for cane cutting is based on Mesa-Lago (1974), pp. 47–52. Also, see Mesa-Lago (1974), p. 49 regarding the KTP-1 factory; he reports that the original capacity figure was revised downward to between 200 and 300. However, in Cuba (1975), p. 55 the 600 figure is reported without qualification.

Castro's report to the Congress is Castro (1976) and the National Bank report is Cuba (1975).

On the age of Cuba's sugar mills, see Economic Intelligence Unit (1976), p. 6. On the number of mills operating at various times since 1969, see Mesa-Lago (1974), p. 47 and *Granma Weekly Review*, 2 July 1978. Data on recovery rates are from Cuba (1973), p. 124.

For his quote regarding livestock, see Mesa-Lago (1974), p. 57. I am grateful to Jean-Pierre Berlan for the comment concerning other countries' experiences with genetic improvement. Data on livestock are from Cuba (1975), pp. 47–50. Data on coffee and tobacco production in the 1970s is from Cuba (1975), pp. 40–1.

Some details on the local rural plans and the peasantry's relation to them is provided by Acosta (1973). Regarding government policy toward the peasantry in the early 1970s, see Castro's speech to the closing session of the 4th congress of ANAP in *Granma Weekly Review*, 9 January 1972. This speech is the source of his statement that the private sector's role will continue for some time.

The data for 1966 and 1971 on share of land cultivated in the private sector are from Acosta (1973), pp. 155–9. The 1975 figure is from Castro (1976), p. 196. The discussion on the size of the peasant sector is based on these same sources. The comments on food self-sufficiency at the end of the chapter are based on various data from Cuba (1973) and Cuba (1975).

CHAPTER 27

On post-1975 growth rates, see Castro's 24 December 1977 speech in *Granma Weekly Review*, 1 January 1978, p. 2, Economic Intelligence Unit (1978), p. 6, and *Economia y Desarrollo* (1977).

The two quotes from Castro are from his report to the Party Congress— Castro (1976), p. 115 and p. 116. The particulars of the industrialisation programme and other details of the plan for 1976–80 are contained in Cuba (1976a); see particularly pp. 92–3.

Information on the progress of mechanisation and other aspects of sugar production, including the labour-force data, have been cited above; see notes for Chapter 26 and Chapter 7. Jean-Pierre Berlan has pointed out to me the importance of mechanisation in reducing the negative implications of sugar's important role in the economy. Data on rainfall are from *Economia y Desarrollo* (1976b), p. 213. The weather issue is also emphasised in Cuba (1975).

For details of the 1976–80 plan, including sector-by-sector productivity and output goals, see Cuba (1976a). Details of the policy toward the peasantry are based on Cuba (1976b); also see Castro's speech to the closing session of the fourth ANAP congress, in *Granma Weekly Review*, 9 January 1972.

See Huberman and Sweezy (1969), p. 118 and surrounding passages concerning their raising the issue of the private peasantry possibly posing a political problem. See Huberman and Sweezy (1967) for an analysis of the USSR and the emergence of post-revolutionary stability.

CHAPTER 28

The quotes at the beginning of the chapter are from Castro (1960), p. 38. See Sweezy (1978) for his statements. All of the particulars concerning investment in and progress of agriculture have been taken from earlier chapters. As examples of statements which attribute Cuba's problems to weather and prices, see Cuba (1975), pp. 30 and 51; also see Castro's 28 September 1976 speech in *Granma Weekly Review*, 10 October 1976.

Data on trade are from Cuba (1973), pp. 186, 208–9, *Economia y Desarrollo* (1976a), and Cuba (1975), pp. 33–6. These same sources provide the basis for statements concerning external assistance. The data on other countries' trade gaps are from United Nations (1977) and the same publication for other years. Also, see Chenery and Syrquin (1975) on this topic, especially Tables S2 and S3.

Castro's statement on the relation of economic ties to government policy is from *Seven Days* (1977), p. 15.

Bibliography

Ackerman, Frank, 'Riots, Populism and Non-industrial Labor: a Comparative Study of the Political Economy of the Urban Crowd', unpublished doctoral dissertation, Harvard University, Cambridge, 1974.

Ackerman, F. and A. Zimbalist, 'Capitalism and Inequality in the United States', in R. C. Edwards *et al.*(eds) *The Capitalist System*, 2nd edn, Prentice-Hall, NJ, 1978.

Acosta, José, 'Las leyes de reforma agraria en Cuba y el sector privado campesino', *Economia y Desarrollo*, no. 12, 1970.

——, 'La revolución agraria en Cuba y el desarrollo económico', *Economia y Desarrollo*, no. 17, May–June 1973.

——, 'Cuba: De la neocolonia a la construcción del socialismo (II)', *Economia y Desarrollo*, no. 20, 1974.

Aguilar, Luis E., *Cuba 1933: Prologue to Revolution*, Norton, NY, 1972.

Amaro, Nelson and Carmelo Mesa-Lago, 'Inequality and Classes', in Mesa-Lago (1971).

Aranda, Sergio, *La Revolución Agraria En Cuba*, Siglo Vientiuno Editores, Mexico, 1968.

Auroi, Claude, *La Nouvelle Agriculture Cubaine*, Editions Anthropos, Paris, 1975.

Barkin, David, 'Cuban Agriculture: A Strategy for Economic Development', *Studies in Comparative International Development*, vol. 8, no. 1, Spring 1972a.

——, 'The Redistribution of Consumption in Cuba', *Review of Radical Political Economics*, vol. 4, no. 5, 1972b.

Bendix, Reinhard, *Work and Authority in Industry*, University of California Press, Berkeley, 1974.

Bengelsdorf, Carol and Alice Hageman, 'Emerging from Underdevelopment: Women and Work', *Cuba Review*, September 1974.

Bengelsdorf, Carol and Michael Locker, 'Perfect Identification of Government and Community', *Cuba Review*, vol. 4, no. 4, December 1974.

Bianchi, Andres, 'Agriculture', in Seers (1964).

Bianco, Lucien, *Origins of the Chinese Revolution, 1915–1949*, Stanford University Press, Stanford, 1971.

Blackburn, Robin, 'Prologue to the Cuban Revolution', *New Left Review*, no. 21, October 1963.

Blumberg, Paul, *Industrial Democracy*, NY, 1969.

Bonachea, Rolando E. and Nelson P. Valdés (eds), *Che: Selected Works of Ernesto Guevara*, MIT Press, Cambridge, 1969.

——, *Cuba in Revolution*, Doubleday, Garden City, 1972.

Boorstein, Edward, *The Economic Transformation of Cuba*, Monthly Review Press, NY, 1968.

Bowles, Samuel, 'Cuban Education and the Revolutionary Ideology', *Harvard Educational Review*, no. 41, Fall 1971.

Bowles, Samuel and Herbert Gintis, *Schooling in Capitalist America*, Basic Books, NY, 1976.

Castro, Fidel, *History will Absolve me*, Impresso por Cooperativa Obrera, CTC, Havana, 1960.

——, 'Report of the Central Committee of the Communist Party of Cuba to the First Congress', in *First Congress of the Communist Party of Cuba*, Progress Publishers, Moscow, 1976.

Castro, Raul, 'Órganos del Poder Popular: decentralización del aparato estatal, *Economía y Desarrollo*, no. 26, November–December 1974.

Center for Cuban Studies, 'Extract of Educational Statistics from Fidel Castro's speech of September 1, 1975', mimeo, NY, 1975.

Chenery, H. B. and M. Syrquin, *Patterns of Development 1950–1970*, the World Bank and Oxford University Press, Washington and London, 1975.

Chonchol, Jaques, 'Análisis critico de la reforma agraria cubana', *El Trimestre Económico*, January–March 1963.

Cuba, Junta Central de Planificación, *Boletín Estadístico*, 1966, Havana, 1966.

——, Confederación Trabajadores Cubanos, *Instrucciones Sobre Trabajo y Salarios*, Tomo 2, Imprenta CTC, 1968a.

——, Ministry of Education, 'Report to the XXI International Conference on Public Instruction, Convoked by the OIE and UNESCO', Havana, 1968b.

——, 'Informe de la Delegación de Cuba al XIII Periódo de Sessiones de la C.E.P.A.L.', Peru, 1969 in *Economía y Desarrollo*, no. 1, January–March 1970a.

——, 'Informe de la Delegación de Cuba a la XI Conferencia Regional de la F.A.O.', Venezuela, 1970, published as 'Dos Años de desarrollo agropecuario cubano', in *Economía y Desarrollo*, no. 4, October–December 1970b.

——, Junta Central de Planificación, *Boletín Estadístico*, 1970, Havana, 1970c.

——, La Delegación de Cuba al Seminario Latinoaméricano sobre Reforma Agraria, 'Una evaluación de la reforma agraria en Cuba', published in *Economía y Desarrollo*, no. 11, May–June 1972a.

——, Junta Central de Planificación, *Anuario Estadístico de Cuba*, 1972, Havana, 1972b.

——, Junta Central de Planificación, *Anuario Estadístico de Cuba*, 1973, Havana, 1973.

——, National Bank of Cuba, 'Development and Prospects of the Cuban Economy', report issued on the XXV anniversary of the National Bank of Cuba, Havana, 1975.

Cuba, 'Las tareas principales del quinquenio 1976–1980', (De la tésis aprobada en el I Congresso del PCC efectuado entre los días 17 y 22 de diciembre de 1975) in *Economía y Desarrollo*, no. 36, July–August 1976a.

Cuba, Departmento de Orientación Revolucionaria del Comite Central del PCC, *Sobre la Cuestión Agraria y Las Relaciones Con el Campesinado*, Havana, 1976b.

Cuba, 'First Congress of the Party Resolution on the Organs of People's Power', *Granma Weekly Review*, 11 January 1976c.

Cuba Review, 'Popular Power: Facts and Figures', *Cuba Review*, vol. 4, no. 4, December 1974.

Cuba Socialista, 'El desarrollo industrial de Cuba', *Cuba Socialista*, April 1966.

Cuban Economic Research Project, *A Study on Cuba*, University of Miami Press, Coral Gables, 1964.

Curbelo, R., 'Tenemos que aplicar la técnica', *Granma*, 28 August 1966.

Debray, Regis, *Revolution in the Revolution: Armed Struggle and Political Struggle in Latin America*, Monthly Review Press, NY, 1968.

Deutscher, Isaac, *The Unfinished Revolution: Russia 1917–1967*, Oxford University Press, London, 1967.

Dobb, Maurice, *Soviet Economic Development since 1917*, International Publishers, NY, 1948.

Draper, Theodore, *Castro's Revolution: Myths and Realities*, Praeger, NY, 1962.

Dumont, R., *Cuba: Socialisme et Développement*, Editions du Seuil, Paris, 1964.

Dumont, R., *Cuba: Est-il Socialiste?* Editions du Seuil, Paris, 1970.

Economía y Desarrollo, 'El comercio exterior de Cuba en el ultimo quinquenio', *Economía y Desarrollo*, no. 35, May–June 1976a.

Economía y Desarrollo, 'La economía cubana en 1975', *Economía y Desarrollo*, no. 38, November–December 1976b.

Economia y Desarrollo, 'La economia cubana en el ano 1976', *Economia y Desarrollo*, no. 41, May–June 1977.

Economic Commission for Latin America, *Economic Survey of Latin America 1963*, UN, NY, 1964.

Economic Intelligence Unit, *Quarterly Economic Review of Cuba, Dominican Republic, Haiti and Puerto Rico: Annual Supplement for 1977*, London, 1977.

Economic Intelligence Unit, *Quarterly Review of Cuba, Dominican Republic, Haiti and Puerto Rico, 1st quarter 1978*, London, 1978.

Fagen, Richard R., *The Transformation of Political Culture in Cuba*, Stanford University Press, Stanford, 1969.

Feder, Ernest, *The Rape of the Peasantry: Latin America's Land Holding System*, Doubleday, Garden City, 1971.

Fraginals, Manuel Moreno, *The Sugar Mill: The Socioeconomic Complex of Sugar in Cuba*, Monthly Review Press, NY, 1976.

Gerassi, John, ed., *Venceremos! The Speeches and Writings of Ernesto Che Guevara*, Simon and Schuster NY, 1968.

Gintis, Herbert, 'Education, Technology and the Characteristics of Worker Productivity', *American Economic Review*, May 1971.

——, 'Alienation in Capitalist Society', in R. C. Edwards *et al.*, *The Capitalist System*, 1st edn, Prentice-Hall, NJ, 1972.

Guerra y Sanchez, Ramón, *Sugar and Society in the Caribbean*, Yale University Press, New Haven, 1964.

Guevara, Ernesto, 'On the Cuban Experience', from *Revolucion*, no. 2, Oct. 1963, as translated and in Gerassi (1968).

——, *Reminiscences of the Cuban Revolutionary War*, Monthly Review Press, NY, 1968.

——, 'Sobre el sistema presupuesto de financiamiento', *Nuestra Industria Revista Economica*, February 1964, translated and reprinted in Silverman (1971).

Gutelman, Michel, *L'Agriculture Socialisée a Cuba*, Maspero, Paris, 1967.

Hernandez, Roberto E. and Carmelo Mesa-Lago, 'Labor Organization and Wages', in Mesa-Lago (1971).

Huberman, Leo and Paul Sweezy, *Cuba: Anatomy of a Revolution*, Monthly Review Press, NY, 1960.

——, *Socialism in Cuba*, Monthly Review Press, NY, 1969.

——, 'Lessons of Soviet Experience', in L. Huberman, P. Sweezy, *et al.*, *Fifty Years of Soviet Power*, Monthly Review Press, NY, 1967.

International Bank for Reconstruction and Development, *Report on Cuba*, IBRD, Washington, 1951.

Jenks, L. H., *Our Cuban Colony*, Vanguard Press, NY, 1928.

Joshua, I., *Organisation et Rapports de Production dans une Economie de Transition (Cuba)*, Centre D'Études de Planification Socialiste, Sorbonne, Paris, 1968.

Karol, K. S., *Guerrillas in Power: The Source of the Cuban Revolution*, Hill & Wang, NY, 1970.

Kenner, Martin and James Petras, *Fidel Castro Speaks*, Grove Press, NY, 1969.

Leontief, W. W., 'Notes on a Visit to Cuba', *New York Review of Books*, 21 August 1969.

Le Riverend, Julio, *Economic History of Cuba*, Book Institute, Havana, 1967.

——, *La Republica: Dependencia y Revolución*, Instituto de Libro, Havana, 1969.

Lewin, M., *Russian Peasants and Soviet Power*, Norton, NY, 1968.

Liebowitz, Michael, 'The Cuban Health Care System', Yale University School of Medicine, doctoral dissertation, New Haven, 1969.

López Coll and Armando Santiago, 'Notas sobre el proceso de planificación en Cuba', *Economía y Desarrollo*, no. 29, May–June 1975.

MacEwan, Arthur, Incentives, Equality and Power in Revolutionary Cuba', *Socialist Revolution*, no. 23, 1975a.

——, 'Ideology, Socialist Development and Power in Cuba', *Politics and Society*, 1975b.

McClelland, David D., *The Achieving Society*, The Free Press, NY, 1967.

Mesa-Lago, Carmelo, ed., *Revolutionary Change in Cuba*, University of Pittsburgh Press, Pittsburgh, 1971.

——, 'Economic Policies and Growth', in Mesa-Lago (1971).

——, *The Labor Force, Employment, Unemployment and Underemployment in Cuba: 1899–1970*, Sage Publications, Beverly Hills and London, 1972.

——, *Cuba in the 1970s*, University of New Mexico Press, Albuquerque, 1974.

Mintz, Sidney, foreword to Guerra y Sanchez (1964).

Morray, J. P., *The Second Revolution in Cuba*, Monthly Review Press, NY, 1962.

Moore, Barrington, *Social Origins of Dictatorship and Democracy*, Beacon Press, Boston, 1966.

Moore, Wilbert, *Labor, Commitment and Social Change in Developing Areas*, Social Science Research Council, NY, 1960.

Nearing, S. and J. Freeman, *Dollar Diplomacy*, Monthly Review Press, NY, 1966.

Nelson, Lowry, *Rural Cuba*, University of Minnesota Press, Minneapolis, 1950.

Nove, Alec, *An Economic History of the USSR*, Penguin, London, 1969.

O'Connor, James, 'The Organized Working Class in the Cuban Revolution', *Studies on the Left*, vol. 6, no. 2, March–April 1966.

——, *The Origins of Socialism in Cuba*, Cornell University Press, Ithaca and London, 1970.

Orris, Peter, 'The Role of the Consumer in the Cuban Public Health System', Yale University, unpublished MPH essay, New Haven, 1970.

Pazos, Felipe, 'Desarrollo insuficiente y depauperación económica', *Cuadernos*, Supplemento del No. 47, March–April 1961.

——, 'Comentarios a dos artículos sobre la revolución cubana', *El Trimestre Económico*, vol. 39, no. 113, January–March 1962.

Pearse, Andrew, 'Agrarian Change Trends in Latin America', in Stavenhagen (1970).

Perkins, Dwight, *Market Control and Planning in Communist China*, Harvard University Press, Cambridge Mass., 1966.

Perlman, Janice E., 'Rio's Favelas and the Myth of Marginality', *Politics and Society*, vol. 5, no. 2, 1975.

Pino-Santos, Oscar, *El Imperialismo Norteamericano en la Economía de Cuba*, Editorial Lex, Havana, 1960.

——, *Historia de Cuba: Aspectos Fundamentales*, Editorial Nacional de Cuba, Editora del Consejo Nacional de Universidades, Havana, 1964.

Polanyi, Karl, *The Great Transformation*, Beacon Press, Boston, 1957.

Pollitt, Brian, 'Employment Plans, Performance and Future Prospects in Cuba', *Prospects for Employment Opportunities in the 1970s*, HMSO, London, 1971.

——, 'Aclaración de datos laborales del Censo Agrícola Nacional de 1946 de Cuba', *Economía y Desarrollo*, no. 14, Havana, 1972.

——, 'Some Problems of Enumerating the Peasantry in Cuba', *The Journal of Peasant Studies*, vol. 4, no. 2, January 1977a.

——, 'Agrarian Reform, Agricultural Proletarians and Semi-Proletarians in Pre- and Post-Revolutionary Cuba—Some Notes', proceedings of a symposium on 'Peasants after the Revolution', Department of Sociology of Leeds University, April 1977b.

Ritter, Archibald R. M., *The Economic Development of Revolutionary Cuba*, Praeger Publishers, NY, 1974.

Roca, Blas, 'Some Aspects of the Class Struggle in Cuba', *World Marxist Review*, vol. 8, no. 2, February 1965.

Rodríguez, Carlos Rafael, 'El nuevo camino de la agricultura cubana', *Cuba Socialista*, no. 27, November 1963.

——, 'The Cuban Revolution and the Peasantry', *World Marxist Review*, vol. 8, no. 10, October 1965.

Romeo, C., 'Acerca del desarrollo económico de Cuba', *Cuba Socialista*, December 1965.

Ruiz, Ramon Eduardo, *Cuba: The Making of a Revolution*, W. W. Norton, NY, 1970.

Schumpeter, Joseph, *The Theory of Economic Development*, Oxford University Press, Oxford, 1961.

Schurmann, Franz, *Ideology and Organization in Communist China*, University of California Press, 1968.

Seers, Dudley *et al.*, *Cuba: The Economic and Social Revolution*, University of North Carolina Press, Chapel Hill, 1964.

Selden, Mark, *The Yenan Way in Revolutionary China*, Harvard University Press, Cambridge, 1971.

Seven Days, 'The Complete Text of Barbara Walter's Interview with Fidel Castro', *Seven Days*, vol. 1, no. 2, December 1977.

Silverman, Bertram, ed., *Man and Socialism in Cuba: The Great Debate*, Athenaeum, NY, 1971.

Stavenhagen, Rudolfo, ed., *Agrarian Problems and Peasant Movement in Latin America*, Doubleday, Garden City, NY, 1970.

Sutherland, Elizabeth, *The Youngest Revolution*, Dial Press, NY, 1969.

Sweezy, Paul, 'The Communist Manifesto after 100 Years', in P. Sweezy, *The Present as History*, Monthly Review Press, NY, 1953.

——, 'Modern Capitalism', in *Modern Capitalism and other Essays* by Paul Sweezy, Monthly Review Press, NY, 1972.

——, reply to B. R. Pollitt on 'War and Soviet Development Strategy', *Monthly Review*, vol. 29, no. 8, January 1978.

Sweezy, Paul and Charles Bettelheim, *On The Transition to Socialism*, Monthly Review Press, NY, 1971.

Sweezy, Paul, 'The Transition to Socialism', in Sweezy and Bettelheim (1971).

Talavera, I. and J. Herrera, 'La organización del trabajo y el salario en la agricultura', *Cuba Socialista*, May–June 1965.

Torres, Simon and Julio Aronde, 'Debray and the Cuban Experience', *Monthly Review*, vol. 20, no. 3, July–August 1968.

United Nations, *Statistical Yearbook 1959*, UN, NY, 1959.

——, *Statistical Yearbook 1970*, UN, NY, 1970.

——, *Statistical Yearbook 1976*, UN, NY, 1977.

Valdés, Nelson, 'The Radical Transformation of Cuban Education', in Bonachea and Valdés (1972).

Weisskoff, Richard, 'Income Distribution and Economic Growth in Puerto Rico, Argentina, and Mexico', Center Paper No. 162, Yale University, Economic Growth Center, New Haven, 1971.

Weisskopf, T. E., 'United States Foreign Private Investment: An Empirical Survey', in R. E. Edwards *et al.*, eds, *The Capitalist System*, 1st edn., Prentice-Hall, NJ, 1972.

Wheelwright, E. L. and B. McFarlane, *The Chinese Road to Socialism*, Monthly Review Press, NY, 1970.

Williams, W. A., *The United States, Cuba and Castro*, Monthly Review Press, NY, 1962.

Wolf, Eric R., *Peasant Wars of the Twentieth Century*, Harper & Row, NY, 1969.

Wood, Dennis B., 'The Long Revolution: Class Relations and Political Conflict in Cuba', *Science and Society*, vol. 34, no. 1, Spring 1970.

Zeitlin, Maurice, *Revolutionary Politics and the Cuban Working Class*, Harper & Row, NY, 1970.

Index